FOSSILS AND FLIES

The Life of a Compleat Scientist
Samuel Wendell Williston

(1851–1918)

FOSSILS
and
FLIES

The Life of a Compleat Scientist

Samuel Wendell Williston

(1851-1918)

by

ELIZABETH NOBLE SHOR

UNIVERSITY OF OKLAHOMA PRESS : NORMAN

International Standard Book Number: 0–8061–0949–1

Library of Congress Catalog Card Number: 77–145503

Copyright 1971 by the University of Oklahoma Press, Publishing Division of the University. Composed and printed at Norman, Oklahoma, U.S.A., by the University of Oklahoma Press. First edition.

This book is dedicated to the descendants of Samuel Wendell
Williston, especially to Sandy, Carolyn, and Donald.

Preface

When, soon after marriage, I learned that Samuel Wendell Williston was my husband's grandfather, I paid little heed. In the next few years I occasionally met a biologist or geologist who commented approvingly on Williston. I met Mrs. Williston only twice, and my memory of her is hazy. She was then in her nineties.

When Annie Williston died, her daughter Dorothy found among the family papers a mislaid typed copy of "Recollections," Williston's own account of his early years. I was asked and readily agreed to type copies of it for all members of the family. Long before I finished, I was intrigued by Williston, and I asked if I could write an account of his whole life, basing the early years on his manuscript. Dottie said by all means, and she began sending and bringing to me family papers as she sorted the accumulation from her mother's house and from that of her sister Ruth. The original copy of "Recollections" finally reappeared, almost illegibly written in ink on tablet paper, and from it I deciphered some of the words missing from the typed copy.

Besides that manuscript, the most valuable material I had to work with was the letters Annie Williston wrote home to her parents in Connecticut from Lawrence, Kansas, from 1890 to 1902. A devoted daughter, and a lonesome Easterner, Annie wrote home faithfully almost twice a week. Her mother, Wealthy Ann Hathaway, saved most of the letters, in the manner of old New England families (who had attics).

When the letters came to me, they were unsorted. They were sent to me in batches, for they first had to be separated from other family letters—from cousins, Hathaway relatives, and friends. Many were in their original envelopes, many were not. Most were dated, others were not. From this marvelous mixture I extracted a living account of the Williston home life over twelve years. Williston's own place in this account was rather small. He was, after all, only one in a family of seven people. He did not change as much from day to day as did the "baby" in the succession of five young Willistons.

The dress sizes of each of the girls were often included and occasionally a sketch of a new dress Annie had just made. Fragments of dress material, sometimes motheaten, would fall from the folded pages. A lock of hair was enclosed in one letter—and a dime in another. Pressed flowers frequently blurred the handwriting. Often a laboriously written note from a child to "Grandma" or "Grandpa" was included. Recipes (then called "receipts," of course) appeared, and Annie reported her success or failure at making an old family favorite dish. When she told of teas, or dinners, or receptions, her major report was on the menu and the clothes of the people present—little about the reason for or the visitor of the occasion. Illnesses ran rampant through the letters, and at times the town seemed in the throes of fierce epidemics. The weather was another favorite topic.

To me, reading these hundreds of letters seventy years later became a fascinating jigsaw puzzle. I laboriously put them in order from the letter date or postmarks, or simply by tying bits of family or social news together. A perpetual calendar, for matching days of the week to dates, proved invaluable. I have sworn never to write an undated letter again, no matter how minor.

I could not help getting involved in the day-to-day life, nor did I try to help it. I enjoyed university gossip tidbits and concluded that state university politics, internal and external, have not changed in seventy years. I read the "receipts" with interest. I mourned the loss of relatives and close friends. I sympathized with all the family during their two five-week quarantines with scarlet fever. I was pleased to discover that Williston, my husband's grandfather, was teaching at the University of Kansas while my grandfather was a student there, and it was a red-letter day when I found brief mention of the "Noble house" in a letter by Mrs. Williston.

Williston, although not referred to as frequently as the children, was ever present in the letters. His devotion to his family was very apparent, and it was obvious that his opinion on the children was not only constantly sought by his wife but frequently expressed and followed unsought. His wife learned to tolerate his laxness in dress, his untidiness in his study, his irregularity in going to church. She appreciated his praise, and she acknowledged his work and his position.

The living scene I found in the letters was of a happy family, a devoted family, and a close family. It made very worthwhile the long task of sorting and reading the letters.

Letters from Williston himself were rare, as they had to find their way to New Haven to be saved. Accounts of his field trips sometimes appeared, but in these letters to his family he wrote more about the flowers, the animals, or the heat than of the fossils. I always welcomed his letters in the assortment, but I winced too —for his handwriting was atrocious. I am now an expert on it, after struggling through "Recollections," family letters, and a quantity of letters written by Williston from the field to O. C. Marsh. I am very grateful to the Peabody Museum at Yale for sending me copies of these latter letters—which I finally deciphered from negatives over a light table and with the aid of a hand lens. Williston's spelling and punctuation have been retained in many instances in order to preserve the flavor of the original.

To fill out the account of Williston, I began writing to people who had known him, especially former students. The list was not long, for many years had passed since Williston's death, but these people all responded very enthusiastically and very helpfully. Time was running out for some, and I mourn the loss of Barnum Brown, Maurice Mehl, and Augusta Hasslock Kemp from my correspondents. I am grateful to every one of the busy people who took time to answer my questions on Williston or on items concerning him. All of these deserve special mention: John B. Atwater, Charles Laurence Baker, Charles H. Behre, Jr., F. R. Blackburn, Margaret Fuller Boos, Carl C. Branson, Ralph W. Chaney, Edwin H. Colbert, Frank R. Cole, D. Jerome Fisher (who deserves honorable mention), Jane Gallena (for whose efforts I am very grateful), William K. Gregory, Arthur W. Hixson, Robert P. Hudson, William D. Johnston, Jr., S. H. Knight, Olof Larsell, Laura Neiswanger (who sent me many useful items), Calvert Norland, Mary C. Payne (who deserves very special thanks), Alfred Sherwood Romer, Walter H. Schoewe, W. Clarke Wescoe, and Richard S. Woodhull. Various chambers of commerce and historical societies were also helpful.

My debt to Williston's children is unlimited: to Dottie (Mrs. George G. Shor), who provided almost all the pertinent family archives, to Genie (Mrs. Walter C. Earle), to Sammie (Samuel Hathaway Williston), and to Ruth, who died in 1963 but who had saved a great many family items. From Ruth's devoted friend, Viola Waskow, much of this material came to me.

I appreciate the permissions given by the following individuals, libraries, and publishers to quote from their works: D. Jerome Fisher, Everett C. Olson, Alfred Sherwood Romer, Beta Beta Beta Biological Society, University of Chicago Archives (University Presidents' Papers), Kenneth Spencer Research Library of the University of Kansas, University Press of Kansas, Yale University Press, and the Division of Vertebrate Paleontology of the Peabody Museum of Natural History of Yale University.

Many of the photographs were from family albums and include a number taken by Williston. I appreciate permissions given to use others from the Kansas State Geological Survey, the American Museum of Natural History, and the Peabody Museum of Yale University.

A special word of thanks goes to the staff of the library of Scripps Institution of Oceanography of the University of California at San Diego, who patiently helped me find old journals and early references, none of which was oceanographic.

To my family I say: Thank you for your patience, and for listening.

E. N. SHOR

La Jolla, California
December 15, 1970

Contents

Illustrations

PART ONE

1851 to 1890

To Set the Sta

Fossil hunting began in America as a gent
the East Coast. When it moved West in mid-nin
became as turbulent as the tornadoes that were a

The restorations of long-extinct dinosaurs, pt
labyrinthodonts that illustrate geology texts and ch
tell nothing of the effort behind those simple pictu
the creatures were found as bone fragments in dusty,
of the western United States—fragments slowly piece
as a jigsaw puzzle with many pieces missing.

Men had to find those fragments: scientists from the E
were too busy to spend much time in uncomfortable trav
Westerners whom they hired to hunt further in interesting p

The finding was not easy. Heat and alkaline water were rou
problems for the early fossil hunters. Weather in western Kans
central Wyoming, and northern Texas was then, as now, hard
predictable. The bone seekers were delayed by June snowstorms
all but drowned by flash floods, pounded by hailstones. They shiv-
ered in spring and fall and baked in summer.

In the 1870's Indians were a nagging worry. Small bands, often
renegades from reservations or braves looking for horses or mischief, could appear anywhere throughout the West. So far as I
know, no fossil hunter was ever an Indian victim (the Indians
may have left them alone as harmless lunatics), but nearby trag-
edies were known to all, so they kept an eye out for trouble. A
night alone, separated from companions, was not restful. Anyway,
the coyotes kept one awake.

As if there weren't enough problems besetting them, the collectors of fossils vied and fought among themselves. Two men,
O. C. Marsh and E. D. Cope, almost simultaneously decided to

r all the fossils in the West and soon ran headlong into each
r. The men they hired were expected to carry on the feud, and
did so with gusto and a certain amount of switching loyalties.
amuel Wendell Williston entered paleontology in 1874 in its
gh-and-tumble days, as a collector for O. C. Marsh. He liked
e "sport" of finding ancient bones, and he thoroughly enjoyed
amping on the plains under dusty canvas or the open sky. He
te antelope, rabbits, prairie chickens, and bushels of beans and
biscuits.

He went on to become an expert paleontologist himself, and he
gathered fossils and honors steadily. He gathered flies too, as a
hobby, and he became an expert on their classification. He devoted
hours to public health, and he helped found a medical school.

There is ever a fascination in the successful man, whatever his
field of endeavor. What brought him to the pinnacle? Was it a
straight line or a zigzag path? Was it smooth or rough?

Williston's path was zigzag and rough. He showed both persistence and uncertainty in his early years, both jubilation and
despair. He wavered over an assortment of professions and let
circumstances lead him to his final choice. In later years he could
easily say that his one ambition had been "to do research work in
Science," but in earlier years the goal had not been clear.

Recognition in science he did gain, but never wealth. Discouraged at times, for his family's sake, he advised two excellent students not to follow his profession—unless money meant nothing
to them. "Science," he once said, "is the slowest and hardest of
professions to make a pecuniary success." To him two pairs of
"galluses" were luxury.

Williston spanned the most interesting era of vertebrate paleontology in this country. Its heyday began when Darwin's *Origin of
Species* was published in 1859, for every new fossil contributed to
understanding evolution. The American West was then becoming
just civilized enough to be studied thoroughly. It proved to have
more spectacular fossils than did Europe—birds with teeth, enormous dinosaurs, anomalous amphibians.

Only three great names preceded Williston in vertebrate paleon-

tology in the United States. By the time he died, there were several dozen professionals, each specialized. There were experts on dinosaurs, on fossil mammals, on fossil fishes. Williston's final specialty was the ancestry of the reptiles. But he had helped to find many other kinds of fossils between his first pterodactyl in 1874 and his last labyrinthodont in 1918.

This is Williston's story. It has stagecoaches and dusty wagons, Indians in breechcloth and borrowed spectacles, mysterious telegrams, early Kansas, young Wyoming, Populists, Sigma Xi, dusty professors, *Diplodocus*, and *Eryops*.

Here is a small chapter in the history of science.

CHAPTER 2

The Young Years

R<small>EMINISCING</small> at a sorrowful time in the late years of his life, in May, 1916, Samuel Wendell Williston wrote an account of his first forty years for his family and friends. He set aside the manuscript, which he called "Recollections," and went back to paleontology. Let us begin with his own account:[1]

As the oldest living student of vertebrate fossils in America and one of the oldest in the world, friends have urged me to write some of my recollections. Not that I am so very old [not quite 65], but because there were so few vertebrate paleontologists in the days when I became interested in the subject—only Leidy, Cope, Marsh and a few other lesser lights in America. Nor were there more than a dozen others in all the world, of whom Sir Richard Owen was the chief, who had published much about extinct vertebrates.

It has never seemed to me that there was much of interest I could say about myself, nor very much about the pioneers in paleontology that I could tell. . . .

I suppose it is the proper thing in one's autobiography to begin his history several hundred years before he was born. Unfortunately, my memory does not go back that far, and fortunately if it did there would not be much of particular interest to recall. I cannot trace my origin to William the Conqueror, nor to any other famous person. Belvin Williston, my cousin in Boston, has traced our immediate Williston family back to about 1650 in Massachusetts. The Willistons were about the usual run of common people, no one famous or even noted, whether for good or evil. There were

[1] In this chapter and the next, Williston's manuscript is presented directly, with the present author's comments, necessary changes, and guesses at the handwriting bracketed. The remainder of the manuscript is used throughout Part 1 in shorter portions, in quotation marks.

some petty town officers, and a few petty criminals among them, but none was hanged, nor sent to prison, nor wrote books. None occupied high office nor were any wealthy or very poor—just a lot of decent, law-abiding, self-respecting, common citizens. Some of them served in the war of the Revolution, and many were fishermen. Prior to 1650 the Willistons of Massachusetts go back to about 1630, but their immediate relations to my father's family have not been traced, though doubtless close.

My father was born September 20th, 1822, in Cranberry Island, Maine. His mother's family, the Stanleys, are still on the island, whither they had come not long before my father's birth from Marblehead, Mass. His father, John Williston, came from somewhere in Massachusetts, Salem—if I am not mistaken, possibly Newburyport, where many of the early Willistons lived, and still live. My grandfather was a fisherman, as were my father and his numerous brothers in their youth. I never saw my grandfather Williston who died in middle life from some acute disease. The family was large, as was usual in those days, fourteen brothers and sisters altogether, I believe. I remember only a few of them— John, Henry, Thomas, Isaiah, William and Aunt Phoebe, who was married to my mother's brother John. [On the occasion of meeting his Uncle Isaiah in 1881, Williston described to his fiancée his father's brothers as being "all alike as peas. . . . They are all frank, blunt, cordial, honest & kind hearted, ruled by their wives and all decidedly wanting in style!"[2] He considered himself to be just like them.]

They knew little of schools. My father, if he ever went to school didn't take kindly to study, for he never learned to read or to write. I have a dim recollection that three months comprised the extent of his school days. It was a great pity too, for my father was a man of far more than ordinary ability as a mechanic—he was noted always for his skill. His life would have been very different had he received even a fair common school education; perhaps also my own would have been different. Of all his children I resembled him the most, both physically and mentally. I was of

[2] Letter of August 19, 1881.

just his height, five feet ten, and during most of my life I weighed the same as he did, about one hundred and eighty-five pounds. I was the only one of his children who could wear his hat, the same size as my own, seven-and-five-eighths. His forehead, like my own, was high and broad. He was kindly in disposition, but of passionate temper when rarely he lost it. His general reputation was that of an honest man and skilful mechanic. He was named after an uncle Samuel, and the name seems to have been a favorite one in the Williston family.

In so large a family it was necessary for him to begin his own livelihood early. When he was sixteen or seventeen, I think, he was apprenticed to a blacksmith near Boston. My grandmother died when my father was about forty years of age, and if I am correct she was well along in the seventies.

My mother's parents came from England, not far from London and settled in New Jersey some time about the close of the war of 1812. My mother, Jane Augusta Turner, was born in Patterson of that state Sept. 22, 1822. My grandfather pursued his trade, that of a weaver for a few years in Patterson, but removed with his family some time in the late twenties or early thirties to Newton Upper Falls, near Boston, where he was engaged till his death, in weaving. I remember his house, on a hill, filled with hand looms. I saw the house again in 1878. And there were plenty of weavers for not fewer than *eighteen* children were born to him and my grandmother, some twelve or more of whom grew to adult life. My mother, Jane Augusta Turner, was well down on the list, but there were at least four or five younger. The youngest, Aunt Carrie, a year younger than my oldest brother, is yet living in Omaha, Nebraska.

My mother had a fair common school education, and her whole life was embittered by my father's lack of an education—she was so conscious of what he lost by his inability to read and write. I have often heard her speak of his lost opportunities because of his lack of an education. But, her early English training she never overcame. All her life, her English accent was only too apparent in her speech.

[In 1884, when writing to his wife's parents, Williston spoke further of his parents: "My mother was refined, and she taught her children to be honest and truthful. My father though without any mean or dishonest traits, had been a rude fisherman and blacksmith and was *wholly* uneducated. There was never harmony, and so when a boy, books and reading gave me a burning desire to go higher in life. I come *honestly* by many of my habits of untidiness. I take after my father in features and traits. He was a man of more than ordinary ability, but he grew up off the coast of Maine beyond the influence of schools—Hardy, muscular, bright and active, he would have made a position in life had he been early brought under training.—He has always however borne an *honest* name, preferring to work, than to get money by questionable means,— and often afraid to demand his just dues. Most of the rest of the family take after my mother more."[3]]

My parents were married in 1844. My oldest brother, John Henry, I never saw. He died when four years of age of "croup." Very clear are my recollections of the silver coffin plate that my mother cherished so long. My two older brothers, Charles and Isaiah, have died within the past three years, the former in Olympia, Washington, where he went about twenty years ago, the latter in Kansas City. I was born in what was then Roxbury, now a part of Boston, July 10, 1851,[4] in a little frame house, which when I saw it in 1879 was used as a saloon. How long I lived there I do not know, but till 1856 I think, for the first and only distinct memory that I have was a torch-light procession with the windows filled with candles to celebrate the supposed victory of John C. Fremont for the presidency. And yet I have distinct recollections of a house in Newton Upper Falls, not far from my grandfather Turner's. I saw that house too, in 1879, and it came back clearly to me. I think we must have lived there till 1855 or early in 1856. And here began my first studies in natural history! My father had

---

[3] Letter of August 25, 1884.

[4] All the memorials of Williston, written after his death, give his birth year as 1852, because the handwritten copy of this manuscript was used by several biographers and is marked over at this point. The author confirmed the year 1851 by getting a copy of Williston's birth certificate from Boston.

a little garden. He was planting potatoes one day with my aid, when several toads were unearthed. I was very curious to know where they came from, and he told me that they grew in the ground. I puzzled my childish brain about them and determined to raise a crop of them myself, so the next day I sedulously collected all the small toads I could find in my little apron and proceeded to plant them as I had seen my father plant the potatoes. My father observed me and asked me what I was doing. I told him I was planting them to see them grow. It caused him so much amusement that I went away crying to tell my mother about it. For years, until I was so old that I resented it, my father always called me "Toad."

I have forgotten to add that I was named Wendell, a name I was always called, because of my grandfather Turner's admiration for Wendell Phillips, then in the height of his fame.[5]

In the spring of 1857 my parents decided to emigrate to Kansas. A colony had left Boston the year before for Manhattan, and the letters that came back had infected many with the desire to go west. My father was then working in a foundry and my mother was not at all satisfied with his prospects and wages. The abolitionists were urging eastern people to colonize the territory in order to help John Brown preserve it to the "Free States." And so, in May, father sold what property he possessed for about $2,500 and with some necessary household belongings started on the then long journey for Manhattan, Kansas, a settlement at the mouth of the Blue River, one hundred and ten miles from the mouth of the Kaw. In addition to us three boys, and my younger sister Eva, my mother's nephew, James Atkinson, a boy of 16, accompanied us. The trip was long and tedious by rail to St. Louis, then a small place, and thence by steamboat up the Missouri River to Leavenworth. There was no Kansas City then. We reached Leavenworth about the 20 of May. Here we remained a few days in a very small hotel while my father bought a wagon and yoke of oxen and such provisions and household things as were indispensable, and we started on the slow and tedious drive of 115 miles to Manhattan

[5] Wendell Phillips (1811–84) was an outstanding orator in Boston and a strong advocate of the abolition of slavery.

through a country but very sparsely settled. For the most part we children rode in the covered wagon, while my father and cousin walked and drove the oxen. My mother was very homesick on the way. I can remember how long and bitterly she cried. One could not blame her. She now realized for the first time in this wilderness what she was leaving behind, perhaps forever. Nor did she see the east again for nearly thirty years, and my father never. We reached Manhattan June 7. The Emigrant Aid Society,[6] under whose auspices this long journey was undertaken, provided a small log cabin, about 15 feet square inside, two and a half miles east of Manhattan for our temporary use till a house could be built in the town itself. [Manhattan in 1857 had 14 or 15 houses.[7]]

My memory of events is now becoming clearer. The house of our temporary occupation had but a single room with a loft reached by a ladder. There were two beds in the room below, screened off by cloth curtains that my mother soon found for them, and we four boys slept in the loft. A big fireplace in one end used for cooking and a rough table and a few chairs comprised the furniture. I do not wonder that my mother was despondent for there were no neighbors within 2 miles. And she needed courage, for the Pottawatimee Indians had a village in the immediate vicinity and the word Indian in the east was a synonym of savage. My father and cousin went each [morning] early to Manhattan across the Blue River where they were building a shop and preparing to build a house, and did not return till late in the evening, leaving my mother, aunt and us children alone. For awhile all the water used by the family was brought by us boys from a spring at "Devil's Elbow," a mile north of the house, and I vividly recall how much we feared the Indians who resorted to the same spring for their water. But my father soon dug a well close by the house, which the squaws were also eager to use to save them trips to the spring. One day, I remember, several Indian "braves" stopped to get drinks. As usual

[6] The Emigrant Aid Society was an organization of Easterners, strongly supported by Amos A. Lawrence (for whom Lawrence, Kansas, was named), the purpose of which was to help Eastern emigrants to Kansas in order to save the state for the north against slavery.

[7] Nyle H. Miller, *Kansas: A Students' Guide to Localized History*, 10.

my mother called the children in and closed the door when she saw them coming and barred it. They rapped on the door and demanded a cup to drink from. My mother told them to drink from the bucket, but they grew impudent and threatened by their actions to beat the door in. My mother hustled my aunt and us children into the loft and took the ladder away, and then seized my father's shot gun which hung over the fireplace, and thrust its muzzle through a crack between the logs, and threatened to shoot them. They went off laughing and saying "heap squaw." But it took courage all the same for my mother, and we children were thoroughly frightened. Like most Indians they were thieves and unreliable, but I do not suppose we were in much danger for our lives.

It was October or November that we moved into the house my father had built in Manhattan. A house of six rooms built of raw cottonwood lumber, unplastered and simply battened outside. There was a dining room, a small kitchen and a small "parlor" on the first floor, and corresponding rooms used for chambers on the second floor, not very commodious accomodations for the eight of our family. Also there was always at least one boarder, two of whom I remember so well, the Rev. Mr. Kalloch, who had been my mother's pastor in Boston, and a very talented but erratic man. Some scandal in his Boston pastorate had induced him to seek the freedom of the west. I can recall how my mischievous older brother and myself once invaded his room and found a treasure in the empty bottles that we threw out of the window. A Mr. Galbraith also I remember because he was a morphine fiend. In addition, there were always a number of day boarders, among whom was a young man, Frank Cole, who married my Aunt Henrietta.

And here I began my schooling. I have no recollection of going to school in Roxbury. Nor can I remember when I could not read, though dimly I do recall learning my letters from the cook stove! "The Beach Stove Co., St. Louis, Mo., patented 1856."

With their New England instincts, almost the first building erected in the village was a stone school house, in the western part of the town. It was of two stories, the first of which was never completed, and served as a fine play house for the younger children. The second floor in a single room about 20 x 30 in size was where my early education was obtained, as far as Algebra and McGuffey's Fifth Reader. My mother took the "Boston Free Flag," a semi-literary paper, and there were a few books in the house the first winter I spent in it. I can recall how vexed some of the boarders were because I monopolized the Free Flag and how indignant I was when they took it away from me. The first book I ever read was a novel whose exact title I cannot recall, except that the heroine's name was "Genevieve," and that name I remember because I persisted in pronouncing it Gen (with a hard g) c-vy-eva, my sister's name is Eva. This book I read the first winter. I have often wished that I might read it again. And my second book, read in 1858, was "David Copperfield." For the next ten years, I simply devoured books.

Among the many more or less useless things that the Emigrant Aid Society sent to Manhattan was a large box—I could just set my arms over the sides when opened—filled with old, second-hand and tattered books. Such of these as were of any use in the school were taken out, leaving it about half full of a most heterogeneous collection, from Baxter's Saints Rest to goody-goody Sunday School books. It was a gold mine to me and I did not cease its exploration till everything readable was read,—and everything was grist that came to my mill. It would have been better had I read less, for I was a rather frail and pallid child, and did not take much part in children's sports. My mother shielded me because she had been told that as a baby I was afflicted with "water on the brain." She let me sleep as long as I desired in the morning, and then always had a bowl of bread and milk saved for me. But my brothers had no such privileges and they had not a little contempt for me.

Another gift of the Emigrant Aid Society to this colony was a small library of a few hundred volumes, of more standard books, that was in charge of the Agent, a Mr. Andrew Mead, who permitted my brothers and myself to make a limited use of it. But I did not find a great deal in it to interest me. They were too mature for my childish comprehension. One only I recall, Stephen's Antiquities of Central America. I read it when I was about seven years old, and although I have not seen the work for many years, I can still vividly visualize its many pictures of Aztec ruins in Yucatan. It directed my interest to Tschudie's Peru, and Prescott's Conquest of Mexico, which a few years later made a deeper impression on me and gave me that fondness for history which formed a large part of my reading for the next ten years. The Sunday School libraries were soon exhausted. I would take home every Sunday all that the teacher would permit. One only I now recall, Adoniram Judson's history of his Missionary experiences in Tahiti.

Another incident of my seventh year stands out vividly in my recollections. Just north of Manhattan is Blue Mont, a steep and high bluff, the termination of a range of hills ending abruptly at the Blue River. In the sand bars of the river, we boys often gathered clams. I was surprised to find on the summit of Blue Mont shells which looked much like clam shells. I asked my father how they got to the top of the bluff in the rocks, for all the clams I had seen lived in the water and couldn't crawl on land. He told me they had been left there by the great Deluge, which once covered all the earth. I took some of the shells to my Sunday School teacher and she told me the same! And so Genesis acquired a new interest to me, and most of the verses that I was required to memorize each week from the bible were chosen from the old Testament. My mother had prohibited us boys from going to Blue Mont and the river for, like most mothers, she was afraid of the water and not till I had surreptitiously learned to swim did she consent to let me go in swimming! Our favorite swimming hole was among large stones filled with fossil shells of Lower Permian age, and they were my first studies in paleontology!

The old cottonwood house was too cold and inhospitable and too small for our large family, and my father built a better house about a quarter of a mile away in 1859. It was full two stories in height, and 20 x 30, a large house then for the village. It was built chiefly of black walnut lumber, sawed by the little "Emigrant Aid Sawmill," and was long known as the "Black Walnut House."[8]

[8] This house still stands, on the property of Kansas State University.

Its shingles and its floors were of pine, brought up the Kaw river in a steamboat, one of the three that ever went so far up the river. I remember especially the boat because its name in large letters spelled to me Col-o-nel something, and it worried me not a little that everyone persisted in pronouncing it "Kernal." The pronunciation of the English language was a very mysterious and incomprehensible thing to me in those days.

We had been in this house but a very short time, not long enough to get settled when there came up one evening one of those "cyclones" for which Kansas was long notorious. It threatened to blow down the house, and did destroy the house from which we had just moved, distributing some of its timbers quite into our back yard. My father and cousin had not returned from the shop which also was blown to pieces, and my mother was greatly distressed and nearly wild in her anxiety for her five children, for my brother Frank was then a baby.

In 1859, my father bought a "claim" of 160 acres nearly adjoining the town and lived on it till the following spring in order to preempt it, in a little frame house that the former owner had built.[9] I attended school while living there, in the unfinished building of the "Blue Mont College." In 1860, he bought the "Emigrant Aid Saw and Grist Mill," trading forty acres of his land for it, and moved back to the Black Walnut house. This was the year of the great drouth, when practically no rain fell for fifteen months and the crops were an almost total failure. Our subsistence for many months was almost exclusively from corn meal and sorghum. There was no coffee, except barley coffee! nor tea, and no [sugar]. I have never been fond of corn bread since that time. When, after more than a year my father obtained a sack of flour, the biscuits that my mother baked linger in my mind as the greatest delicacy and luxury of my life! [A favorite dish of Williston's in later years—both at home and in camp—was boiled potatoes with onions. He explained this to his family as another result of the 1860 Kansas drought, when cabbage was the only vegetable for months. In the

9 This was before the Homestead Act of 1862. The senior Williston bought the General Land Office warrant of a veteran of the War of 1812.

spring, when his father was finally able to buy potatoes and onions, his mother boiled the potatoes, mashed them with a fork, and sprinkled them with raw chopped onions.]

My father needed all his boys to help him run his mill, and it was my duty that year (1860–61) to sit on a high seat and turn the throttle of the engine on and off for every board made by the circular saw. It became very tedious for so small a boy.

Thanks to my mother—who felt bitterly my father's lack of an education—we boys were kept at school. She insisted that we should have an education. My own school work was too light to keep me out of mischief. It took me but a little while to learn my lessons and moreover, I preferred to read books rather than to study lessons. Whenever I could get books, and I searched the town for them, I was hidden in the barn or out of reach of my mother's voice, immersed in them. For awhile Beadle's dime novels and the New York Ledger furnished my chief mental papulum, but when I could not get these anything else was grist that came to my mill.

It was during this time that I got my second lesson in natural history. My father was very fond of fishing and hunting. He went fishing every Sunday in the Blue river, and among the fishes that he brought home, chiefly cat-fish, shad, and "buffaloes," were river sturgeons. I usually helped him clean and prepare them for cooking. I observed that the sturgeons had no "back bone" like the other fishes, but instead a long fibrous rod—the notochord. I puzzled greatly over it but no one could give me any enlightenment. It was one of the things that later directed my interest to natural history.

Blue Mont College, founded by the Methodists in 1859, became merged into the State Agricultural College in 1864, and I was a very happy boy when in 1866 [age 15] I was permitted to enter it.

Of the beginning of the Civil War, my memory is vague. I recall the excitement in the little town when the news came of Quantrell's Raid in Lawrence in 186[3][10] and for awhile there was not a little

[10] William C. Quantrill, with 400 Missouri "bushwhackers" killed 150 people in

fear that the "bush-whackers" would come as far west as our town. From time to time there had been "scares" of Indian depredations and every one capable of bearing arms was trained for defense, and signals were planned to call the citizens together. But we were fortunately spared from both Indians and bushwhackers.

The famous "Butterfield Overland Express" route was established in 1859, and my interest in it was great because it was all that connected us with the outside world. Mr. Butterfield had once been a boarder at our "Cottonwood House," and my father was the official blacksmith for the company at Manhattan. We boys were sure, when possible, to be on hand when the "Express" came, and watched with curiosity and awe the passengers that alighted at the hotel, one of whom I remember was Horace Greeley.[11]

But my memory is clearest of a certain book that one of the passengers left at the hotel. The hotel keeper's son was a chum of mine, and he got it for me surreptitiously or otherwise, but I could have it only for a day. Such an opportunity was not to be missed, for it was a famous book even then, and so I sat up all night to read it by the light of a tallow dip. I finished it as the sun arose to receive a chastisement from my mother. The influence it made upon me, a boy of ten, was intense, for it was "Uncle Tom's Cabin." I became an ardent, a fire-eating abolitionist, as were most of the inhabitants of the village. War news did not reach us very promptly. There were few or no daily papers in the state, and a telegraph line did not reach in till the railroad did, in 1866. My father took us boys a few times to the neighboring garrison Fort Riley, 16 miles west of Manhattan. When I was about twelve years old my desire to enlist as a drummer boy became very strong. I even secretly contemplated running away from home to offer my valuable services to the United States Government! My father was not eligible as a soldier, for he suffered most of his life with a chronic

Lawrence in August, 1863, and burned much of the town, during the bitter border raiding between "slave" Missouri and "antislave" Kansas.

11 This paragraph is confusing. Greeley did indeed pass through Manhattan May 27, 1859, on the last stage of the Overland Stage Line, the route of which was then moved north. The Butterfield line did not run through Manhattan.

ulcer on his leg, and my oldest brother was too young. The second Kansas regiment was partly made up in Manhattan and among the volunteers was a hired man who had been in the family for years, "Charley Lewis," a Swede, and in his furloughs he found an eager audience in us boys.

Perhaps the strongest impression of my whole life I received when the news came of the death of Lincoln. The news that peace had at last been declared was received in our town as everywhere else with jubilation and public rejoicings, to be followed so soon by the news of Lincoln's assasination [*sic*]. No one who reads these lines, unless he should happen to be older than I am, can realize, even feebly, how great was the love of the people for Abraham Lincoln at the close of the war. He was worshipped as I believe no other man in the world's history has ever been. My father brought home the news, the day following his assassination, about six oclock [*sic*] in the evening. My mother was in the kitchen finishing the preparations for supper with all the children, there were five of us then. My mother sat down and wept and we all, father, brothers and sisters wept with her. Every detail of the scene is burnt into my memory. I even remember what was upon the stove and where each of us stood when my father opened the door and exclaimed, "President Lincoln is dead." Every house, every store, every church was draped in mourning for thirty days, and the world sorrowed with us.

About this time I was learning a trade. From the countless books I had read I became ambitious to write books myself, and, as the nearest approach to an author in our village was the editor of the weekly paper, I decided to be a printer. My mother's consent was obtained, and Mr. Pillsbury the editor gave me a job in his office, where he did nearly all the work himself of editing and publishing the small weekly paper. I was not strong enough to manage the "Washington" hand press, but I inked the rollers, cleaned the type, and learned to set type till I became fairly proficient. And I have not yet forgotten all I learned there. Five years ago, I set all the type for my "Bibliography," some twelve or fifteen pages. And in fact, here dates my first attempt at authorship! Secretly I set up a stickful of a supposedly humorous account of the capture of Jefferson Davis, and Mr. Pillsbury allowed it to appear in the paper as a contribution from the "Printer's devil." I was about thirteen years of age when it appeared; it is not included in my bibliography!

However, after a few months my mother concluded that the emolument of $2 a week would hardly compensate for the loss of time and I was sent back to school, to the Agricultural College some [of the time], where I considered myself a real college student because I was studying Latin and Greek. I am sorry to say I was a heedless boy. All that I wanted to do was read, and I seized every excuse to avoid work. In despair, I suppose, I was left more or less to my own devices, and my father considered me as the type of laziness. Nevertheless, although I was not called upon to plough or harvest, I had plenty of things to do on the farm,— too many I [thought] then, not enough I think now. I had four or five cows to milk morning and night, the cows to get up, the pigs and chickens to feed, and the wood to bring in. I was not strong enough to do the heavier work.

It was about this time that I became deeply interested in some phases of Theology. My mother had become a convert from a Baptist to Spiritualism. There were many spiritualist "seances" in our house, and I naturally became a believer too. But my belief began to waver when for some strange reasons to me the "spirits" called up seemed to forget their own life experiences. Indian chiefs talked English, and I wondered where they learned it. From my early boyhood I was fond of foreign languages. Every year I collected all the Almanacs I could get from the merchants in foreign languages, especially German and French. So I had begun to get a smattering of the languages. At the seance a German was supposed to be speaking with the medium, and partly to show my own erudition—I suppose—I asked a question or two in the German language, which were unintelligible to the medium. It is very probable they would not have been had she been a native of Germany, but it finally convinced me there was something wrong. However the Spiritualist literature that came into the house during those years had something to do with my future life. Among the books I remember one on the "Preadamite Man," another by Robert Dale Owen, who, while an able geologist was also a spiritualist. And the "Banner of Light," a spiritualistic organ, I read every week.

It was about this time when I was fifteen years old that Professor Mudge loaned me Lyell's Antiquity of Man. I remember the night I brought it home there was a dance at our house, in which I was not interested, but it gave me the opportunity in an upstairs room to read the book till the guests departed in early daylight hours. I was thoroughly convinced when conviction meant antagonism to the church's teachings. And Professor Mudge about this time lectured on the subject and on Evolution, to which he remained opposed till his death. It was my first introduction however to the doctrine to which I soon after became a devoted disciple.

And these things went on till I was about seventeen years old. My father wanted to take me out of school and set me at some useful work "earning my salt," for times were growing less prosperous in the family. I remember how long I had to plead in Sept. 1867, to be allowed to go back to school, and not till the fall term had actually begun did I get my parents' consent. [Williston's mother was no doubt responsible for the decision.]

At college I did pretty well, I think, though I was more interested sometimes in the library than in some of my text books. There were about a thousand books in the college library, possibly a few more, but to me it seemed to contain the treasures of the world. At first I conceived the plan of reading it through shelf by shelf, which I felt sure I could accomplish in three or four years! But I quickly abandoned that idea, after attempting some that were far beyond my comprehension, and made a selection of those things I liked best. But I must have read more than two hundred of the books, including much of the fiction and most of the history and general science.

I was very fortunate in my teachers, especially the teacher of science, Professor B. F. Mudge. I have published a brief sketch of his life. . . .

[Benjamin Franklin Mudge[12] was another Easterner who chose Kansas as his home because of strong antislavery views. Born in Orrington, Maine, on August 11, 1817, he was educated in Massachusetts and Connecticut in science. His professional life began as a lawyer in Lynn, Massachusetts, where he also became mayor and was curator of the collections of the Lynn Natural History Society. In 1859 he became a chemist for oil refineries, first in Chelsea, Massachusetts, then in Breckenridge, Kentucky. At the beginning of the Civil War his opinions on slavery led him to move to Wyandotte (now Kansas City), Kansas, where he taught and lectured.

In 1864 Mudge became the first state geologist of Kansas, but the next year he left that post to become professor of natural history at Kansas State Agricultural College in Manhattan, until a change in administration in 1873 forced him to leave. He then became a fossil collector for O. C. Marsh of Yale, and worked for the Kansas State Board of Agriculture until his death in 1879 in Manhattan.

Mudge was always an active collector, especially in geology, mineralogy, paleontology, and botany. Williston said: "His extensive collections of mineralogy and paleontology were presented to the Agricultural College, but, unfortunately, from lack of appreciation by the political head of that institution a large part of the 'bones and stones' that he had so painfully collected were destroyed or thrown out into the yard after his resignation."

One of the first professional geologists in the state, Mudge made the first geological map of Kansas, and explored the western part of the state in the 1870's, "when explorations meant real dangers and hardships of the most pronounced kind. . . Nearly every summer found him in the midst of Indian country usually wholly without protection from the danger of hostile Indians save such as his own rifle and revolver afforded." Of his work, Williston (who later himself revised the state geological map) commented: "In general it may be truthfully said that his pioneer work in Kansas geology was important and extensive, though now largely

[12] Summarized from S. W. Williston, "Prof. Benjamin F. Mudge," *American Geologist*, Vol. XXIII (June, 1899), 339–45.

superseded by more detailed and accurate studies. He saved the people of his adopted state many thousands of dollars by his skilled advice, so freely given that he died a comparatively poor man."

Mudge published only twenty-nine scientific papers, but he unselfishly provided specimens and his own knowledge to many others. "His extensive collections in the whole field of Kansas geology and paleontology have greatly enriched scientific literature. Especially will his name be found with great frequency in the published works of Lesquereux, White, Cope and Marsh as the discoverer of very many of the new forms described by them. . . .

"His work in life, however," Williston continued, "has chiefly borne fruit as a teacher. He was widely known as an enthusiastic and able lecturer, and his courses were always in demand by the teachers and scientific men of the state. . . . In his later years, the kindly faced, plain old gentleman, as ready to talk with the uncouth farmer as with the aristocrat, interested in everything that affected human happiness or human morals, was known from one end of the state to the other, a welcome guest everywhere; and while his enthusiastic eagerness in the discovery of a new fossil or a new fact in geology might occasionally bring a smile to the unscientific, he was loved and revered by the people of Kansas as perhaps no other citizen has ever been."]

I doubt not that my life [Williston went on in "Recollections"] has been chiefly devoted to natural science was largely due to his [Mudge's] influence. I studied every subject that he taught, and they were many. "Natural Philosophy," chemistry, botany, geology, zoology, veterinary science, mineralogy, surveying, spherical geometry, conic sections, calculus, etc. Mudge had a considerable collection of fossils and minerals, that filled a long case. To me it was a wonderful museum. There were no laboratories of any kind, no microscopes and but few instruments. The college catalogue of about that time in enumerating the equipment, gravely mentions an electrical machine, three Leyden jars and six test-tubes! The electrical machine was a never-ending source of delight. The professor occasionally got it out and charged the Leyden jars, and then with hands joined in a circle gave us a shock. He prophesied that some day electrical light would take the place of other illuminants. My ambition was to make a machine myself, and I nearly succeeded, but I found no way of boring a hole thru the glass plate for the shaft. The oxyhydrogen light was another great wonder. My greatest interest was given to physics or Natural Philosophy as it was then called. I read every book on the subject that I could find in the library. Chemistry had second place, while biology interested me but little, though I never tired of reading books on domestic medicine, Beach's Eclectic Home Doctor, and a domestic book on Homeopathy,[13] in which my mother was a firm believer, were my chief sources of inspiration. I too was an ardent believer in the efficacy of the little sugar pills that I thought were unmedicated. My mother called in the doctor in great alarm when she discovered it. But he laughed and said he guessed they wouldn't do me any harm! My faith in them thereafter was utterly destroyed, and I ridiculed the whole thing, especially after I had read the history of the "art" and the life of Hahnemann [the founder of homeopathy].

During 1868 I began to be restless, and as usual I suppose, a girl was at the bottom of it. I was infatuated with a young lady school teacher some six years my senior, and became at once unduly conscious of my rusticity. My clothes were poor, and I had no spending money. I blamed my father, very unjustly, for not providing better for me, and I tried to earn some money for myself. The summer of 1868 I taught a country school near Manhattan for my board and ten dollars a month. But thirty dollars did not go very far in supplying me with what I thought were my needs. My chief memory of that summer is my study of Shakespeare. I filled a large blank book with what I thought were the "gems" of his plays. It is about the only thing that has come down to me from those early days—it amuses me now.

In October of 1868 I helped disrupt the old "Blue Mont Literary Debating Society" of the College, of which I had been a zealous

[13] Homeopathists believe that a disease may be cured by treatment with drugs which produce in healthy individuals symptoms similar to those of the disease.

member since the beginning of my "College" days, and to found the Webster Society. There were six or eight of us dissafected who helped found this new Society [at this point Williston's handwriting is illegible, but a booklet of the Webster Literary Society published in 1914 gives the founders as: F. Hines, J. F. Johnson, M. R. Mudge, J. P. Shannon, C. O. Whedon, W. F. White, S. D. Huston, Sam Kimble, J. B. Reynolds, F. H. Wharton, A. J. White, S. W. Williston]. I suggested the name and drafted the constitution, working all one Sunday, Oct. 11, upon it. I am glad to say that the Society still flourishes.

CHAPTER 3

From Survey Rod to Fossils

IN FEBRUARY, 1869 [Williston continued], I had some hard words with my father, which I have always regretted and determined to leave home. I remember the day, Feb. 19, because I marked it in all my books. I fear that I was getting a little too wild and too fond of wild companions. We indulged in pranks to the annoyance of some of the College professors. They were not vicious, nor of evil habits, but I fear that if all had been known, my relations with the College might have been abruptly severed without my consent! for putting the President's buggy in the College Chapel, purloining some of the professors' chickens and frying them in the College, locking in some of the goody-goody students care [keepsakes?] of the college did not meet the faculty's approbation. In fact, the faculty had me under their surveillance for awhile though I was never called before that august body to answer for my sins—perhaps because I had two or three friends among their number, especially Professors Mudge and Lee. My "best girl" went back on me, and I thought nobody loved me any more!

And so with a few dollars that I managed to get, not very creditably I fear, tho' not really dishonestly, I packed up what few things I had and took the train for Junction City, a town of about a thousand inhabitants twenty miles west of Manhattan, to seek my fortune. A branch railroad was building there, the U. P. Southern Branch as it was then called, later the M. K. & T. I was too full of conceit for my own good. I felt sure the town was waiting to welcome me with open arms. A clerkship in a store was my ambition, because I could then wear my Sunday clothes every day and always have a clean collar, even if a paper one. I thought the height of affluence was to have two suits of clothes and two

pairs of suspenders! Strangely how little things will impress one—
Even yet, two pair of "galluses" seem a luxury to me!

But I was grievously disappointed in a very few days to find
that no one seemed eager to employ me. After several days of
fruitless applications, and my money all gone, I was perforce compelled to seek more humble employment. And this I found as a
laborer at $1.50 per diem, shovelling dirt for the buttress of a
bridge then building across the Smoky Hill River. I little dreamed
then how intimately the river was to be associated with my future
life [in fossil collecting]. I was but 17 years old and not very
vigorous, weighing about 140 pounds. The bridge foreman after
a few days gave me a lighter job, pumping water with a hand pump
from a coffer dam of one of the piers. But, this was a very monot-
onous and dirty job, and I fear that I "loafed on it." Suffice it to
say that after a few days of it I was very peremptorily "fired" by
the foreman, and my dismissal was accompanied by some very
lurid remarks about my worthlessness by the foreman—and he
was something of an artist in profanity. His name was Kitchen,
of whom more later.

Thoroughly disheartened and ready to cry, after the first feeling
of anger, I picked up my tin dinner bucket and started back to the
town. As I walked through the main street of the town in my muddy
clothes and with my dinner pail, a sudden impulse for which I
could never account, turned me into the office of the Chief Engineer,
Mr. A. P. Robinson. Perhaps it may seem incredible, but as a boy
I was always shy and timid in the presence of men, especially of
men whom I thought belonged to a higher class in society than
my father's family. I remember the incident very clearly now.
As I stood before his desk he looked up in some curiosity and asked
me what he could do for me, in a rather stern voice. I was tempted
to turn tail and run, but I managed to stammer out, "Do you want
a clerk?" I suspect that the singularity of the request aroused his
interest, and that he would have answered my request with a curt
No had I appeared more boldly and in conventional clothes. He
began questioning me and I told him that I had left College at
Manhattan to earn some money. He seemed especially curious to

know why I left school, and what I had studied. I almost feared that he guessed the real truth—that I had run away from home. However, after some questions he surprised and delighted me by telling me that he would want a clerk in about two weeks and that I might try the place. But he advised me to go back home and wait till he wrote me. In later years I recognized clearly that Mr. Robinson took a human interest in me, and wanted to put me on the right road. He knew too well what the dangers were in that town, with all its roughness and disorder for a boy in a tough boarding house.

I left his office the happiest boy in the State of Kansas. I did not have quite enough money to pay my board bill, so I left my valise with my landlord,—and walked back to Manhattan, twenty-one miles. During the next week or two I bragged, I fear over much of my high prospects as clerk to the Chief Engineer of the Southern Branch Railroad. But two weeks went by and no letter came. My heart went way down in my boots. I thought that all Mr. Robinson wanted was an excuse to send me home. And I had many explanations to make to my friends to whom I had boasted. The ridicule was so much that I kept out of the way.

My hopes were about gone when the Postmaster one day gave me a letter, with an expression of regret that the letter had been in the office nearly a week but had been lost in a crack. He knew how anxiously I had been waiting for it. He was the former editor, Mr. Pillsbury, under whom I had started to learn the trade of a printer.

With a few dollars that my brother gave me I took the next train for Junction City, only to find that the much desired clerkship had been given to a college mate, who had applied for the position with influence to back him. However, Mr. Robinson gave me a place as axman in the construction corps of the first division with a salary of thirty-four dollars a month. Mr. Walker, whom I many years later knew at Lawrence, was the division engineer. In a few weeks the second division of twelve miles was put in charge of a young engineer just from Union College, Mr. Carpenter, with Bob Freeman as rodman and me as axman. Bob had been sent from

New York to get him out of the way of temptations. With but little education and no ambition to advance he shirked his work, which so far as possible was transferred to me. He held the rod during the day and I spent the evenings with Carpenter doing the office work that was properly his duty. Mr. Carpenter after a month or two on his return from a visit to Junction City, reported that we were to take charge of the third division in addition, and for the extra work we were to receive extra pay. This was good news to Bob and me, and we or rather I willingly undertook the extra work—out in the field at day-light, staking out earthwork and stringers and working till late at night in the office. Unfortunately, when pay day came around we found to our disappointment that only Mr. Carpenter's salary had been increased.

On the completion of the work on the second division, Mr. Carpenter was ordered to go to the fifth division, and another engineer, Mr. Pinney, was placed in charge of the third. I mustered courage one day, when Mr. Robinson was at our camp, to ask to be transferred to Mr. Pinney's party, a request that was granted for both Freeman and myself. Mr. Pinney was an older man and [an] able and experienced engineer, an Oxford man. Unfortunately, his love for the bottle had prevented the advancement that his ability would otherwise have secured for him. Finding my eagerness to learn he willingly resigned into my hands so far as possible the work of the division, overseeing and directing my work. With transit and level Bob and I staked out the earthwork for cuts and fills and laid out the buttresses for stringers and breasts, and with Mr. Pinney did the office work. I was grateful for the opportunity.

It happened a little later that Mr. Robinson suddenly resigned his place as chief to take charge of a new road building between Little Rock and Fort Smith, Arkansas, and a general manager, Mr. Stephens, was appointed to take charge of the S. B. Mr. Stephens was not an engineer, who was to be appointed later. Almost immediately after his assumption of the control of the S. B. he appeared at our camp in some excitement and called for Mr. Pinney. Mr. Pinney unfortunately was away for a few days.

I hardly knew where, but I told Mr. Stephens that he had been called to see his family in Leavenworth. It appeared that by over-sight or negligence $300,000 in bonds voted by the adjoining county Morrison would lapse unless the track was laid within its line by a certain date, which was only a few days away. A few rods from the county line, a small bridge, or rather a 30-foot stringer had not been begun or even staked out. When he found that the next engineer was thirty miles away, after a little vigorous language, he suddenly asked Bob and me if we could lay out the stone work for the stringer. I would never have presumed to do it myself, but Bob promptly replied yes we would lay it out immediately. Where-upon, Mr. Stephens drove away telling us that a large force of men would be there the next morning and we must have the stakes driven ready for them! I was bewildered and indignant at Bob, but when Bob told me we could do it, I realized that if the work was not ready for the men we would all get fired. We might as well try anyway, for if we failed there would be nothing worse than discharge. I spent most of the night in our tent making the plans. Mr. Pinney had taught me to draw plans, and I had a set of instruments I had just bought. It was a very simple piece of work, merely the computation of the batter, but I was only a boy yet, and was overwhelmed with my responsibility and the knowl-edge of the certainty of my discharge if I failed. However before breakfast next morning Bob and I were at the ravine with transit and level and the work was ready for the men when they appeared. Suffice it to say that the bonds were saved and I was called to Junction City to lay out some town sites.

However, most of the engineer corps of the S. B. had followed Mr. Robinson to Arkansas, and I too asked for a position with him. He promptly told me to report to Little Rock, Arkansas, to take a rodman's place with Mr. Pinney in the third division of the L. R. & F. S. R. R. [Little Rock and Fort Smith Rail Road] at $75. a month. I returned home then for a couple of weeks vacation, and then left for Little Rock in December. The journey by way of St. Louis and the Mississippi river to Little Rock was an event-ful one for me, for it was the first time in my memory that I had seen a town of more than two or three thousand people. I was charged to bring Mr. Pinney's dog with me! One incident, a boy's first experience in a city, I must relate. After buying my ticket and leaving the dog on the boat, I wandered about St. Louis to see the sights. I observed a museum of horrors that I decided to investigate. After looking about the room filled with waxwork criminal atrocities, I was invited, together with two other equally green appearing countrymen, to step into a private room back of the museum by the proprietor to see some things that were not usually shown to the ordinary sightseers. Then he did show us some vile waxworks, but pretty soon he drew us to a show case filled with a marvellous display of wealth in bills and coins. He explained to us a system by which any one could become wealthy by investing a few dollars. I had been taught to be distrustful of such things, but still I was curious. But one of the "greenies" became greatly excited. He invested a dollar and won ten by the shake of the dice. Again he tried it and won another ten. The third time he proposed to go halves with me for the grand prize of $2,000, and this time I agreed and put up two dollars and a half. And sure enough, it won the $2,000 prize! For just a few minutes I thought I was rich, and all sorts of visions of wealth appeared before my eyes. Unfortunately, the proprietor explained that there was a commission of 10% due him. I expostulated but he was firm and I seized the bunch of bills and was about to count out his two hundred dollars when he reminded me that the prize was not my property till I had paid the commission. The "greenie" then became eager for me to advance the whole $200, and even began to search my pockets for the money. Fortunately, I had spent nearly all that I had for my ticket to Little Rock, and they had no further use for me. $2.50 was what my experience cost me! But, had I visited the museum before I had bought my ticket I do not know where I would have spent the night! I have always since thought that my experience was cheap. I was not so trustful of strangers after that.

When I reached Mr. Pinney's camp 24 miles out of Little Rock in the Palamie Bayou I found Bob Freeman there also, only he was now axman and I was rodman. And we had a third assistant in Mike Mengher as teamster and chainman.

I liked Pinney because he helped me to learn the profession which I had now decided was to be my life's work, but I can hardly be grateful to him for his influence. To celebrate our re-union he had the contractors of the division in that evening. I had been reared with an abhorrence of liquor by my mother. I hardly knew its taste yet, though I had occasionally indulged in a glass of beer at Junction City. But he had prepared a large bowl of punch and it seemed good to me that evening, and before the night was over I was drunk—for the first and last time in my life. I rather liked the experience and for the next month or two I began to get a liking for whiskey. The day before I left Manhattan I visited my old friends and teachers at the College, to bid them good bye. As I parted with Professor James H. Lee whom I loved with Professor Mudge most of all he took my hand, and with deep feeling said "May God Bless you, Williston." I thought of those words one night as I lay in bed, and wondered whither I was going. What were my ambitions to become a famous man? I drank no more whiskey. I had been homesick, and my "best girl" had gone back on me and married. I saw her one afternoon in 1898 at Lawrence.

I was eager to be an engineer and studied all the books that I could get. And Mr. Pinney was as willing as before that I should relieve him of the more tiresome duties. Bob, Mike and I staked out the earthwork and gave grades and lines for the contractors, only calling upon Mr. Pinney for advice, or for the more difficult [stone] work. About a mile from this camp there was a long marsh that required a half mile or more of trestle-work. One morning we received notice at camp that a contractor was there with a force of men to begin work upon the backs or foundation and wanted lines and grades. Bob, Mike and I appeared on the scene with our instruments, and after staking out sufficient work for several days, I turned to the contractor who had been watching and chatting with us and said, "Mr. Kitchen, I guess you don't remember me?" "No, where have I seen you before?" "At the coffer dam in the

31

Smoky Hill just a year ago," I replied. "***—was that you?" "'Tis," I said, "shake." We were good friends. He thought I was the engineer in charge of the division!

There was comment, I heard later, along the line about the way Pinney was running his division. One day, along in April or May, Mr. Robinson in his light Concord wagon and negro driver appeared at our camp and asked for Bob and me. Mr. Pinney was anxious to serve Mr. Robinson, but he replied there was nothing but what Williston and Freeman could do as well. He told us to bring level and rod and drove with us a few miles up the line and then told us he wanted us to test some levels. From the location notes he directed Bob to a "bench mark" nearby and told us to run the levels along the completed earthwork. He drove along the hump and took our readings of the rod as I called them out to him. I was greatly worried, for I had not adjusted my level as recently as I should have done, and so, as soon as I was out of earshot of Mr. Robinson I impressed upon Bob the necessity of care, and in pacing his turning points in order that any errors of adjustment in the level would be counterbalanced by foresights and hindsights. I levelled my instrument with great care. After a mile or two another Bench was reached upon which Bob held his rod, and called out the elevation. Mr. Robinson figured a few minutes and then put his notebook in his pocket and told us to get in the wagon. I was too tired to question him, but he gave us cigars and seemed in good spirits. We drove back to camp where he left us without any explanations.

His actions puzzled me much and Bob and I discussed for several days what the "Old Man" wanted. I began to suspect after a while that he wasn't testing the location survey so much as he was testing me and my work, and I was anxious for awhile, fearing that I might be discharged. I had nearly forgotten the incident in a few weeks when I was ordered to report to Mr. Carpenter, my old engineer, on the sixth division.

This was very unwelcome news for I didn't like Carpenter. Like myself, he was too conceited I thought. I was tempted to resign, but I hadn't saved much money and was too proud to go home.

32

And so I obeyed orders. We got along very well, however, but I didn't have as much freedom as with Mr. Pinney.

In a few weeks I received an order to report at the location camp up the line to take charge of the level with $100. a month and expenses. Major Preyer, the locating engineer, was a stern disciplinarian, and my lot for a while was not a happy one, especially as I was ill part of the time with malaria. However, his reports of me must have been favorable, for in about a month, Mr. Brown, the transitman, was ordered to Van Buren on a preliminary survey, and I was promoted to his place with $125. a month and all expenses, equivalent to $150. It was just sixteen months from the time I had applied for a job on the S. B. at Junction City and I was not yet nineteen years old. A young Cuban, Mr. Escobar, took my place at the level.

I remained as transitman till November, surveying the line thru to Van Buren, when we were ordered to return to Russel to make some changes in the line, and do some construction work. Meanwhile, my health had suffered greatly from malaria in all its forms. I weighed less than 135 pounds. Discouraged and worn out, I resigned in December. I had not saved much money, some I sent home to my mother, some I loaned never to get it back, and the rest of it I had spent thoughtlessly. I was paid my last two months' salary in small bills, and at the suggestion of a merchant in Russelville, I exchanged the most of it to large bills only to find a few days later when I reached Van Buren that they were counterfeit. I reached home in utterly broken health, and at Junction City I had to borrow enough money to pay my railroad fare to Manhattan. I finally, after months, recovered $50. of the money I had thought was lost for good.

[A journal kept by Williston during his year in Arkansas gives a revealing picture of his youthful ambitions. Exposed to the typical relaxations of the surveying crew, he quickly decided not to participate in the often-heavy drinking parties, but he very much enjoyed the evening card games (not played for money, apparently). He began there his lifelong habit of smoking, first with a pipe and occasionally cigars. On Sundays he liked to hike the countryside, where he learned new shrubs and trees, and he sent specimens back to Mudge. He also read a great deal, finishing most of the works of Sir Walter Scott and Charles Dickens, and sadly he noted the death of Dickens that year. He matured enough to accept philosophically the marriage of the girl he thought he loved. The most unfortunate consequence of his year in Arkansas was contracting malaria, some thirty years before the role of the mosquito was known. It plagued him with chills irregularly for the rest of his life.

But the most remarkable theme of that year's journal was his ever-recurring yearning to return to college. Typical of the entries, often no doubt influenced by the style of the authors he was reading, was his cry of June 30: "O happy happy days of student life, may they hasten speedily & passing quickly & joyously fit me to take an exalted place before the world to battle for fame & wealth."]

I was too ill [he continued in "Recollections"] to do much, but went back to college for a few months and then went with my brothers to Cowley County, Kansas, where they had taken claims in the newly opened land. I recovered my health sufficiently to return to school the following autumn, graduating in March, 1872, with the degree of B. S. because I did not feel sufficiently interested in Plato and Herodotus to make up the back work necessary for the degree of A. B.

The previous autumn some merchants of Manhattan had undertaken to promote the building of a railroad from Manhattan to Lincoln, Nebraska. Just why a local company should have undertaken so large an enterprise I do not know, but I suspect it was largely to get control of the best right of way for future control. An engineer had been employed to make some preliminary surveys. It was a hasty survey, with high sounding plans, to impress the people. As the only person in the village who knew the least about railroad location I helped a little in the field work. But the engineer did not take kindly to the plans and resigned in the spring. An attempt was made to secure some one else to take charge of the work, but the inducements were not very great for a really

Samuel Wendell Williston

Williston's mother, Jane Augusta Turner Williston, in 1882.

Williston's father, Samuel Williston, about 1880.

Benjamin Franklin Mudge, professor of sciences and "natural philosophy" at Kansas State Agricultural College. Caption on back of original reads "Taken on his first visit to Lawrence after severe sickness."

Harry A. Brous, Williston's field partner when he began hunting fossils for Mudge and the man who interested Williston in entomology, in a picture taken about 1874.

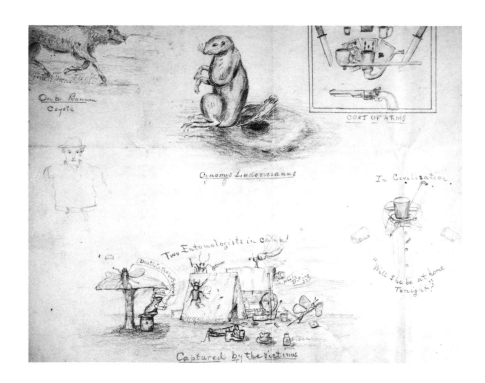

A page from a sketchbook Williston kept on the plains in 1875.

Buffalo Park in western Kansas, where rival fossil hunters met in peace to share good water, as sketched by Williston in 1877.

O. C. Marsh, about 1880.

Annie Isabel Hathaway, about the time she met Williston in the early 1880's.

Connecticut Board of Health in 1887 or 1888.

A syrphid fly, *Milesia virginiensis,* in a photo from the third edition of Williston's *Manual of North American Diptera.*

Francis Huntington Snow, about 1896.

Williston in the field in western Kansas in 1891, checking his watch. "As you know we dont wear broadcloth out here."

Geological Survey of Kansas, Vol. 4, Paleontology, Pl. 69, 1898.

Skin impression of *Tylosaurus proriger*, found somewhere in Kansas about 1891, in a picture taken by Williston.

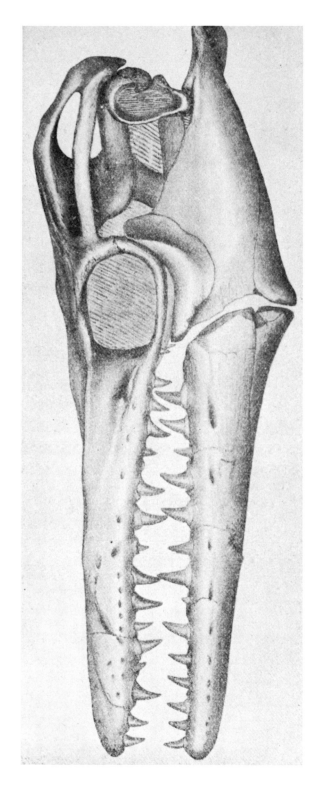

Mosasaurus horridus Williston, one of the group of reptiles that Williston studied in detail.

49

E. C. Case in the field in 1891.

competent engineer. I lamented my youth, for I was conceited enough to think that I might have been chosen for the position had I been a little older. It was not to be supposed that a boy of 20 would do to take whole charge of so important an enterprise as the "Blue Valley Railroad!" However, a young man from abroad was employed to begin the work, and I was instructed to make up a party for the location. In a few days I trained two of my college classmates, C. O. Whedon and Albert Todd, the former later a prominent attorney of Lincoln, Nebraska, the latter an officer in the U. S. Army, to handle the level and rod, while I took charge of the transit. During the spring of 1872 we located the line as far as Beatrice, Neb. where the party was disbanded and the engineer resigned, and I was called back to superintend the construction of the first part of the road, for a few miles out of Manhattan. Affairs were in a doubtful condition when in November I sought a settlement of what was owing me for salary. For several months past I had been getting such things as I needed and small sums of money from the store of the "President" of the road, Mr. Purcell. They refused to pay me what had been agreed upon, $75 a month, telling me that a few months before the "Board of Directors" had reduced my salary to $65. a month, but through an oversight had neglected to inform me of the fact! There was a difference of thirty dollars between us and that method of business vexed me. It happened, however, that I had in my possession all the engineering notes on the construction work, grades and plans, so I concluded I would take a little vacation—I had had none for nearly a year, previously taking the precaution, however, of securely hiding my note-books in a hay-stack. There was consternation when I did not show up in camp on Monday morning, to lay out work for the laborers, some fifty or more. I tramped out into the country to visit my friend. C. O. Whedon had been a student of law the previous winter at Ann Arbor. The sheriff was promptly sent after me, and demanded permission of my landlady to go to my room after my books, which she reluctantly conceded. There were many dire threats as to what would be done to me, even intimations of the penitentiary. But Whedon had told me that a civil process was all that they could do, but that they could seize the books whenever found. I told the officers they were welcome to the books, if they could find them, but that I would deliver them only on the payment of my salary, to which the secretary finally agreed. I waited till the office was clear and no sheriff in sight and with one hand received the thirty dollars and with the other delivered the books! The company went into bankruptcy soon after.

And this was my experience as a civil engineer, a little less than three years. The panic of 1872 and 1873 was then on. I sought in various places for a job, but railroad work had ceased everywhere in the United States, and better engineers than I were idle. I had very little money left after paying my bills, some of them for the previous winter when I was a student, and "bached" it. I went to southern Kansas where the family was, and spent the winter, earning a few dollars playing at country dances. It was in the latter part of November of that year that I went with a local party of young men a hundred miles or so west on a buffalo hunt.

Early the following spring I returned to Manhattan and began the study of medicine with our old family physician, Dr. Patee. There seemed to be no opportunity to follow engineering, and by this time I had become a little tired of the prospects and its continuous change. I wanted more opportunity for study. I remember about this time that my sister Eva once asked me why I studied so much. I told her that it was my ambition to be the "most learned man in the State of Kansas"!

Ever since I was a child and had been so interested in "Beach's Family Doctor" I had been ambitious to be a physician, and had constantly the vision before my eyes of a shingle over my doorway with "S. W. Williston, M. D. Physician and Surgeon" inscribed upon it! Just how I was to become a doctor I had little idea, but my mother encouraged me, and Dr. Patee had often told me he would take me as a student. In those days the student of medicine "read" in some preceptor's office for three years, meanwhile taking two courses of lectures of four or six months each, the second merely a repetition of the first, before coming up for his degree.

And so, in April, 1873, I began the study in Dr. Patee's office, boarding in the house two miles away at the farm. There it was my duty to compound the doctor's prescriptions in his little pharmacy and keep his books, and "hold down" the office in his absence. I had the free use of his library, with but very little advice or direction in my reading, except that I was told to study anatomy and physiology first. By excavating an old Indian burial ground in the vicinity, I got a collection of bones, and perhaps chiefly because of that collection I am now chiefly an osteologist. I had no money and but few clothes. A few dollars I picked up in one way or another to pay for my tobacco and clean collars—paper collars, but the next two years were very hard.

And yet things might have been easier had I chosen. In 1873 Professor Kedzie, a young man, was appointed to take charge of Chemistry [at the Agricultural College]. He established a laboratory, the first of any kind that I had ever seen. I became deeply interested in it and entered it as a graduate student, spending my afternoons there for several months, in qualitative analysis,—and I had almost decided to become a professional chemist when an incident occurred that put an end to such aspirations.

Not a little dissatisfaction had arisen in the state about the College. Nominally the Agricultural College it was still practically the Classical College that it had been when under Methodist control. Here and there innovations had been made, as concessions, a "professor of agriculture," etc., but in reality the ancient languages were still the chief part of the curriculum. In 1873 President Dennison who had served from the foundation of the institution was peremptorily dismissed and the Rev. Mr. Anderson was installed in his place. There can be no doubt but that he made many salutory changes in the policy of the institution, tho' it is much to be feared that Mr. Anderson's motives were more political than educational. The languages were abolished, even German and French, and industrial training was made a permanent feature of the school. All these changes caused much hard feeling and bitter opposition on the part of the old regime and their friends. Of all the teachers remaining none was more deeply respected and beloved than Professor Bj. F. Mudge, the professor of the sciences. Anderson was much opposed to him as a friend of Dennison and seized the first pretext that was offered, a day's absence from his duties—to summarily and arbitrarily dismiss him. Not knowing that he had been dismissed I accepted an invitation to teach his classes, for the short time that [I] supposed he was to be absent. In a few days, however, we learned of the summary action of President Anderson. I joined in a mass meeting of the students, as its chairman, to protest vigorously against his dismissal. We locked and barred the chapel door and drew up some vigorous resolutions. Professor Kedzie had urged me to keep out of the trouble, hinting that I might be appointed permanently in Mudge's place if I kept still. But my love for Prof. Mudge was too great to see him disgraced with equanimity. I was requested next day to confer with the Faculty and explain my action. I did and was relieved by the president from further duties! I left the building very angry. As I left the building I turned and shook my fist, and said, "Some day you will want me and can't get me." You see I had plenty of self-confidence! Sixteen years later I declined an urgent invitation to join its faculty! [And forty years later, according to his daughter, he refused to consider an appointment as president.]

In the spring of 1874 I was elected the first president of the K.S.A.C. Alumni, and chose for my address a tirade against the study of the ancient languages.

Meanwhile, I had become an enthusiastic disciple of the Darwinian doctrine. The works of Darwin whose Descent of Man had recently appeared, of Huxley, Tyndall, and especially one by a German author Buechner, I absorbed with delight. From the reading [of] Lyell's Antiquity of Man years before I was already prepared to accept the theme of evolution. In my study of human anatomy the many anatomical anomalies that I had hunted out, represented by normal structures in other animals, had been a conclusive proof. I accepted Darwinism as a demonstrated fact and was, I fear, more or less impatient with those who denied its truth. And because of my rather bold exposition of the doctrine, I acquired a sort of obloquy from the staid, orthodox people of the village. For years past, I had been very fond of debating societies, and in the village society of which I was a member, I tried one evening to sustain the side of Evolution from some rather sneering criticisms that came up incidentally. Perhaps because of the earnestness with which I spoke I was invited to deliver a lecture at the next meeting on the subject, an invitation that I accepted with utmost pleasure. With the cocksureness of youth, my address lacked neither in positive and dynamic statements I doubt not. It was given in the Congregational Church, and was the first public lecture I believe ever given west of the Mississippi River in favor of Evolution! in February, 1874. Few can realize at the present day the ridicule and opposition with which the Darwinian theory was received in those days. Few, very few periodicals dared to uphold it or apologize for it. Nevertheless, I was a little shocked at the severe criticism I received for my lecture in the next number of the village paper, and in the pulpits.

Professor Mudge in 1872 and 1873 had extended his geological explorations in western Kansas. In 1872 he had found the famous specimen of Ichthyornis, which suddenly brought Professor [Marsh] fame. Almost by pure accident he sent the specimen to Prof. Marsh, rather than to Professor Cope, for whom he had intended it. [Actually, Marsh had written to Mudge asking about his summer's collecting and offering to identify specimens for him.] Upon the severance of his relations with the Agricultural College, Professor Marsh promptly engaged him to collect fossils in western Kansas for Yale College. He left in May [1874] taking with him from Clay Center a young man as teamster and assistant. They collected in northwestern Kansas for a few weeks. But the chalk outcrops in the more settled regions were not extensive, and Mudge determined to go south to the Smoky Hill Valley. He reckoned without his host, however, for his assistant refused to go because of his fear of the Indians who were more or less rampant in those regions. He [Mudge] therefore wrote to one of his former students who had just graduated at the college, Harry A. Brous, and who was an enthusiastic collector of beetles and other natural history specimens. He told him to get a team and outfit and drive out to where he would wait for him. As the way was long and dreary, about 175 miles, he told him to get some one to accompany him, who might return as soon as they reached the railroad, and suggested me. Brous and I had long been chums. He had determined to study medicine and used frequently to drop in my office on his way home to discuss plans and ambitions. Upon the receipt of Mudge's letter in the latter part of June he invited me to accompany him. I gladly accepted the opportunity, for it had been now nearly two years since I had had any camp life. I was engaged to play a concert in a band of which I was a member in a fourth of July celebration. We left on the fifth. It was this accidental and thoughtless decision that led to my life's devotion to Paleontology! Had I not gone with him in all probability today I would have been practitioner of medicine somewhere in Kansas! We joined Mudge about the 14th and started almost immediately south. In a few days I found a good specimen of a pterodactyl and became an enthusiastic lover of the "sport" of collecting fossils— for sport it seemed to me.

I had planned that autumn to borrow a couple of hundred dollars and go east to a Medical College. And so I returned to Manhattan by rail in September, but did not succeed in getting the necessary funds. Mudge thereupon asked me to return, which I did, about the first of October, and remained till we all returned in late November. It was in October of this year that I had my first real experience of the plains by getting lost on Hackberry Creek. I slept out a couple of nights, with nothing to eat and with a constant serenade of the coyotes and wolves, finally reaching the station 25 miles north pretty thoroughly exhausted. I thought that the Indians had captured Mudge and Brous. They thought that the Indians had scalped me! But they turned up safely the next day.

[From this time on Williston never liked "the sneaking, disreputable, cowardly, and in general abominable, coyote." Years later he told the Geographical Society of Chicago: "I once spent a night, long years ago, lost and alone, far out on the plains, surrounded by a hungry pack of these cheerful imps and I have never forgotten them. If all the coyotes now in existence could be corralled on the top of Mount Pélé, and I could start off the old volcano just long enough to annihilate them it would give me glee."[1]

For my season's work Mudge paid me $25, which bought me a suit of clothes and other things sadly needed. My total cash income this year was not more than $50; it was the hardest year of my life. My board I worked for in part, in part I had it from my parents, but I did not have a second whole shirt and when I gave my address [on evolution or to the K.S.A.C. alumni?] I had to borrow clothes to wear, for my clothes were ragged and patched.

Times now began to improve. Professor Marsh and Professor Cope as is well known were rivals and very jealous of each other. They had been quarrelling with each other for two or three years, with mutual criminations and recriminations. Because of the discoveries Marsh was making in the Cretaceous of Kansas, Cope grew eager to participate in these, but could find no one to undertake these collections, but Marsh was afraid to have too many learn about the region for fear that Cope would seduce some of the assistants by the offer of higher pay. He therefore instructed Mudge to retain his assistants of the previous summer. Brous and I were engaged for the following season at $35. a month and our expenses. We accepted the offer gladly and started for the field ourselves in early March [1875], meeting Mudge at Ellis on the railroad. We stipulated that [we] should quit in September to allow medical lectures.

It was this season that an incident occurred that I have often related, but will bear repeating. It was in the latter part of May. Prof. Mudge had forgotten his handpick one Saturday afternoon while working in an exposure or "slide" as we called them—about three miles south of the Smoky Hill River, a little west of south of Trego. Sunday morning he directed Brous and myself to drive our ponies and light half-spring wagon for three or four miles till we found a suitable camping place and then wait for him. [A sketch map was in the manuscript here, to which the following letters refer.]

[1] "The Great Plains," *University of Chicago School of Science and Mathematics*, Vol. VI, No. 8 (November, 1906), 649.

We stopped under a low bank (B) and waited for an hour or more till we thought it about time for Mudge to show up. Looking in his direction (D), we could see nothing of him, but, a few miles off to the south in the divide (E) we did see something that excited our deepest interest, what appeared to be thirty or forty horsemen, riding loosely. We hoped at first that they were soldiers from Fort Wallace, sixty or seventy miles to the west. They occasionally scouted over the plains for Indians, but it had been several weeks since we had seen the last. But the disorderly array of the horsemen immediately convinced us that they [were] Indians on a foray from the south. Watching them without much concern for ourselves, we were soon horrified to see Mudge appear around a low hill to the west. We knew only too well Mudge's absent mindedness. We each of us carried our Smith & Wesson 45 revolver on all our tramps, and in addition much of the time a Spencer or Sharp's rifle, but Mudge had gone off that morning without any arms, and it would have mattered little had he had a revolver, for he stood about as much in danger from it himself as would any enemy. We saw that he would soon appear in the open plain in sight of the Indians and our anxiety became intense. What we should do we did not know, but we decided that if we did nothing Mudge would surely lose his scalp. We were not quite as brave as it might appear, for long experience in the borders of civilization had taught us the habits of the Indians pretty thoroughly. We knew that such forays as the present were merely for game or marauding. We knew that they will kill wantonly for the sake of booty, but that like most other people they were not inclined to expose their own lives recklessly, with little to gain thereby. Furthermore we knew that with our rifles we were in no great danger from poorly armed Indians. Nevertheless we did not feel entirely comfortable. We opened up the mess chest and got out all the cartridges we had, rifle and revolver, and there were plenty for we had only recently reloaded all our shells. Mr. Brous took the reins with a rifle by his side, and I got in the top of the bedding back of him with another rifle. Our revolvers we always belted on when we arose in the morning and took off only as we went to bed. And we started to intercept Mudge at full gallop. For about a half mile or more we had to cross a low valley of a ravine out of sight, both of the Indians and of Mudge. When we drove up on the opposite side, we found that Mudge and the Indians had stopped and were parlying at some distance. And we were delighted also to see that there [were] only eleven Indians in the party, the remainder being loose ponies they had stolen, and apparently not a single rifle among them. They were armed with bows and arrows only.

They were a party of Apaches from the Indian Territory accoutred in primitive Indian fashion with skins and bows and arrows, and with an extremely limited English vocabulary. But that vocabulary included three words that every Indian early learned, "Whiskey," "tobacco," and "How?" After much gesticulating and protestations of peace we all met. And their first demand was for whiskey and tobacco. All that we had of a spirituous nature was a quart bottle of alcohol half filled with beetles, and I was the only one who used tobacco in the party and I was not disposed to part with my limited supply and go without myself till we should visit the station a couple of weeks later. So, I kept very quiet about it. Mudge, however, who stood by the wagon, after repeatedly shaking his head and reiterating "No tobac" thoughtlessly took out his false upper teeth to show that he did not use the weed. Were I to live for a hundred years yet I should not forget the excitement and consternation that this action produced among those wild men of the plains. That any man could take his teeth out of his mouth was to them as a miracle would [be] to us. They discussed the matter earnestly among themselves for a long while all of them on their ponies crowding close to the professor, who, however prudently kept close to the wagon. They tried to work the teeth in their own mouths, a proceeding provocative of much laughter among them, and by many signs tried to learn why all his teeth were movable, for by this time he had also removed his lower teeth for their inspection.

When their curiosity had been satisfied so far as it was possible to satisfy it, the leader of the party drew a small copper medal attached by a leather thong about his neck for Mudge's inspection. How he had come by it I do not know, probably from some government agent. On it was engraved "Little Dog Chief." The professor naturally took out his spectacles to read it, and again the simple red men were filled with astonishment for they probably had never seen such things before. It must be remembered that in their limited intercourse with the whites in those days they had come in contact only with young men, pioneers in the west. They had to try these also with many comments. A wild Indian clad in a breech cloth, skin leggings, mocassins [sic], feathers and spectacles was a sight to make a horse laugh. The whole scene is so vividly impressed upon my memory that when I am asked I can now picture [it] in every detail.

By this time we were all in good spirits and [I] relented so far as to give them my tobacco, and went without myself for a week! We parted with many protestations of peace and good will on their part, which would have left better impression on us had they not surprised a party of cowboys the next morning and captured their ponies and scalps. So we were told later. We did not sleep much that night.

We collected chiefly along the Smoky Hill Valley that season [1875], as far west as Fort Wallace, and got many valuable specimens. One other incident of the season is deeply impressed upon my memory. This time Brous and Mudge got lost in the vicinity of Monument Rocks. It was my work to drive and care for the team, Brous doing the camp work. They left me after breakfast with instructions to go around the head of the canyon and meet them at the first exposures east. But they strayed to the north on Hackberry Creek, while I was hunting for them in the east. As the evening approached I drove to the top of the divide and unhitched and got on one of the ponies and rode everywhere I thought they could be. They saw the horseman from a hidden place a mile or two away, and when I fired my revolver a time or two to attract their attention, they concluded that I was an indian and hid themselves till dark, when they started afoot for the railroad 30 miles north. At nightfall, becoming alarmed I built a fire on the divide from such wood as I could gather, and went away a few hundred yards and tried to sleep with the halter straps of the ponies fastened to my wrists. I was afraid of the Indians also. Abandoning my search the next morning I drove to Buffalo Park, 35 miles, and got there just a little time before Mudge and Brous appeared on a freight train from the west. They had reached Monument Station where there was no telegraph station and waited for the first train to take them east, there to organize a party to hunt for me!

The last 18 miles I had ridden on horseback, leaving the other pony to follow. But he did not follow. I started out the next morning to find him, thoughtlessly without water, expecting to get him in an hour or two. The thermometer was 106 in the shade. I wandered all that day till four in the afternoon till I turned up where I had left the wagon at a water hole, about 4 in the afternoon. It is a day that stands out from all others in my life, as a day of suffering. I returned the next day in a rain, without the pony, which did not turn up for several months.

That closed our season's work in mid-September. My six months' wages netted me $195 and Brous $205, for he did not use tobacco! We bought a pony of Mr. Chas. Sternberg who had been collecting that season in the region and travelled overland to Manhattan and thence Brous and I almost immediately to the University of Iowa for our first course of medical lectures.

Up to this time I had always been rather slender in bodily stature never weighing more than 160 pounds. When I reached Iowa City I weighed less than 150. On the first day of January following I weighed 190. We got board and lodging with Billy Green the janitor for $3.50 a week, but even those moderate terms left not a great surplus to invest in a new suit of clothes made necessary by my increased girth. I was absolutely penniless when the term ended on the 19th of March [1876].

That season by Marsh's directions we had each signed his name to the specimens he had collected. Perhaps that was the reason why he invited me in February to come to New Haven. I promptly accepted his invitation, and sold my watch and borrowed enough to take me there, in March.

[Williston apparently never knew of Mudge's recommendation to Marsh. In reply to a query from Marsh, Mudge wrote on October 3, 1875: "In relation to an assistant 'capable of making Science a study,' I think Mr. S. W. Williston will answer your purpose. He was a student in some of my classes for several years and has taken his degree of A. B. He is 24 years old, and has just gone to attend medical lectures at Chicago [actually at Iowa]. He excels in Mathematics and the Natural Sciences. Has not paid much attention to paleontology till the past year or a little more, but is now quite interested in comparative anatomy. He has said to me that he only made medicine a study, hoping to become a professor of Natural Science. He made all the drawings which were sent you this summer."[2]]

I had lived practically all my life [Williston continued] where either scientific men and authors were almost unknown. I had always been a book worm of the most accentuated type. I had grown to reverence, almost to worship the writers of books, and especially of scientific books, as ideals of [the] way I would like to be myself. Such men as Huxley, Darwin, Dana, Gray and Marsh were my ideals of all that was great and good. I thought them impeccable and almost infallible. My greatest ambition was to follow humbly in their footsteps—to write a book sometime myself and to make discoveries. Of my first attempt at writing for publication, when I was fourteen years old, I have already written. While in Arkansas I had occasionally written letters to the local Manhattan paper, and that season on the plains I had written for the Kansas City and Topeka papers, becoming almost a regular contributor to the Star. It was in one of these papers while I was at Iowa City that I urged the founding of a medical school at the Kansas State University that I helped twenty years later to realize.

It was thus with feelings almost of awe that I met Professor

[2] Charles Schuchert and Clara M. LeVene, *O. C. Marsh: Pioneer in Paleontology,* 184.

Marsh for the first time at New Haven on March 19 or 20, 1876. My heart was in my mouth when I knocked at the basement door of the old Treasury Building, and heard the not very pleasant invitation to "come in." There was a frown on Marsh's face, accentuated by his nearsightedness, as he waited for me to state my business. No doubt he thought me a wild and woolly westerner in my military cloak, slouch hat and cowboy boots as I stammered my name. But he quickly made me feel more at ease.

CHAPTER 4

The Antagonists

WHO was this man who so awed the young Westerner? Othniel Charles Marsh was this country's first professor of paleontology, the man chiefly responsible for establishing a study of vertebrate fossils in American universities. His biographers, Charles Schuchert and Clara M. LeVene, say that Marsh amassed an outstanding collection of fossils, that he began many modern collecting techniques, that he trained many paleontologists, and that he provided valuable evidence to confirm Darwin's theory of evolution. Marsh's major paleontological contributions were in fossil horses, toothed birds, dinosaurs, very early and later fossil mammals. In character, he was strong-willed, suspicious, opinionated, and a law unto himself.

Marsh's beginnings were as humble as those of Williston, but his connections were excellent. He was born October 29, 1831, in Lockport, New York, where his father owned a farm. When Othniel was almost three years old, his mother died just after the birth of her second son, leaving also a daughter two years older than Othniel. Two years later their father remarried and tried several businesses before returning to farming. Othniel was expected to help with the farming, though he often slipped away to roam the fields and woods to hunt. The farm was only a mile from the Erie Canal, then but recently built and later widened. The construction exposed new minerals and a variety of invertebrate fossils—trilobites, crinoids, brachiopods, and bryozoans—which the young Marsh began to collect.

The most important influence on Marsh's life was his millionaire uncle, George Peabody, his mother's brother, who took an interest in Othniel's life from the moment the boy was ready for serious schooling. Peabody paid for his education at Phillips Academy at

Andover, where Othniel continued his interest in mineralogy and graduated as class valedictorian. It was then fairly easy for the young man to persuade his uncle to finance his college career at Yale, which he had chosen for its emphasis on science and its new Sheffield Scientific School.

Marsh's attachment to Yale continued for the rest of his life. He was one of the first graduate students in the Sheffield Scientific School, again thanks to his generous uncle. His chief interest was still mineralogy, but he had found some fossil vertebrate remains while hunting minerals in Nova Scotia, and he became much interested in these. Peabody, fully convinced by many favorable reports of the young man, paid Marsh's expenses on a museum tour of Europe and allowed him to purchase a library and a large number of paleontological and mineral specimens. While Marsh was gathering this material in Europe and studying, he also persuaded his benefactor that Yale desperately needed a proper museum for its scientific collections. The result was a gift of $150,000 to Yale by George Peabody for the Peabody Museum of Natural History. As a corollary of this gift, Marsh was offered a professorship at Yale, to be endowed from his uncle's gift, but without salary. Marsh's income came directly from his uncle for many years.

Upon his establishment at Yale as the country's first professor of paleontology in 1866, Marsh entered into a study of this country's fossils. He began with fossil mammals in New Jersey and with fossil footprints in the Connecticut Valley, but he soon heard reports of interesting discoveries in the West. His first trip west, a field trip after a meeting of the American Association for the Advancement of Science in August, 1868 (before the completion of the transcontinental railroad), was an eye-opener to the Easterner, and he vowed to devote himself to the geology of the great plains. On his brief trip he acquired from Antelope Station, Nebraska (Territory), fossil remains of eleven extinct vertebrates, one of them a miniature, three-toed horse—the first of the complete series he was to bring to light, thus helping to confirm Darwin's recent theory of evolution.

young professor looked at his meager collections from the ains and yearned for more. Funds for expeditions were as) find then as now, but Marsh conceived the idea of inviting Yale students and recent alumni to accompany him on collecting trips—at their own expense. The students were eager; George Bird Grinnell, who went on the first trip, said that none of them "had any motive for going other than the hope of an adventure with wild game or wild Indians."[1]

In the 1870's Indians still dominated the West enough to be considered, but Marsh arranged to have an Army escort accompany his party everywhere. Marsh's life was always simplified by his knowing the right people in Washington. On his expeditions he could count on obtaining supplies and troops at any Army post. Williston in later years made much of the fact that Marsh was always accompanied in the field by soldiers. Williston was a Westerner who looked upon the Indians as cowards and thieves; Marsh was an Easterner who looked upon the Indians as vicious savages. Both men were partly right for their period in history, but neither would have accepted the other's viewpoint. To justify Marsh's opinion, one need only read of the clashes between whites and Indians throughout the plains country during the 1860's and 1870's. Marsh was a cautious man.

He led four student trips from 1870 to 1873 and brought back, among the tons of material, the first known fragment of an American pterodactyl—from the Smoky Hill River in Kansas. He was especially interested in western Kansas because he had received from Mudge early in 1872 pieces of the first-known bird with teeth, which Marsh named *Ichthyornis dispar*. In the same summer Marsh's group found the second toothed bird, penguin-like *Hesperornis regalis*. These quickly publicized finds gave Marsh instant worldwide recognition.

He was never one to discourage publicity. His fame spread, and many people began sending him fossils. His acquaintances among the Army escorts proved valuable as occasional collectors and informants on new fossil localities. Buffalo hunters, frontiers-

[1] Schuchert and LeVene, *O. C. Marsh*, 100.

men, and scouts were useful too, and among these Marsh could hire collectors seasonally and locally. He paid their expenses readily, and some of them knew him through bison hunt and over campfire, where they had listened with fascination to his tales of extinct monsters.

But the quantity of material pouring into Yale's museum prevented Marsh from further fieldwork himself. He hired laboratory assistants to help him remove the fossils from the rock, and he hired steady collectors to work for him in the field, among whom was Benjamin F. Mudge.

Marsh's scientific life would have been quite different without another ambitious entry into the new field of paleontology, Edward Drinker Cope. Cope was a great naturalist, in the nineteenth-century style of Charles Darwin, Thomas Huxley, and Louis Agassiz. He was very probably a genius. His interests covered all of natural science, in all aspects of which he was a keen observer. He published extensively on fossil vertebrates, modern fishes, and modern reptiles and amphibians—and his work has stood the test of time. In temperament, he was jealous, resentful, and aggressive.

Edward was born July 28, 1840, on his father's farm near Philadelphia. Like Marsh's, this young boy's mother died when he was three years old. Eight years later Cope's father remarried. The Cope family was well off financially, its predecessors having done well in the young American colonies and having become public-minded philanthropists, in spite of some stigma in earlier generations in regard to their Tory views and adherence to the Society of Friends.

Edward's early education was in Quaker schools, and he continued in the Society, though with some soul-searching. He was very fond of the outdoors and showed an early, remarkable interest and ability in nature studies. For four years, at his father's urging, the young man worked on several kinds of farms, which taught him a great deal about plants and the local small animals, but he did not take to farming.

Through extensive reading, traveling to museums and institutions of this country, and studying briefly under Joseph Leidy at

University of Pennsylvania, Cope acquired the equivalent of ɔllege education. His father accepted his son's leanings toward natural history, provided him with the funds to buy many valuable books, and allowed him to take courses and visit museums as the young man chose. In 1863 and 1864 Edward toured the institutions of Europe, eager to meet the famous scientists whose books he had read. Marsh was completing his own education in Europe at the same time, and the two became acquainted.

On his return from Europe, Cope took a position as professor of zoology at Haverford College in Pennsylvania. He taught for three years, but he found himself not suited to it, as he simply wanted to be a naturalist. Such a situation took a considerable fortune, which at first Cope had.

Cope became interested in fossils while he continued his life-long interest in the lower vertebrates. He traveled throughout the eastern United States at first, collecting and publishing descriptions of fossil and modern vertebrates (plus a few invertebrates). He was then living in Haddonfield, New Jersey, one of the first areas of fossil vertebrates found in this country. He made frequent trips to the nearby marl quarries to collect fossils, including one especially interesting visit in view of later events:

"After the work of the winter [he wrote to his father on March 17, 1868] I have been taking a little outdoor exercise as it has come conveniently in the shape of a trip through the Marl country. I had intended making it this season but not so early. My friend, Prof. Marsh of Yale College, had however planned to go a little earlier, so I accompanied him. . . . Prof. Marsh had studied and travelled in Europe for three years and is very familiar with their invertebrate fossils. We have procured three new species of Saurians. . . ."[2]

This may be the only time that Cope ever spoke kindly of Marsh.

He first went to Kansas for fossils in 1871, perhaps because of correspondence with Mudge on identifications of fossils from there. We wish we knew, for by 1871 Cope apparently already considered himself in severe competition with Marsh, as shown

[2] Henry Fairfield Osborn, *Cope: Master Naturalist*, 157–58.

in a letter to his wife from Topeka, Kansas (September 6, 1871):

"I am now in a country which interests me greatly and the prospects are that I will be able to do something in my favorite line of Vertebrate Palaeontology. . . . Thee remembers Richardson at Indianapolis. He wanted to go with me to Kansas, and now that I find such splendid opportunity to collect in the middle and west of the state I have telegraphed to him to meet me at Manhattan. Marsh has been doing a great deal I find, but has left more for me, and one of his guides is at Ft. Wallace, *left behind*, and in want of a job. Prof. Mudge wanted to accompany Marsh [on one of the Yale student trips] and Marsh wouldn't let him go! I'll let him go!"[3]

Cope found a 75-foot mosasaur on his first Kansas trip. From then on his life became one of summer expeditions to the West and winter study and publication of the finds, first in Haddonfield, New Jersey, and then in Philadelphia. Until 1889 he never had the funds nor the organization backing, such as a university or museum, necessary to hire many employees to help him with the tedious chore of removing large fossil specimens from the rock in the laboratory. He did hire some collectors throughout the West, but Cope himself traveled far and wide to gather specimens.

Vertebrate paleontology was in its infancy in America when Marsh and Cope entered it. Europe's large fossils were known and so were a few from the American East; but along the eastern sea coast of the United States the fossil record is very incomplete. No one yet knew that dinosaurs of tremendous size had ever existed. The western plains represented one huge prehistoric burial ground, unrecognized by Indians, scouts, Army troops, farmers, and buffalo hunters—the few who lived there before 1850. Civilization had to reach the West before anyone had time to look closely at the rocks and stream beds.

The study of the West had begun before the Civil War. The push was slowed by the war and then resumed even faster. Kansas, for example, was settled rapidly by New Englanders trying to hold it as a non-slavery state. Colorado had minerals, and so cen-

[3] Osborn, *Cope*, 160.

ion sprang up there. Railroads were the key, and
ly pushed across the plains, mostly to connect with
California. The government felt the need of sur-
out the vast inland plains and sponsored a long
the 1860's and 1870's.

...., both vertebrate and invertebrate, from the eastern states
had been found and studied before 1800. Some were in young American universities and museums, and many had gone to Europe to be
identified (and kept). In the early 1850's Joseph Leidy became
the country's first recognized paleontologist, although his official
position was professor of anatomy at the University of Pennsylvania. The few schoolteachers and Army people who knew what
to do with unusual fossil specimens they had found began sending these to Leidy for identification. Thus he had the first inkling
of the rich fauna of the territories, the midland area that had once
been the floor of a shallow sea. Leidy described and classified specimens, often fragmented, as completely as possible and in 1869 published *Extinct Mammalian Fauna of Nebraska and Dakota*. His
1865 "Cretaceous Reptiles of the United States" had provided a
meager beginning, from fragmentary material, on that group.
Leidy's publications provided to Cope and Marsh a starting point
for their future work.[4]

Cope's biographer, Henry Fairfield Osborn, contends that the
first conflict between Cope and Marsh began in Fort Bridger, Wyoming, in 1872:

"Marsh disputed Cope's right to enter the Bridger field and
put every obstacle in his way. Thus began the intense rivalry in
field exploration and the bitter competition for *priority of discovery and publication*, which led to an immediate break in the previously friendly relations between Cope and Marsh."[5]

It must have been a hot summer in Wyoming. Not only was
Cope working there, almost alongside Marsh's student group, but

[4] For an account of Leidy's life and accomplishments, see Henry Fairfield Osborn,
"Joseph Leidy," *National Academy of Sciences Biographical Memoirs*, Vol. VII
(1913), 339–70.

[5] *Cope*, 177.

also Leidy was there on his own first trip to collect fossils. The three field parties dug out specimens frantically, named fragments on the spot, and telegraphed the names to Eastern scientific journals—tacitly assuming that everyone was finding the same species. They left a legacy of confusion that took many years to unravel in the taxonomy of the bulky extinct mammals called uintatheres. As Williston remarked much later: "The pioneers in paleontology were often justified in naming small and obscure fragments of bones, or single bones. . . . Nevertheless, the custom is a very reprehensible one when indiscriminately followed."[6]

The controversy was so distasteful to Leidy that he stepped out of vertebrate paleontology completely—a great loss to the new profession—and returned to his earlier studies of rhizopod protozoans.

Williston entered the fray as soon as he began working for Marsh in 1876. His first contract, in Marsh's handwriting, dated March 28, 1876, indicates his duties:

"I hereby agree to work for Prof. O. C. Marsh in the Yale Museum or in the field collecting, as he may direct, for the next three years and a quarter, or till July 1st 1879, for forty dollars per month. If sent away from New Haven collecting, my RR or stage fare to be extra."[7]

He promptly began studying his new employer too, for he continued in "Recollections":

"He [Marsh] found me quarters in a little building in the yard of Peabody Museum, then approaching completion. The next day he set me at work studying bird skeletons with Owen's Comparative Anatomy as a guide. He was then deeply interested in his Odontornithes [birds with teeth] and wanted more specimens, especially of the smaller forms which were very difficult to find in the Kansas Chalk. For recreation I helped a few hours every day to carry trays of fossils to the museum.

"After a few days he quizzed me about my past and my future

[6] *Water Reptiles of the Past and Present*, 186.
[7] Letter in the library of the Peabody Museum, Yale University.

ambitions, and shocked me by telling me to forget all I had learned about human anatomy! Shocked me because I was a little proud of my accomplishments in that line. My chief interest at Iowa City had been in the dissecting room. And right here I may mention that Prof. Marsh's chief defect was narrowness. A man of really remarkable ability he had a sort of contempt for all knowledge that did not bear directly upon his own special work. He was a man of extraordinary detail, with profound visualization powers, but lacked in generalization. He made many important discoveries in science but never formulated a single broad generalization. He was just the opposite of Prof. Cope, a man lacking in detail, wholly without powers of visualization. Perhaps as a pioneer in American Paleontology such a man as Marsh was more needed, for his work was always reliable when not [dictated] too much [by] his personal prejudices.

"By the first of May [1876] I was again in the field in Kansas, this time in a larger party in the charge of Mudge. For two or three seasons, a young man, then known as L. W. Field, had been collecting fossils occasionally for Marsh in western Kansas, in the intervals of his other work. He had been a buffalo-hunter engaged to get skins for the market. As the bisons disappeared from Kansas —the last we saw was in 1876—he collected some specimens which he sold to Marsh. This year he became a regular member of our party. In addition, a young man from Topeka, George Cooper, an entomologist had been employed, largely to do camp work. I regret much that I was somewhat unjust to Mudge this season. Brous had been given a decided [refusal] by Mudge's daughter, and was sore not only at her but unjustly to her father. We had no trouble, but thru Brous' influence I harbored some unkind feelings toward the professor for which I have always been sorry. He was not a very good collector—old men never are as I have learned from experience. I was a good collector then, and thought I did not receive my full share of credit. Toney and conceited, I thought he was an 'old fogy' and a long season wore us all out. Seven continuous months in the hot plains of Kansas was almost enough to drive any man to desperation. We collected that season till November. I visited the Centennial Exposition at Philadelphia on my return."

Schuchert and LeVene described the difficulty between Williston and Mudge in another light.[8] Williston was now a full-time employee of the honored Professor Marsh, and quite possibly a favored one. He had stepped beyond being an assistant to his former professor Mudge. Williston, who was self-assured, quite probably felt himself to be a man of the world after his short stay in the Yale laboratory.

The season of 1876 became the second round in the Cope Marsh feud through the participation of one more collector, Charles H. Sternberg, who worked for Cope.

Sternberg was born in 1850 in New York, where his father was principal of Hartwick Seminary. The family moved to Iowa when Sternberg was fifteen and two years later the young man joined an older brother on a ranch in Kansas. The outdoor active life of the early West appealed to him, and an early introduction to evolution directed him to collecting fossils, inspired by the discovery of fossil leaves in the Dakota sandstone near the ranch. Sternberg became the foremost collector of all kinds of fossils, which still stand as memorials to him in a dozen museums in this country and several in Europe. Not really a taxonomist in vertebrates, he nevertheless became an excellent collector, and, when not in the employ of one museum, would collect and sell specimens wherever there was a market.

In 1875 Sternberg sold some fossils to Cope. The following winter he attended Kansas State Agricultural College, where, in the spring, he learned of Mudge's summer collecting plans:

"I made every effort in my power to secure a place in the party [of Mudge, Sternberg wrote], but failed, as it was full when I applied. . . . Almost with despair, I turned for help to Professor E. D. Cope, of Philadelphia. . . . The Professor responded promptly, and when I opened the envelope, a draft for three hundred dollars fell at my feet. The note which accompanied it said: 'I like the style of your letter. Enclose draft. Go to work,' or words to the

[8] *O. C. Marsh*, 186–88.

...e effect. . . . As soon as the frost was out of the ground, having secured a team of ponies and a boy to drive them, I left Manhattan and drove out to Buffalo Park. . . . Here at Buffalo I had my headquarters for many years. A great windmill and a well of pure water, a hundred and twenty feet deep, made it a Mecca for us fossil hunters after two weeks of strong alkali water. At this well Professor Mudge's party and my own used to meet in peace after our fierce rivalry in the field as collectors for our respective paleontologists, Marsh and Cope."[9]

[9] Charles H. Sternberg, *The Life of a Fossil Hunter*, 32–34.

CHAPTER 5

Collecting in 1876 and 1877

Kansas

A LIVELY picture of early fossil collecting, more detailed than his brief account in "Recollections," appears in Williston's letters from the field to his new employer.[1] He arrived in Manhattan, Kansas, on April 2, 1876, to prepare for the field with Mudge. There he also learned of Sternberg's preparations and promised Marsh that he would "write immediately should he [Sternberg] get onto good ground."[2]

Marsh's party was instructed to find more bones of the toothed birds particularly, and to look for saurians (mosasaurs and plesiosaurs), pterodactyls, and crinoids.

Basic items needed for the months of work were a heavy wagon and team of horses, with a driver who usually doubled as cook, plus a tent and riding ponies for the collectors. Food supplies were mainly flour, bacon, salt, and beans; the abundant antelope provided most of the fresh meat. Bison, seen by Cope and Marsh by the thousands in 1871 in Kansas, were completely gone by 1876, and their bones lay in heaps along the rail lines. Flour sacks and cigar boxes were carried for fossil containers. Heavy specimens were crated, wrapped in straw or buffalo grass.

In the field the collectors set up camp at some source of not-too-alkaline water, fairly near a railroad station, and worked out from there to explore for fossils. They generally stayed two to four weeks in the same location, sending one member of the party to the station about once a week for mail and to ship specimens.

Mudge's group in 1876 was delayed by a late spring snowstorm,

[1] These letters, as indeed all correspondence, were saved by Marsh and became the property of the Peabody Museum at Yale upon Marsh's death. Unfortunately Williston did not save his letters from Marsh.

[2] Letter of April 4, 1876.

By April 21 Williston reported to Marsh, from the locality of first-known *Hesperornis*:

"I have the pleasure of sending by express tonight much more of the Hesperornis than I had expected though less I fear than you had anticipated. I am sorry to have been delayed so long but it was unavoidable. The heavy storms prevented the Prof. [Mudge] from getting here till day before yesterday. I have been here a week but could get no horse and not caring to venture out so far alone on foot as the Northern Cheyennes are all about— two parties of 80 have passed here within two weeks onto the Smoky [Hill River]. We reached the locality yesterday morning —I find that it is about 18 miles out, on the *Hackberry* [Creek] a short distance *before* the mouth of the Mulberry.

"I followed your directions strictly—marking out the spot & looking over it inch by inch lying flat on the ground, and afterwards working over the wash and loose soil as thoroughly with the knife. I think we have gotten *every* fragment—there are *certainly* no large pieces. I also dug out further on the old horizon.

"Though from finding what we did after our last years search has rather shaken my confidence—The wash is quite precipitous—though otherwise the locality is very close to what I sketched as I recollected. The other portions that you expected must be irrecoverably lost in the sand stream.

"I have put in every fragment I found that had the slightest resemblance—not pretending to discriminate so that you will probably find some foreign fragments, washed in from other places. . . . I hardly thought according to your instructions they were of sufficient value to telegraph—but I sincerely hope they may be of high value—at any rate I looked for them as if they were diamonds. . . ."

Into the sack went eighty fragments of the toothed bird and undoubtedly other animals—a frustrating puzzle for the preparator.

The hunt continued, successfully, as Williston reported on April 25:

"Prof M[udge] takes in tomorrow [to the railroad station] two specimens of Hesperornis which I think will please you. Mr Cooper brought in in his satchel a fragment of the shaft of No 1 which thanks to the knowledge I obtained in the laboratory I immediately recognized from its deep groove as a portion of the tarso-metatarse. I went back with him to the locality.

"We went over all the soil to the bottom repeatedly and I hope have got all that was there. Please let me know what portions of this and No 2 we might yet expect. I would like to re examine after a heavy rain whenever we get a chance. Cope's party was camped not more than half a mile from the locality and Brous stood guard to keep them from seeing or getting it for several hours till one of us happened along. We came into the spot and cleaned it out getting all the birds within a mile and half of their camp. They got belligerent immediately and left. They are now camped about a mile from us. The boys are all very cautious in preventing their getting any idea of what we are doing. I do not think they will have any success in pterodactyls or small birds. One or two excellent ones they had struck carelessly with a pick and abandoned. Bird No 4 was partially crushed by their feet. Turtle (?) No 7 they had thrown away for a worthless fish! They have however got one or two large turtles that are good and some pretty good saurians.

"They will soon get into ground that has been well examined by yourself and our own party, and we will have a decided advantage in knowing where to look. We are now about 8 miles west of Monument—four miles North of the river. We shall *all* try our utmost to prevent any good specimens going elsewhere but to Yale. . . .

"Professor I am anxious lest I have forgotten or am neglecting any of your directions. I want to do the best I can.

"So far Brous Field & Cooper are having the best success nor in fact do I expect to compete with them. Brous & Cooper have had years of experience in collecting insects. They keep me pretty well employed inspecting their 'birds' which mostly turn out turtles or saurians. I hope to continue our success. Nor do I see any reason why we should not. The pterodactyl head I found was injured in getting it to the station. I have studied it so thoroughly however that I think I will be able to replace every fragment when I return."

Marsh was pleased with the party's specimens, to Williston's gratification:

"I am *more* than glad to know [wrote Williston on June 1] that the specimens we have found have been so good and am *determined,* especially now as I know what pleasure they afford you, that there shall be more of them." The Marsh party discouraged Sternberg's group away from the area of Monument Rocks. Williston guaranteed: "*Not* a *soul* knows *anything* of our success or even where we are save of course the telegraph operators . . . . Mr Field & myself worked nearly two days on it [a large pterodactyl] removing with much labor a number of nicely marked slabs & then were caught in a rain that sadly damaged & destroyed them. How can we measure bones that have very large or irregular outlines? Could we use tracing linen? If so will you please send us a yard or two for such delicate specimens? . . . I am conscious that we injure specimens occasionally with the knife when they perhaps might be avoided but it is sometimes impossible to uncover from the top & with the pterodactyl bones often so irregular in position and the thermometer at a hundred will perhaps excuse us somewhat, but we shall earnestly try to observe your directions. . . .

"I shall try to have your directions in collecting and shipping well observed. From the relations I have borne to the Prof. [Mudge] for so long makes it hard for me to direct or dictate in any way, so that we may make some errors. But please be explicit about any mistake.

". . . Sternberg & one assistant is down on the Smoky. . . . I ascertained his plans but kept my own counsel. He doesn't know what a pterodactyl looks like & hardly what a saurian is. He has had directions from Cope to collect all vertebrates—and we will take pains to leave him plenty of fishes. . . ."

Because of Marsh's lack of interest in fishes, Cope was soon to become the country's leading authority on fossil fishes, for there were many in the Kansas chalk beds.

In the same letter of June 1, Williston referred briefly to the party's getting caught in a flash flood, but he told the story more completely later to his own paleontology students:

"We pitched camp in the river bed, over the protest of the more experienced member of the party. There was grass for the horse, and he was pegged out to graze. The only concession we made was to pitch the tent with the opening downstream, and well we did. The rushing of the approaching water woke us up, and we grabbed our guns and crawled out into four inches of water and made for the bank. The last man had to swim to make it. It was then a choice of shivering in the cold in our wet clothes or exercising on the cactus-studded bank. Those who chose the latter turned the night blue with their expletives.

"As the daylight began to come we observed that the bend in the river made a great eddy in the water, and a mass of sticks, trees, dead animals and debris went continuously round and round while the current went by on the other side. Finally someone spotted the grub chest. When it came around near the bank we fished it out and had some soggy coffee. Then we began to look for other things. There was a boot, and then another, the tent, the wagon, and finally we rescued everything important but one boot and the drowned horse."[3]

The collectors moved on to Butte Creek in Wallace County, Kansas, where at first collecting went slowly. On June 18 Williston reported:

"There is shipped this time bird 11 ... found in the grey siliceous chalk on the south side of Butte Creek about 4 miles below Twin Buttes. There was nothing visible but the thin edge of the sternum & I did not once surmise its character finding it where it was & saw the keel of the sternum. I then found the upper end of the coracoid sticking out about six inches from the point of the sternum. You will on that acount [sic] please excuse the rather rough usage that the ribs received. Expecting to find the remainder of the coracoid I spent a considerable time over the wash—after looking it over with the knife—I removed the soil to a clean place & sifted it through a mosquito netting; after going through several bushels I found the two larger fragments but nothing more. It seems to me there ought to be more but I cant find them. . . .

[3] Recounted by his daughter, Dorothy Shor, July 25, 1967.

"We are all much obliged for your offer to repair the damage of the flood. The Professor however is the only one who lost much. He had only gotten his horse about two weeks previously & will have another just as soon as he can get one. The rest of the party lost clothing mostly & you know we dont wear broadcloth out here."

Sternberg, it was rumored, was thoroughly discouraged over his own lack of success and finally left the vicinity.

Working conditions in the field were often difficult for various reasons. On August 24 Williston commented:

"I am *very* sorry the collection of the pterodactyls displease you —especially as I must take my full share of the blame on No. 61. The rock containing it was tilted near a fault 20 or 30° and covered so deeply that last year I would hardly have attempted to remove it at all. Please write to Prof. Mudge about the packing and shipment he takes entire charge of them and I seldom know how they are sent. I always read what you write about the collecting and shipment to the rest of the party, but I can only suggest.

"Please write explicitly just the best way to remove a slab when the rock is sufficiently solid. We have been in the habit of uncovering to about three inches with the pick—then work a ways further with our large knives and then within an inch only with the small blade of my pocket knife. We are only seldom able to get up a slab containing more than 5 or 6 sq. feet of surface. If we try to take up a rock without channeling around it, it breaks into very small fragments, and in cutting around we are almost sure to injure some bone. Does a fracture in the bone hurt it as much as a tool mark?

". . . We are again getting into the pterodactyl and bird strip. I do not think that region near Monument will afford good specimens now to any save yourself. I feel quite sure there is more of the same kind of ground on the S. fork of the Solomon near the head which we expect to examine yet if the Indians do not prevent. The soldiers have nearly all been taken from the state, and without the present Fall proves an exception, the indians will be at their former tricks."

Interestingly, Williston made no reference to Custer's catas-
trophe during that summer of 1876.

Western Kansas was still part of the Wild West, as Williston
wrote from the railroad station on September 3:

"A party of horse thieves & desperadoes made a raid on the
station yesterday morning attempting to steal horses. A special
train brought up a sheriff and men from Hays who captured them
all last night with a large amount of plunder, and they are now
on the way to the station. There *were* 14 of them but one—for
whom there was a standing reward—exchanged compliments with
the sheriff—His funeral services will be very short!!"

The summer's work had been of distinct value to both Marsh
and Williston. Marsh had been provided with a great many pieces
of pterodactyls, of toothed birds, of mosasaurs, of plesiosaurs,
and of crinoids. The party did a reconnaissance of a considerable
area of western Kansas, tracing the fossil-producing horizon across
the valleys of the Smoky Hill River and its tributaries. Williston,
whose enthusiasm and keen observation rode high that summer,
pondered the characteristics of the geologic formations and wondered over the variations in the structure of bones from differing
species. As the season's collecting approached an end, he wrote on
September 29:

"The snow has made its appearance and frosty weather makes
it so uncomfortable that the party will probably break up about
the 15 of Oct. I should like to rest a few days at home and then
will be *very* glad to get back to work in the laboratory where I
anticipate a great deal of enjoyment learning something about these
fossils.

"I do not know how well I have done my summers work—but
I *do* know that I am far from satisfied with it myself, when I see
how many of the specimens might have been improved and perhaps
another season I can do better, and I desire above all to assure
you of my willingness to do any kind of work that will aid you in
your scientific researches, and sincere thanks for your many kind-
nesses."

Disillusionment had not yet set in.

Williston's final postscript from the field (October 13) showed his interest in the specimens:

"Professor if not inconvenient will you please all[ow] one of the freight boxes to remain till I return so that I can see it unpacked. I would like to see in what condition they arrive, where the specimens are injured and how they could be prevented."

On this eager note Williston returned to New Haven in the fall of 1876 to work on the collected specimens and to prepare for his next season of collecting, when he was to be in charge.

Among his preparations, which indicate the cloak-and-dagger atmosphere of the profession then, was a note listing the code words to be used in communications, especially telegrams. Telegraph operators or station agents could tell the kinds and numbers of fossils shipped, or the trials and tribulations of the search. One of Sternberg's brothers, for example, was agent at Buffalo Park, where the clean water attracted the rival collecting parties. On Williston's list, *B. Jones* was the code word for Cope, *Jones* for Brous (Harry Brous, who had worked with Marsh's party the previous year and had now changed sides), *health* stood for collecting success, and *ammunition* for money. Specific fossils were coded as *hornis* for Hesperornis, *iornis* for Ichthyornis, and *drag* for pterodactyl.

Williston arrived in Manhattan again on March 9, 1877. There he learned that his former companion Brous was working in Texas for Cope and that Sternberg would soon be hunting fossils for Cope in western Kansas. He was quickly dismayed over the details of outfitting a collecting trip, and was further set back by sending off a wagon and a team of horses in the care of a driver, just in time for a late snowstorm that "ruined" one of the horses. Apologetically, he wrote Marsh on April 7:

"I shall try to do the best I can & I hope will do satisfactory. I sometimes get perplexed and would gladly have someone to take the worry of provisions & outfitting, so that I could have nothing to do but attend to fossils." He even asked for Mudge, but the professor was unavailable.

When Marsh did not reply promptly to pleas for money to pay

for supplies, Williston sent off a coded telegram on April 22 that must surely have puzzled the telegraph operator at Trego, Kansas: "Send hundred ammunition health poor B Jones nothing going south."

News of Cope's field parties filtered through to Williston. Harry Brous was definitely in Texas and Cope would join him there later. Sternberg and two assistants were hunting in the Monument Rocks area, but they too had lost a horse and had to wait another; they were finding nothing, except fishes. Williston learned that Sternberg "entirely avoids our last year's washes,"[4] apparently considering them completely cleaned out.

For Marsh's party the area of Russel Springs proved rich in fragments of pterodactyls and birds. Williston could not find suitable packing boxes locally so he requested one-quarter-inch pine strips from New Haven to make his own small packing boxes fitted to the size of the museum trays.

At Monument Rocks the group found saurians and turtles, then moved to Wallace where they found more birds. At Buffalo, Williston met Sternberg and learned that he had shipped few fossils. Sternberg was en route for Nebraska by the end of July.

Marsh's chief interest continued to be the toothed birds and he must have repeatedly urged his party to search for every fragment. Williston replied on August 9.

"We rely far more on *texture* in determining a fragment than shape—so that I dont think there is any more danger in leaving the head than any other part of the skeleton—[birds numbered] 25 & 24 were found by the driver (a younger brother [Frank Williston]) who knows and cares no more about the anatomy than a girl, but as soon as he had learned the peculiarity of texture to distinguish birds from shells he found & recognized them close by camp."

On August 26 he described the method they were using for finding bird fragments:

"When birds come up so thickly as they have twice now there is some fun in looking—but at other times even when we think there must be birds in a wash—it is hard to get them for a few

4 Letter to Marsh, June 12, 1877.

hours of bird looking gives one an aching back and eyes. The best success we have is by stooping over with the eyes about 3 feet from the ground, and going along foot by foot. Ten or 12 hours of such work is tolerably certain of bringing a bird when the ground has not been hunted too closely, especially if a bird before has been found in the region.—I think that *all* the ground west of Monument Rocks will produce bird—There seems to be a great deal (at least with myself) in an unconscious training of the eye in birds & pts [pterodactyls]—two (birds) that I have found this year were in a manner that simply astonished me—the first as I was riding *on a galop* [*sic*] across a little wash while looking for a camping spot—the second as I was jumping down a bank. I am pretty confident we will bring the birds up to 40 before quitting. We haven't had two weeks' work this whole season on absolutely new ground (new to us)—all the rest of the time on ground that had been hunted from one to five times—Probably a third of the pts have been newly washed out—and most of the rest those that didn't show up much or in places partly concealed or spots where no one but Brous or Mudge had looked. There are none of us even now but what often leave specimens behind us—especially when they are probably concealed—and there always must be fossils here for the hunting—at this work getting is many times what it was, two years, that is with the same experience.

"I like to work in the field if there is only the novelty of something new to see, and study over, and if some one else will only direct."

Williston's collecting desires were very soon to be realized, for on September 13, as he was making arrangements to conclude the summer's work in Kansas, a telegram from Marsh started him in an entirely new direction where there was certainly something new to see and study over.

The Battle of the Dinosaurs

The competition between Marsh's and Cope's workers continued in Colorado, through a series of coincidences which brought to light the enormous dinosaurs of the western United States. Dinosaurs were known, but just barely, in 1877. When Richard Owen of the British Museum coined the word *Dinosauria* in 1841 for an extinct group of reptiles different from any modern group, he had only nine different genera to work with, mostly fragments of animals. Joseph Leidy had described the first American dinosaurs, from teeth brought back from the Judith River, Montana, by Hayden's 1855 expedition, and from a considerable assortment of bones found in Haddonfield, New Jersey, in 1858. Leidy named the latter *Hadrosaurus*, one of the duck-billed dinosaurs about twenty-five feet long, but unfortunately his specimen was headless.

Brontosaurus, Stegosaurus, Allosaurus, Diplodocus, Ceratosaurus, Morosaurus, Laosaurus, Atlantosaurus, Camarasaurus: these newly discovered dinosaurs, the aristocrats now familiar to school children, first came from the ground in 1877 from Cañon City and Morrison, Colorado, and from Como, Wyoming. It may be fitting that the rebirth of these behemoths should have been in the throes of the rivalry between Cope and Marsh.

Many years later Williston commented:

"Most great discoveries are due rather to a state of mind, if I may use such an expression, than to accident. The discovery of the immense dinosaur deposits in the Rocky Mountains in March, 1877, may truthfully be called great, for nothing in paleontology has equalled it, and that it was made by three observers simultaneously can not be called purely an accident."[5]

In March, Arthur Lakes, a teacher in the School of Mines at Golden, Colorado, while hunting fossil leaves in the Dakota sandstone near Morrison, Colorado, came across a tremendous vertebra, partly exposed in a block of sandstone. Not long afterward he found a femur more than six feet long nearby.

Also in March, O. Lucas, a school teacher in Garden Park, near Cañon City, Colorado (about eighty miles south of Morrison), was hunting botanical specimens near his home when he came across some large fragments of fossil bones. Lakes wrote to Marsh

[5] "The First Discovery of Dinosaurs in the West," in W. D. Matthew, *Dinosaurs*, 124.

of his find and Lucas wrote to Cope. Marsh was slow in replying, so Lakes wrote to Cope also, and the race was on.

Marsh hired Lakes to quarry for more bones, and he sent Mudge from collecting in Texas to help Lakes. Later in the season, Williston was sent to Morrison also. Cope hired local men in Cañon City to start quarrying where Lucas had found the bones. Another of Marsh's collectors, David Baldwin, learned of Cope's project and left his digging in New Mexico to check the rumor. He worked near Cope's crew but missed the biggest bones because he looked in the wrong horizon. (Baldwin had been working in Permian "red beds" in New Mexico, and he searched the same horizon in Colorado; the dinosaurs were in Jurassic deposits higher.) Williston and Mudge both went to Cañon City to try to wrest fossils away from Cope's area.

Marsh's first paper on the Colorado discoveries, based on the big bones found by Lakes, came out in July, 1877. It introduced *Titanosaurus montanus,* fifty to sixty feet long (estimated from the femur), larger than "any land animal hitherto discovered."[6] (The name was later changed to *Atlantosaurus.*)

Marsh was very pleased with his announcement, but it was a short-lived record, for Cope was able to introduce the even larger *Camarasaurus supremus* from Cañon City in August, which he said "exceeds in proportions any other land animal hitherto described, including the one found near Golden City by Professor Lakes."[7]

The third great fossil area of that year had actually been known to a few local people long before. But some time in the winter or spring of 1877 William Reed found some large fossil bones as he was hunting game near Como, Wyoming. He and the station master, W. E. Carlin, wrote to Marsh in July, offering to sell him fossils and the secret of the location. Marsh bought the bones, which did not reach him until October, and found them worthy of investigating. He wired Williston to go to Como, Wyoming, immediately.

Thus Williston was actually at all three of the 1877 discovery

[6] Schuchert and LeVene, *O. C. Marsh,* 191.
[7] *Ibid.,* 193.

sites—the only paleontologist who saw all of them during the quarrying. Marsh was at Como briefly in 1878 and in 1880; Cope visited Cañon City and Como in 1879.

Williston's part in the dinosaur race was partly recounted in his letters to Marsh in the late summer of 1877, after he had ended the work of the party in Kansas. A telegram from Marsh in September instructed him to go to Cañon City, where Cope's discovery had been made, and where Mudge was already at work. Williston found himself on the same train with Sternberg to Denver. Typically of the atmosphere of the day, each plied the other with questions and evaded replying. Sternberg was actually en route to eastern Oregon for Cope and was not part of the dinosaur seekers that year.

On his first look at the Cañon City locality, Williston reported sadly on September 21, 1877:

"I am very sorry to find that Cope is getting by far the best lot of fossils. The locality that the man Lucas first discovered is in a heavy clay or shale and the bones are well preserved and many of them entire. Where we are at work the sandstone renders the bones less accessible and when uncovered they are so extremely friable and broken that it seems almost useless to ship them. . . . Fragments of bones are scattered all through the hills—the point is to find them in good material. Now I dont [sic] propose to see Cope get better specimens from the farmer than we can get. Prof Mudge thinks we had better work out these than use time in the risk of not finding better—but I *am* agoing to find better.—It seems to me too there ought to be birds and mammals and possibly (?) pterodactyls in this.

"May we glue together fragments when it will save you time in hunting them out there. Also please explain how to make measurements & outlines so that they will be of the most service.

"I think there must be a number of new species of those dinosaurs if we can only get good bones. I think I know the scapula & coracoid & the different vertebrae—Will you please give me a little idea of the pelvic bones?—and of the skull—as soon as I can see a bone once and know what it is I will be a little more at home. . . ."

The small party continued digging out the "bird in the hand," finding the bones better as they went deeper.

By direction from Marsh, Williston went to Morrison, Colorado, in October. He summarized his exploration of the Cañon City area from there:

"Not being able to go on with the quarry at Cañon without blasting I spent a week in exploring the whole basin—finding several localities that promise well that had escaped Lucas. . . . The basin containing sedimentary rocks is six miles wide and extending 12 miles north of Cañon. The west ridge running around on the north (about 1000 feet high) is covered so far as I climbed it with regularly stratified grey limestones (and marble) with a few fossil shells resembling closely Dana's figure of *spinifer* niagarensis (pg 226) and I called it Silurian. This covers the side of the range at about 30° or 35° dip. At its base and lying upon it the coarse red concrete sandstone Triassic? (puddingstone) shows itself at about the same dip—I estimated it to be all of 200 feet thick. This follows the ranges alround [*sic*] the valley but on the East side I did not see the Silurian between it [and] the granite. Everywhere thereabouts the fossiliferous material (Wealdon) lies right upon it without the intervening limestone as there is here [Morrison]. The strata in the valley are much broken up, on the west side they dip slightly toward the east & vice versa. The fossils appear within *not more* than 50 feet of the Triassic—small bones especially turtle fragments I think are more abundant in the lower strata.

"There are certainly not less than 100 feet of fossiliferous material as they outcrop directly above each other & I think 200 feet would be nearer. The formation is over three hundred feet in thickness to characteristic (there and here) [i.e., Cañon City and Morrison] capping sandstone stratum. I found fossils nearly ten miles apart and the whole region contains them. —It took me a day or two to learn how to find fragments and as much longer to find the outcrops from the clay—I certainly think that the fossils will turn up almost anywhere between here and Cañon City."[8]

One of the major finds at Cañon City, quarried out by Williston, Mudge, and a local man named Felch, was the first specimen of *Diplodocus*—the eighty-foot-long monster that once lunged through swamps. Williston described the find many years later:

"The hind leg, pelvis and much of the tail of this specimen lay in very orderly arrangement in the sandstone near the edge of the quarry, but the bones were broken into innumerable pieces. After consulation [*sic*] we decided that they were too much broken to be worth saving—and so most of them went over into the dump. Sacrilege, doubtless, the modern collector will say, but we did not know much about the modern methods of collection in those days, and moreover we were in too much of a hurry to get the new discoveries to Yale College to take much pains with them. I did observe that the caudal vertebrae had very peculiar chevrons, unlike others that I had seen, and so I attempted to save some samples of them by pasting them up with thick layers of paper. Had we only known of plaster-of-paris and burlap the whole specimen might easily have been saved. Later, when I reached New Haven, I took off the paper and called Professor Marsh's attention to the strange chevrons. And *Diplodocus* was the result."[9]

It may well have been this fossil which resulted in a sudden gift to Williston by the unpredictable Marsh. According to a family story, once when Williston showed Marsh an unusual specimen in the laboratory from the summer collecting, Marsh was so pleased that he pulled out his own watch and presented it to the young man. The Williston family still has this silver, key-wound Longines watch, though it may have brought a wry smile to Williston occasionally in later years.

Of the Morrison, Colorado, area, Williston had very little to say in his letters to his employer, but his stay there was brief. His restless employer had by then learned of the Como, Wyoming, discovery and wired him to go there immediately to "collect and learn all possible."[10]

[8] Letter to Marsh, October 28, 1877.

[9] "The First Discovery of Dinosaurs in the West," in W. D. Matthew, *Dinosaurs*, 129–30.

[10] Undated telegram in Marsh's handwriting in the Peabody Museum collection of Williston letters.

Heavy snow at Morrison, a collapse of rock in the quarry there, and the accumulated tiredness of nine months in the field had combined to send Williston home just before the telegram was sent. His disillusionment with Marsh had actually begun before this. In "Recollections" he summarized briefly the long season:

"The following year, 1877, Mudge was sent to Texas in quest of Cretaceous fossils and I was placed in charge of the Kansas party, which this year consisted of Guild (Field), Cooper, my younger brother Frank, and myself. Mr. Brous severed his relations with Marsh and collected for Cope in Texas.

"My faith in Professor Marsh had begun to fail. The previous year I had begged permission to study the fossil Fishes of Kansas, with the expectation and hope of doing some research work for myself, knowing that Marsh had no desire nor intention of ever doing any work upon them himself. He assented [apparently] and set me at work studying fish skeletons, done in my own time of course. After some months work upon the recent fishes I suggested that he let me take some of the specimens I had collected to my room to work upon evenings and holidays. But he declined, giving me to understand that he did not want me to do any paleontological work for myself, that it would distract my attention too much from my regular duties. I recognized then, or a little later, that I would never have the opportunity of doing any independent research work in paleontology as long as I was his assistant.

"In September I received instruction to disband my party and join Mudge & Lakes in Colorado to collect from the newly discovered Morrison deposits. I remained with Prof. Arthur Lakes at Morrison only a few weeks and then joined Mudge at Cañon City to work in the Felch quarry.[11]

"As October and November passed I was getting tired of so much field work, having been in camp since March. In November I took my own lief and went back to Manhattan. I was somewhat discouraged, as I saw before me only field work collecting fossils for others to study and no opportunity to advance myself in Science.

[11] This sequence, written years later, does not agree with that in the letters Williston wrote to Marsh in 1877.

An incident that I need not relate here disturbed my faith in Marsh's honor, and I felt that I had nothing to expect from him in the way of advancement. Guild, who had spent the winter at New Haven, rooming with me, urged me strongly in September to sever our relations with Marsh and begin collecting on our responsibility as a commercial business. But I had signed a contract with Marsh in March of 1876 when I had implicit confidence in him, to remain with him at a salary of $40. a month for three years, and although I felt that he [had] taken advantage of my inexperience, I did not feel justified in breaking my word. But I did feel justified in quitting my work in November, at Cañon City [actually Morrison], without his permission, giving as my excuse that I was tired and worn out.

"I had scarcely reached Manhattan, however, at Thanksgiving time than I received a telegram from Marsh followed by a letter directing me to go at once to Como, Wyoming, to investigate the recent discovery there of Jurassic fossils. I obeyed, reaching there about the first of December [actually November 14]."

The air was full of intrigue in Como, for the original discoverers of the bones, station agent William E. Carlin and section foreman William H. Reed, had used assumed names in writing to Marsh. Williston's first letter from Como on his arrival was very optimistic:

"I have seen a lot of the bones that they [Carlin and Reed] have ready to ship & they have taken them up pretty well. They tell me the bones extend for *seven* miles & are by the ton.

"The point will be to get into & ship as soon as possible, for the men have got pretty exaggerated ideas of what they are worth. I read a *purl* of your letter to them. I think for three months the matter can be kept perfectly quiet & by that time I hope you will have the matter all your own. I have engaged Reed to go to work upon the day after tomorrow—*if I see nothing to make me hesitate* guaranteeing an increase of wages on what he is now making ($60) but not saying how much. The bones are right by the station but there are only 4 or 5 persons that know about them. . . . The bones are very thick, well preserved and easy to get out. . . . I will send a ton a week gotten out good. They have a lot of Belemnites here which will be sent by first box. I of course do not know the species but they are new to me. It is agoing [*sic*] to be pretty hard to get them down to reasonable terms—but meanwhile I can send the fossils."

Two days later he was still enthusiastic:

"Work can be prosecuted every day this winter with success and from the accessibility and great quantities there will be great danger next summer from competition—At present but *seven* persons here have seen or know about the fossils but it will be almost absolutely impossible to prevent tourists to know about them in the spring. Cañon City & Morrison are simply nowhere in comparison with this locality—both as regards perfection, accessibility, and quantity. Where I shall commence work is about 250 *yards* from the NW shore of the Lake—a mile & a half from the station & a third from the R.R. track. I choose that spot because it is in a sheltered little basin (a ridge being between it and the Lake) shut in warmer—South exposure—and not requiring much digging.

"I should certainly call this the same formation as the Colorado localities. The ridge south (¾ mile) is very steep consisting mostly of clay shales—precisely similar to those in Colorado interspersed with thin strata of sandstone. *Exceptionally* the bones are in the sandstone but mostly in the clay, *magnificently* preserved and scattered all along for 6 or seven miles. The shales are exposed & clean, *& it will be the grandest place imaginable to hunt for small specimens*, but it has a northern exposure & but little if anything can be done there in the winter. The fossils extend over a hundred or more [*sic*]. 50 feet or so below the lowest I found what I take to be the Jurassic about 200 or 250 feet in thickness. This is made up of *mealy* yellowish sandstone and shales and almost literally *filled* with belemnites—in some places bushels might be expected —but no vertebrate fossils. Below this is the red Triassic or what I take to be the same as the red stained pudding stone at Morrison &c. It is however a little lighter color & finer—in one or two places only approaching the conglomerate character. This red stain is seen at one or two places on the N. side of the lake where it is pushed up slightly. Above this the Jurassic (?) makes the bank of the lake & running back a hundred or a hundred & fifty yards the strata dipping 30 or 40° away from the lake into the Rock Cr valley—a projecting ridge of sandstone (hard & grey) marks what I think is the Wealden—below which are found the belemnites and above the saurians.—About 100 feet above this (stratigraphically) are the deposits which I propose to start into tomorrow.

"The bones are beautifully preserved & will probably admit of being taken up whole. The ground is not much inclined and I propose to get a tent (9 x 9 wall) which will not cost over $25—nail it to a Scandling frame, allowing it to be lifted & readily moved & in cold stormy days place it over the work—& if very cold get a sheet iron stove and work comfortably. The shortness of the day will however only allow about 5 [number uncertain] hours work —but that will be more effective than July & August work. Board at the section house which will not be over ¾ of a mile when the lake is frozen. The fossils will be taken to the track on a hand *cart* & brought in on a hand *car*—making no expense except for packing material. . . ."

A reconnaissance of the area indicated the extent of the fossils:

"There are five hundred square miles of fossil country—They have found bones 15–18 and more miles from here in different directions. Friday I found an entire foramen lying exposed above the ground *seven* miles east from here & literally acres of clay wash covered with fragments! Whenever a surface is exposed there are fragments. . . ."[12]

The three workers set up the tent and stove over the diggings and worked in comparative comfort. Carlin made a trip east to negotiate terms with Marsh and after some delay the shipment of tons of fossils began to Yale. Years later Williston said of the early digging at Como:

"Inasmuch as the mercury in the thermometer during the next two months seldom reached zero—upward I mean—the opening of this famous deposit was made under difficulties. That so much 'head cheese,' as we called it, was shipped to Professor Marsh was

12 Letter to Marsh, November 18, 1877.

more the fault of the weather and his importunities than our carelessness. However, we found some of the types of dinosaurs that have since become famous."[13]

Once Williston had set up the digging operations at Como and taught Reed how to pack and label the material, he was ready to leave. It had been a difficult year, as he recounted in "Recollections":

"The work there was very painful and hard. A scratch of a pin on my left hand had developed into so serious a condition that by the first of January I was compelled to carry my arm in a sling. Early in January I requested permission to return to New Haven, but Marsh, hoping to induce me to remain through the winter sent me a hundred dollar bill in a letter as New Year's present, which I promptly used to buy a ticket to New Haven. I reached New Haven discouraged after ten months consecutive work in camp. But I saw no way to better my condition."

It was a short winter's stay in the laboratory, for by April 18 he was back in Como to continue the quarrying. He arrived in a severe snowstorm to find his brother Frank, then working on the bones with Reed, very ill with mountain fever, and to learn that a knowledgeable stranger had visited the area to ask about the fossils. The stranger was assumed to have been sent by Cope.

The snow slowly melted, his brother improved, and the stranger did not reappear. After checking the area, Williston reported on April 25:

"The first quarry was a particularly fortunate one. I doubt whether another will ever be found like it. They have opened up spot after spot, only to leave them. . . . The work is immense to get the bones to the station. They have pack [sic] them all *up* a steep hill & nearly ¾ mile to the R.R. on their shoulders, & there can be no way of avoiding much of this shoulder work."

Williston made a reconnaissance of a considerable area in southern Wyoming and then returned to New Haven to continue work in the laboratory. A party under Reed and later E. Kennedy went

[13] "The First Discovery of Dinosaurs in the West," in W. D. Matthew, *Dinosaurs*, 129.

on quarrying bones at Como for several years. Frank Williston continued in this party until 1880, when, undoubtedly to the equal dismay of his brother and Marsh, he switched sides and began sending fossils to Cope. He compounded the felony by also shipping fossils to Alexander Agassiz at Harvard.[14]

The year 1877 yielded a bumper crop for Marsh:

"In the *American Journal of Science* for December of that year," wrote Schuchert and LeVene, "Ringmaster Marsh 'trotted out' some of the amazing animals in his three-ring dinosaur circus of 1877: *Stegosaurus,* most bizarre of land animals, with small head, body heavily armored with large bony plates, two rows of huge plates standing erect along its back, and tail bristling with huge spikes—an impressive defensive armament for a harmless plant-eating creature; *Apatosaurus,* a dinosaur of the same general type as *Atlantosaurus,* between 50 and 60 feet long; *Allosaurus,* a fierce carnivore, half the size of the foregoing, but much more terrible in claw and tooth; and, in striking contrast, the graceful little *Nanosaurus* and the tiny 'leaping' *Hallopus.*"[15]

The three 1877 dinosaur localities were worked extensively for several years more, but Williston did not return to them until many years later, and then but briefly. The most spectacular of all time was Como, from which Marsh acquired many specimens and, later, so did the American Museum of Natural History.

Como now appears much as it must have in 1877. There is no town at the site, for the railroad tracks were moved south many years ago. A hogback, the Como Ridge, extends for some miles as a relief to the flat plains. The attractive lake is a haven for ducks and red-winged blackbirds—and mosquitoes. Belemnites can still be found in great quantity, but dinosaur bones are definitely rare. Now only an occasional geologist stops by on a historical pilgrimage. One small building adjacent to the only house at Como Ridge is a private museum; the building is made entirely of dinosaur bones.

[14] For an account of this and the years of collecting at Como, see John H. Ostrom and John S. McIntosh, *Marsh's Dinosaurs.*

[15] *O. C. Marsh,* 198–99.

Cañon City, Colorado, is a charming quiet town of about 9,000 people, very different surely from the old-West town of 1877. Not much now indicates its part in the dinosaur discoveries, for few fossils were left for the local museum to take out after Marsh's and Cope's workers had left (though the Cleveland Museum of Natural History in recent years found a fine specimen of an overlooked *Haplocanthosaurus*). In 1953, the citizens of Cañon City placed a monument near their town that, in understatement, says: "Garden Park. Type locality of dinosaurs. The first remains of several species of dinosaurs were found within a two-mile radius of this point in 1877 by Prof. O. C. Marsh of Yale University, and Prof. E. D. Cope of the Academy of Sciences of Philadelphia. This discovery of extinct giant reptiles in the western hemisphere received world-wide acclaim." Listed as type specimens from the area are: *Tyrannosaurus, Stegosaurus, Diplodocus, Brontosaurus,* and *Ceratosaurus.*

Morrison, Colorado, is now a very small town huddled in an attractive canyon setting, surrounded by red and gray massive sandstones. No evidence of the quarrying of dinosaurs can any longer be found there.

Fossil Collecting Techniques

Fossil collecting has always been hard work. Modern mechanical equipment helps considerably now, but in the 1870's picks and shovels were the major implements. Carving out a large bone laboriously with hand picks, wrestling it onto a wagon or ox-drawn sledge while trying to make certain it held together, and hauling it to the railroad—all took weeks of strenuous back-breaking labor. One wonders what kept the field crews at work, especially in the heat of mid-West summers.

The intensive collecting of the three new fossil localities in 1877 led to a sudden refinement in the methods used to remove specimens from the field. Marsh is generally considered to be the one most responsible for modern methods of collecting, but it was actually his assistants and field men who devised the methods he claimed as his own. Sternberg also contributed to new techniques.

Williston has been credited with the idea of bandaging specimens like broken bones in the field. From Cañon City on September 21, 1877, he wrote Marsh, "Will it do to paste strips of strong paper on fractured bones before removing?" Five days later he added, "Those strips are put on with ordinary flour paste and can be removed I think easily."[16]

Also in September Arthur Lakes wrote Marsh from Morrison, Colorado: "I do not know whether you wish us to use plaster of paris but if it is not an obstacle in your final clearing up of the bones it would be often a great assistance to us in keeping together very fragmentary bones."[17]

David Baldwin, working in New Mexico for Marsh during 1876 and 1877, cut pieces of wood to fit along the bones, tied them with hemp, and thus devised a rough splint.

Sternberg, possibly referring to 1876 on his trip to Montana with Cope, said: "We found [the bones] very brittle . . . and we were obliged to devise some means of holding them in place. The only thing we had in camp that could be made into a paste was rice, which we had brought along for food. We boiled quantities of it until it became thick, then, dipping into it flour bags and pieces of cotton cloth and burlap, we used them to strengthen the bones and hold them together. This was the beginning of a long line of experiments, which culminated in the recently adopted method of taking up large fossils by bandaging them with strips of cloth dipped in plaster of Paris, like the bandages in which a modern surgeon encases a broken limb."[18]

It is uncertain whether Sternberg adopted the rice-paste method before Marsh's collectors made their pastes and splints. Various collectors, including Williston, developed similar methods almost simultaneously, so that the bones traveled more satisfactorily and the preparator had an easier task.

When Cope and Marsh were rivals, there were no collecting

[16] Edwin H. Colbert, *Dinosaurs,* 37.
[17] Schuchert and LeVene, *O. C. Marsh,* 175.
[18] *The Life of a Fossil Hunter,* 88.

ethics. Marsh prevented Cope's men from entering an area he considered his own in 1872, but in 1877 Marsh's crew moved right into Cope's area in Cañon City. Apparently the only rule then was: Don't work right in someone else's quarry. At least be on the other side of the hill.

The arrangement of present paleontology was recently defined by Romer: "It is customary in vertebrate work that a gentlemanly division of territory be made to avoid overlap of effort and a stepping-on of toes."[19] In practice, an area belongs to the discoverer until he has abandoned it completely. Only then may others try their luck. Some of the fireworks have gone out of collecting, but at least since Cope's and Marsh's day paleontologists will talk to each other.

[19] Alfred S. Romer, "Review of *Late Permian Terrestrial Vertebrates, U.S.A. and U.S.S.R.,* by Everett C. Olson," *Copeia,* No. 1 (1964), 251.

CHAPTER 6

Distractions from Marsh

WILLISTON's years in New Haven, from 1876 to 1890, from age twenty-five to thirty-nine, were difficult ones for him. Happy moments there were, but his growing dislike of Marsh and his indecisiveness about his own future often depressed him. He could not see his way to fame as clearly as when a youth.

While struggling with his inner turmoil, he set himself to work diligently. Casually at first, he began a new hobby to take his mind off Marsh. In "Recollections" he explained the beginning:

"I had long given up any hope of doing any independent research work in paleontology and had been seriously considering some other branch of Natural History, where I would be unhampered by Prof. Marsh. In 1876 we had been flooded out by the river one night and when we came to recover our camp equipage that had been covered by a dense layer of drift, we found many beetles. Brous had been a collector of beetles for years, and it was a harvest for him. We had a few days to wait till the river went down and I helped him to collect specimens. There were so many that they attracted my interest. Brous gave me a box and pins and I undertook to see how many species I could find. The result was that I began a collection of beetles for myself. And I continued the fad till I had got together about twelve hundred species. When I began to study them, however, for mere collections did not satisfy me, I found that the literature was extensive and access to a considerable library would be necessary to prosecute my studies very far.

"I reluctantly then turned to something else while keeping up my collection of Coleoptera. The next season, 1877, I bought a copy of Coues's Key to N. A. birds[1] and Guild and I collected and

[1] The *Key to North American Birds* (1872) by Elliott Coues was the first bird book

99

identified about one hundred and fifty species in western Kansas, while I meanwhile made a small collection of spiders and living reptiles. I was thoroughly imbued with this collecting fever. I published one or two papers on the habits of beetles, one especially on Amblych[e]ila cylindriformis Say, whose habits I discovered by observing their remains in the excrement of owls as crepuscular —and that they lived in holes in clay banks. They had sold for as high as $20. a specimen. When we left Kansas they were a drug on the market at 50 cents! The results of my bird collecting were published in a list of the birds of Wyoming, the plumage of Wilson's phalarope, etc."

Amblycheila cylindriformis, "a sort of double-jointed, back-action beetle," nearly precipitated its own scientific controversy. Fellow-collectors Harry Brous and Williston both claimed credit in print for discovering its obscure habits, and D. H. Robinson of the University of Kansas later attributed the discovery to Francis Huntington Snow, entomologist and chancellor. In what was probably his first scientific paper, Williston objected strenuously to Brous' taking all the credit in an earlier published paper and emphasized the accuracy of his own observations.[2] Snow almost simultaneously gave the credit to both Williston and Brous. Williston himself caught five hundred of these elusive beetles in 1876 and 1877.

"When I returned to New Haven in January, 1878 [Williston continued in "Recollections"], I was still more determined to find some independent field for research. I desired some field in which not so much had been done but that the libraries and collections would be within my reach. The only opportunity I thought for me would be in some western college, where I knew I would have to provide my own facilities for research. So, after deliberation, I began the study of flies. And that is how I happened to be an entomologist."

---

to use the artificial key for identification and was a remarkably useful field guide, with a great deal of information on habits of birds.

[2] "On the Habits of *Amblychila cylindriformis*," *Canadian Entomologist*, Vol. IX (1877), 163–65.

J. M. Aldrich commented in more detail about Williston's entry into the study of flies:

"His interest in the flies began to be serious about 1878. At this time Osten Sacken[3] had returned to Europe, and there was not a single American student of the order [Diptera] but Edward Burgess, the Boston yacht designer, who published only one small paper. So Williston was virtually alone on the continent. In the absence of guidance, he plowed his way by main strength (as he often narrated to the writer) through descriptions of species until here and there he made an identification, which served as an anchor point for a new offensive. He had few definitions of genera, so had to work backward from the species. After a year or two of this tedious and time-wasting effort he came upon Schiner's Fauna Austrica, in which the Austrian families, genera and species of Diptera as known up to 1862–4 are analytically arranged and succinctly described. To his immense relief and satisfaction, he now found that all his American flies could be traced to their families, and most of them to their genera, in this fine work. He was so impressed by the saving of time accomplished that his own publications coming later show the effect of this early experience on every page; everywhere he has the beginner in mind and is clearing the way for him."[4]

Williston's "Recollections" continues with the spring of 1878:

"When Professor Marsh began talking about my going into the field again I readily acquiesced. I laid in a stock of birdshot, alcohol, insect pins and went back to Como, Wyoming, in March. I had given loyal service to Professor Marsh for four years, had given up my medical career, with no prospects before me but those of a field collector, with a present salary of $40. a month and a possible one years hence of $100, with an opportunity of doing all the research I desired to be published by him! [This last phrase was

---

[3] Carl Robert Osten Sacken (1828–1906) was a Russian diplomat who studied insects actively as a hobby. From 1856 to 1877, while consul general of Russia in New York, he collected and classified insects, especially flies, extensively throughout the United States. In 1877 he went to Germany.

[4] "Samuel Wendell Williston," *Entomological News*, Vol. XXIX (November, 1918), 323–24.

crossed out by Williston in the original copy of "Recollections," but I feel it can remain after all these years.] I concluded then that I would take things a little easier. [William] Reed, [E.] Kennedy [a local railroad man] and my brother were to assist me. But I had other plans. I advised and directed their work, spending a few hours with them each day to earn my salary. The rest of the time I devoted to collecting bird skins and insects! When the specimens began to reach New Haven, the absence of my name as a collector attached to the specimens, and the suspicion that I was not very contented gave him a hint, and he told me to return to New Haven. I spent a few weeks prospecting for new locations in the vicinity and on the third of July I took the train for the east. And that was practically the end of my field work for Marsh [except one trip in 1884]. I was interested in the collections of dinosaurs and worked upon them in the laboratory for the next few years.

"In January 1879, before the expiration of my 3 years contract I told Prof. Marsh that I was determined to complete my medical course. Brous had graduated in Philadelphia and had begun practice. Marsh knew and I knew that Cope would employ me with a salary sufficient during the season to pay my expenses at College the following winter. A new agreement was made whereby I was to receive $66. a month for the following three years with the opportunity to complete my studies in the Yale Medical School. [The contract also stipulated that Williston would work only three hours daily in the museum during this time, and that he would have three weeks of vacation each year.] I immediately began my medical studies so long interrupted. In brief, I received my M.D. degree the following year, in June 1880.

"At my graduation, Prof. Marsh had me officially appointed 'Assistant in Osteology' in Yale College. In 1881 I was placed on the government payroll as 'Assistant Paleontologist' at $1200 a year [from Geological Survey funds under Marsh's direction], and I was married."

Because Williston was writing the above account for his family (who were presumed to know the story) and for other paleontologists, we can understand his lack of detail on his own courtship.

According to his daughter, Dorothy, Wendell rented a room in a double house on Lyon Street in New Haven in 1880, and his future wife, Annie Isabel Hathaway, lived in the other half with her family. She had completed high school the previous year or two, and was teaching school; she was twenty.[5] The two young people passed on the steps of the double house occasionally, and Williston much later told his family that he on first sight considered Annie a very beautiful girl. That she was.

In the early course of their acquaintance, Annie reported to her family on the first time she saw Wendell's collection of beetles: "If you chance to say 'bug' while you are in the room you are at once corrected and told that they are beetles. I saw a lady bug there and I happened to mention it and I was informed that it was a lady 'beetle' *ahem*."[6]

By January of 1881 the courtship was in full swing, and was at times stormy. The major disagreement centered around Williston's religious beliefs (or lack of them). Annie wanted him to become a member of her Congregational Church and this he firmly refused to do. In a letter to her, postmarked February 1, 1881, he explained his position:

"Your mother said not long ago [that any] man shows only his best qualities, and conceals his bad, to a girl he loves—you have seen in me all my good and bad qualities as well as you would, after years of acquaintance.—Shall I confess them? I am perhaps a little inclined to be egotistical, or possibly others might say *conceited* in my own abilities. I am sometimes prone to exaggeration; my lonely life is, I am afraid, making me more and more selfish —not in money—but in the comforts of life that I would dislike to give up. I am often dogmatic, 'for the sake of being contrary,' —and what *you* would add as the worst of all—a '*Unitarian*' in belief. No person has ever dared whisper a word against the purity of my morality. I have no vices (for I do not smoke and will not again [he tried a number of times, but he never did give up smok-

---

[5] Annie was born November 6, 1858.
[6] Letter of May 26, 1880.

ing]). Eleven years ago I went far away from home among strangers alone and unknown; temptation encompassed me everywhere, and I tremble as I think now that I might have become a drunkard —*tobacco*! and a good resolution saved me. I kept a full journal for the year. . . . One page in February is the dearest of all to me, for it contains the resolution that I would be *master* of myself.[7] —I have been, I trust I have shown you that I can be now. —An unkind word or a word to intentionally hurt one's feelings I never allow to pass my lips, and an angry one very, very seldom. I will not say I have done nothing in my life to regret. I do regret *one* unintentially [*sic*] cruel thing I have done from the bottom of my heart —causing to love me a pure noble hearted girl whose love I could not return. I am candid with you. Oh that you had been so with me and saved me all those months. You knew before I said one word of love, what my religious beliefs were. . . . Let me relate an incident. A college friend and half way chum was continually in hot water with the Faculty, and especially the President, who suspended him twice. A little later he fell in love with the President's daughter—he told me that he was bound to marry her and if necessary to do so would turn 'preacher.' He afterwards 'got religion' and joined a Church, won the consent of the President and married his daughter. He tried hard to convert me, for he was afraid I had the opinion of him that I had often expressed of such. Years passed, he is a famous and prosperous lawyer, and his *wife is unhappy* (or so I have been told). The last time I met him, I heard him use an expression to a client that struck me as hardly suitable for a church member. I said, 'How's this, W————, I thought you were a church member.' His reply was, 'To hell with the Church, a man cant be a lawyer and pious too'! Do you wonder that I was disgusted! He undoubtedly won his wife by professing that which at heart was only pretence. —Did the ends justify the means? pardon me but I have too high an opinion of the religion of morality that Christ taught to wish to imitate such procedures. One of the brightest ambitions of my life (a professorship—at a

[7] In his journal of 1870 in Arkansas he vowed in February never to drink again, after having joined a few times in the festivities of the surveying crew.

104

time when I was bitterly struggling to learn my profession—I threw away when already proffered to me, rather than to be untrue to what I thought right [the offer from Kansas Agricultural College to take Mudge's place], and, much as I love you, I will not promise to become an orthodox Christian. But you nor no one else *ever* hears me ridicule or make light of religion, anything that tends to make humanity better has my best wishes. Sincerely I would give five years of my life to be a conscientious Church member (except the belief in universal punishment) but I never expect to be, God has given me *reason* and I would be untrue to Him by refusing to obey its dictates."

Armed with his new medical degree that year, Williston considered setting up in practice in Kansas, to be near his own family, for his mother was ill, but Annie's family was reluctant to have her live so far away. He tried to persuade her (letter postmarked March 31, 1881):

"I can enter into a physicians life with love and enthusiasm, I have abilities that especially fit me for a physician. I have had *seven* years of *scientific* training. I am happiest when I work the hardest. I am at home in the west, and have more influence there. The position I have occupied here, my fluency as a lecturer, and my scientific studies, together with the friends I have there will give me better start.

"On the contrary, the position I occupy here, is dependent. Science is the slowest and hardest of professions to make a pecuniary success. My employer is a man I can not respect, and my work is such that I can acquire very little enthusiasm in. To work for fame alone will not satisfy me longer."

But he stayed in New Haven, chafing. In November, his wedding date set, he bearded the lion in his den:

"I came very near having a quarrel with the Prof. last Saturday. . . . I talked pretty severely to him, about money matters and the way he was trying to prevent me from acquiring any sort of independent reputation. I got decidedly angry and he seemed pretty well annoyed at me. . . . It seemed to do him good to get talked up to—he was apparently more anxious than ever to keep all straight with me on the following Monday."[8]

Despite his uncertainties, Williston had a remarkably pleasant year, thanks to the congeniality of the closely knit Hathaway family, at whose house he spent many a cheerful evening. The elder daughter Genie was engaged and she married in September, 1881,[9] and the two couples often picnicked and attended concerts and lectures together.

James T. Hathaway had a keen interest in the world about him, evidenced by the great variety of news clippings he meticulously saved and mounted, and by his years of journal entries. He had been a printer and intermittent newspaper editor; he began as an apprentice on the New York *Tribune,* and later himself published the Fair Haven *Tribune.* Hathaway contracted tuberculosis and after his recovery settled in New Haven as a printer. He and his wife were a very devoted couple and doting grandparents. Mrs. Hathaway saved all letters that came into the house, in bundles tied with ribbons and bits of string. The family thought highly of Williston, whom they called "the Doctor," and they sympathized with his problems with Marsh. Annie strongly encouraged his extracurricular work on flies.

The wedding date was finally set for December 20, 1881, and Williston joyfully—and with supreme self-confidence—planned their honeymoon trip in a letter to Annie (November 30, 1881), who was visiting Genie in Washington:

"I am almost wild with joy and anticipation when I begin to realize that the time is so soon. 'The 20th' 'the 20th' keeps ringing in my ears, all day long (when the Prof. isn't talking to me!). I

---

[8] Letter of November 24, 1881, to Annie, who was visiting in Washington.

[9] Genie's husband was Franklin Hathaway Trusdell, a cousin of James T. Hathaway. He was a newspaper reporter, became the head of the Associated Press bureau in Washington, and was one of the founders of the Gridiron Club. After the shooting of President Garfield in 1881, Trusdell occupied a corner room in the White House while reporting on the president's condition, and he later covered the trial of Charles J. Giteau for the assassination. He was an excellent reporter and writer—but not a faithful husband. Genie left him after five years of marriage, taking their only child Harold back to New Haven with her. Ironically, Mrs. Hathaway had been more uncertain over Annie's husband-to-be, Williston, than over Genie's.

have a number of scientific friends in Boston with whom I am personally, by correspondence or by reputation acquainted. You will want to see the city with me, and wont [*sic*] I take pleasure in showing you about the Museums, especially the Harvard Entomological collection—the largest in America. The Professor of Entomology is a friend. There is no pleasure I feel so deeply as to meet scientific men who are acquainted with me through my writings. You have had a strange effect upon me the past year. I have lost *very* much of the diffidence that I had, and I dont feel the least hesitation now in meeting and talking freely with men of even worldwide reputation."

On the evening of December 19, "Prof. O. C. Marsh of Yale College drove down in his carriage and brought a beautiful set of Chambers' Encyclopedia, bound in elegant style."[10]

And so at last came December 20, 1881. "The sun shines warm; a blue haze bathes the distant hills in beauty. . . . It is a delightful, October day of the Indian summer type." So wrote the bride's father after the morning wedding ceremony and the departure for Boston of Dr. and Mrs. S. W. Williston, where we hope the bride enjoyed the museums.

Annie later told her family that at the time they were married Wendell had only two shirts to his name—and the other one was dirty! He also owed ten dollars, for flies he had bought.

In July, 1882, Williston signed his third contract with Marsh, agreeing to work for him for five years, forty hours a week and one month's vacation each year, for $1,500 annually. For the next three and one-half years he did so, studying his collection of flies on many evenings and relaxing in a happy home life in New Haven. He and Annie lived with her parents. Their first child, Ruth, was born November 5, 1882.

In the summer of 1884 Williston did his last field work for Marsh, on the hot plains of Kansas. Although the trip gave him a chance to visit his parents, he found the work tiresome and discouraging, and the separation from his family hard to bear. But he

10 Journal of James T. Hathaway.

was pleased to add new flies to his growing collection. In letters to his wife he presented a new possibility:

"I am going to write Marsh a long letter . . . and demand $1800 or else permission to leave him this fall. If he gives me $1800 I shall agree to give up the study of Entomology entirely and devote myself to the anatomy of reptiles."[11]

But Annie disagreed:

"When you write to Marsh dont [sic] say any thing about giving up your flies, for you have spent so much time and money on them that it seems a pity, and you are just getting so well known in that line. What I mean is dont [sic] offer to give them up, but get $1800 without, if you can."[12]

He did not broach the suggestion to Marsh.

Williston had much to do in solving the field problems at the fossil locality at Long Island in north-central Kansas. Sternberg had been working there, for Marsh, for some time, and J. B. Hatcher was working with Sternberg. Personality problems had developed, and relations with the land owner were strained. Williston resolved this diplomatically by setting up two quarries, one under Sternberg on the east side of the ravine, the other under Hatcher on the west. The fossils were very well preserved Tertiary mammals:

"The material is a clean heavy sand and the bones are in remarkable preservation, cleanness and abundance, as an instance it was said not long ago several loads were dug out and sold for old Buffalo bones for $30 per ton! The outcrops now, however have been dug in so far that it is simply folly in removing earth by shovel, that can be done so much more expeditiously by horse-power.

". . . Sternberg assures me that in travelling this whole region there is no locality *that any ways* compares with it for abundance, perfection, and *cleanness* of specimens. The bones have dried, and hardened in the sun can be brushed and cleaned and made to look like the best recent bones. Usually the limb bones are complete and without a fracture, but there appears to be almost no relation be-

[11] Letter of August 9, 1884.
[12] Letter of August 15, 1884.

tween the bones. The animals appear to consist chiefly of noceros of two kinds, mastodons, large tortoises, and camel., S[ternberg] says also of Carnivores.

"There is no reason why with good packing the bones should not reach New Haven in absolute safety, but I will assure you that you never will succeed *in* getting *specimens packed well by Sternberg* OR *anybody else when the matter of packing material becomes an object of personal economy!* What is needed is *small* and *more* boxes, but they cost about 30 to 50 cents each and owing to the large number of boxes required you see it is a matter of Economy to Sternberg to scrimp on packing material."[13]

Williston continued two days later:

"My advice to Sternberg and Hatcher is to make strong boxes of moderate size (costing 50 cts each), and, in the case of limb bones, to wrap and tie and label each bone separately, then to cover the bottom deeply with hay, put in a layer of bones, filling the interstices carefully and completely with hay, then another good heavy layer of hay, a second layer of bones and remainder with hay. In this way I am confident nearly every bone will reach you in as perfect condition as recent bones, and cleaner. The jaws, of which I have seen several, are admirable specimens. The bones can not be sacked immediately, they require thorough drying to make them harder, but the ground above the quarries affords good drying places. . . ."

Shortly before leaving the field area, Williston summarized the collection:

"Sternberg [has] taken out four beautiful skulls (Rhinoceros, &c) several of them that will be as white, as perfect and as clean as recent osteological specimens. I am satisfied there is a greater variety of forms that [*sic*] one at first supposes. Hatcher has taken out several mice more or less complete, several snake vertebrae, the bill of a small bird, and a bone of a larger one. I am chiefly engaged in wrapping specimens. Two men can remove all that one person can wrap and pack as they ought to be. . . ."[14]

[13] Letter to Marsh of August 9, 1884.
[14] Letter to Marsh, August 29, 1884.

"I remained with Prof. Marsh till 1885 [Williston went on in "Recollections"], though discontented. Discontented chiefly because I did not have the opportunity to work as I desired. Professor Marsh's methods were such that his assistants were forced to waste much of their time. In February of 1885 I had a controversy with him because of a letter that I wrote to the Director of the U.S.G.S. complaining of the delay in the payment of our salaries. He was angry, perhaps properly so, and on his return from a trip to Washington, accused me of things that were not honorable. In my anger I accused him of various things of the past not very creditable to him, that he thought I did not know, and suggested that it was about time for us to sever our relations. To this he agreed, but asked me to remain till the first of July that there might be no outside talk. I applied for, and received the degree of Ph.D."

The letter Williston had written to Director John W. Powell of the Geological Survey was brief:

"Funds for the payment of salaries for the employes in the Palaeontological Div, for the quarter ending Sept. 30 have, I believe, not yet been received here. As the frequent delay of the quarterly payments causes much inconvenience, may I beg, on the part of us all, greater promptness?"[15]

Williston may or may not have known that the Geological Survey funds under which he was employed at Yale were provided directly to Marsh for his disbursement and that the tardiness of payment was Marsh's laxness in money matters. Powell merely returned the letter to Marsh. The laboratory employees often chafed under Marsh's careless handling of salaries and field expenses. Marsh had never married, and he received regular income from his uncle's estate.

Among the memorabilia of Marsh in the Peabody Museum is Williston's final letter to his employer:

"From a review of all the circumstances, and after mature deliberation, I have finally and definitely resolved to sever my relations with you. I beg that you will accept this without further

[15] Letter filed with the Williston correspondence to Marsh in the Peabody Museum at Yale, dated October 15, 1884.

110

discussion. I do not wish to have any trouble nor to leave in an unfriendly spirit. My duties are too irksome, and it is impossible for me to do justice to them. To remain longer is simply to postpone the day when I must seek another occupation, and I cannot afford to lose more years of my life. . . ."[16]

Thus Williston left Marsh after eleven years. He had lost his awe after the first few months of working for Marsh, but he held a grudging respect for him throughout his life. Under his direction Williston learned how to find, to collect, and to study paleontological material—a background he found invaluable in later years. When his own publications in paleontology began a few years later, many references appeared to Marsh's work, some disparaging but others praising the insight into animal relationships. The characteristic that he could not accept was Marsh's lack of recognition for the professional work done by assistants, including himself.

In what was undoubtedly a fit of pique he turned his back on paleontology and, inevitably, turned to his flies. His Ph.D. dissertation was "A Synopsis of North American Syrphidae." He had a Ph.D., he had an M.D., he had a family—and he had no job. In "Recollections" he said:

"I did not know what I was to do, but I determined to give up science in which the prospects for success seemed so poor, and go to the practice of medicine. On learning that I had given up my place with Prof. Marsh, Prof. Riley of Washington, the U. S. Entomologist, made me an offer of the position as his chief assistant at $1800 a year. I thought it over and declined his offer, much against the advice of my family. Had I accepted the place perhaps I would now be the U. S. Entomologist."

Although Genie's husband did some negotiating with C. V. Riley in Washington over the possibility of Williston's working for him, Williston declined apparently because he "entertained a shrewd doubt as to whether he could be happy in a position subordinate to Riley."[17] Family letters indicate that he feared finding himself working for another tyrannical employer.

[16] Letter dated February 17, 1885.
[17] J. M. Aldrich, "Samuel Wendell Williston," *Entomological News*, Vol. XXIX (November, 1918), 326.

The Hathaways pitched in to help. Mr. Hathaway enlarged his printing business (and later did considerable printing for his son-in-law), and Mrs. Hathaway began renting rooms, often to paying relatives and friends, especially Yale students. Early in 1886 Genie left her husband and returned home with her son. She and Annie helped with the extra housework entailed in roomers.

Williston tried various approaches. In "Recollections" he went on:

"But, I had reckoned rather hastily. Filled with the best resolution to practice medicine I hung out my shingle in New Haven in July 1885, but my specimens had not ceased to attract and I finally waked up to the fact that my habits had been too strongly fixed after ten years to be broken or given up.

"I went to Washington to do some work for Professor Riley in the autumn and then accepted an offer from Mr. Scudder to act as an assistant editor of Science in New York for a salary of $125 a month. In September I had accepted the place of Demonstrator of Anatomy in the Yale Medical School. For six months I went to New York daily and returned in the evening to act as demonstrator at the school. The work was arduous from 6:30 in the morning till 10 or later in the evening. In July, 1886, I was appointed assistant Professor of Anatomy, and resigned my work on Science. Unfortunately, the place carried little salary with it, only $300., but I managed to make a living by other work, tutoring in anatomy, writing definitions for the Century Dictionary, as 'town physician' and a very little in the practice of medicine. The next year I was appointed health officer of New Haven with a salary of $600. Altogether, I was now earning for the first time a larger income than I had had since I was a boy of 19 on the Arkansas railroad.

"An epidemic of small-pox in 1888 I carried through so successfully that the Town Council gave me a vote of thanks and increased my salary to $1200. but I resigned to undertake special work in the water supply of the state for the State Board of Health.

"In 1887 I had been made full professor of Anatomy."

Medicine had become Williston's chief interest again. The epidemic of smallpox in New Haven was apparently more a case of prevention than treatment, but at the same time Philadelphia had 176 cases of smallpox and all the Eastern cities were very concerned over the spread of the disease. Williston ensured that the disease did not get beyond one family in his town. From the present Director of Public Health in New Haven came this comment: "During Dr. Williston's brief tenure as Health Officer, the Board adopted the first regular rules and regulations relating to the control of contagious diseases, which regulations in my opinion represent a degree of public health sophistication not generally prevalent in those days."[18]

For the Connecticut Board of Health, jointly with Dr. H. E. Smith and Dr. T. G. Lee, Williston made a study of stream pollution by sewage and industrial wastes, one of the first in the country.

"It was expected," wrote the Principal Sanitary Engineer for Connecticut recently, "that the results obtained from this investigation would serve to indicate the general characters of the water of the state and serve as a rational basis for efforts looking toward their improvement. . . . Previous to this survey no systematic examinations had been made of the state's water supplies.

"The study provided data from microscopical, bacterial and chemical examinations which were made for the water supplies serving Hartford, New Britain, Meriden, Middletown, New Haven, Rockville, Willimantic, Norwich, Thomaston, Waterbury, Bridgeport, Danbury, and Stamford, these being the larger public supplies in use at that time. All of these water supplies were untreated at that time and Doctor Williston was collecting the needed basic data looking toward the possible need for treatment and improvement of the water. . . . This work also included the obtaining of data on the water temperature at New Haven and also the temperature of the ground."[19]

In a small brown notebook of Williston's, dated 1887, are comments on interviews with farmers and factory owners, on odors of streams, places where cattle refused to drink, amounts of sewage

[18] Letter to the author from John B. Atwater, October 10, 1963.
[19] Letter to the author from Richard S. Woodhull, October 10, 1963.

and chemicals being emptied into streams by paper mills, hat factories, and other manufacturers, and attempts to relate cases of typhoid fever and malaria to polluted water. The malaria and the typhoid organisms had both been identified finally in 1880 in Europe, but not until 1898 was the mosquito's role in malaria pinpointed. Williston must have been especially interested in the cause of malaria, for his own—contracted in Arkansas as a youth —bothered him intermittently throughout his life.

In his simultaneous work as a professor of anatomy at Yale, Williston was popular. At the end of his final year there, twenty-eight of his students presented him with an engraved gold watch. "Professor Williston was completely surprised and overcome, so much so that he was unable to respond."[20] He then gave to his father-in-law the watch Marsh had given to him earlier, which was a prized possession of Hathaway's for many years.

As a prelude to his later interest in high-quality medical practice, it is worth noting that Williston was president of the Yale Medical Society for the winter of 1887–88. This was a fraternal organization of graduates and senior undergraduates of the Medical School of Yale University.

From an old notebook of Williston's, most of the pages of which are filled with descriptions of flies, it appears that he may well have been one of the founders of this society a decade before. The heading in the notebook says "Organized Nov. 1, A.D. 1878," and the following pages present the by-laws of a group to be known as the "Associated Medics." Signatures of the founding members follow, and these include Williston and several names that appear in the 1888 list of the Yale Medical Society.

Although at one time Williston had considered giving up his keen interest in entomology, in order to gain higher favor from Marsh, he never did slacken his work in this field. As noted, Annie recognized the value of her husband's work in entomology and encouraged him to continue it. Only a year after they were married,

[20] Undated newspaper clipping, mounted in a scrapbook of Williston's, in which his new position is also announced.

when he had bought a new guitar, she threatene[d]
he had completed a paper in progress. During th[e]
of his New Haven days, he published fifty-one
Some of these, "On the Classification of North A[i]
(three papers) foreshadowed his most valuable
entomology. He collected specimens whenever he
and he bought specimens and studied those sent [t] ~~~~ ~~~~~.

The recognition from his hobby was welcome to a man who still
yearned for fame. Annie reported once: "At the Naturalists meeting [in New York] yesterday W[endell] was introduced to a great
many and most of them said they had heard of him before and it
has made him so stuck up that there is nothing here good enough
for him."[21]

Unfamiliar with the banquets of the day, Williston at that meeting went through a six-course dinner (for two dollars), thinking
each course was the last and therefore eating "everything up clean"
until he was "as full as a tick." He no doubt soon became an expert
in banquets as well as in flies.

The publication of his Ph.D. dissertation on Syrphidae was the
first monograph on flies by an American. The syrphus flies, some
of which look like small wasps, "contain among them many of the
brightest-colored flies," wrote Williston later. "None are injurious
in their habits to man's economy and many are beneficial. . . .
They are flower-flies and feed upon honey and pollen, loving the
bright sunshine."[22]

Entomologist J. M. Aldrich defined Williston's contribution to
this family: "His work showed high taxonomic ability as well as
a clear preception [sic] of the needs of dipterology in that day,
for it was carefully adapted to beginners; —almost too much so,
for . . . it created the impression that the family is an easy one,
thus encouraging many beginners to publish in it before they were
really prepared."[23]

[21] Letter to Genie, December 28, 1883.

[22] *Manual of North American Diptera,* 3rd edition, 247.

[23] "Samuel Wendell Williston," *Sigma Xi Quarterly*, Vol. VII, No. 1 (March,
1919), 20.

In 1888 Williston published a "Synopsis of the Families and Genera of North American Diptera," the first of the taxonomic manuals that were to become his outstanding contribution to American entomology. His father-in-law printed it for him.

CHAPTER 7

Into the Newspapers

ALTHOUGH he had removed himself from paleontology after 1885, Williston could not help being drawn into the public clash between Marsh and Cope in January, 1890. Williston's was a small part in the notorious feud. As one of several disgruntled assistants who had worked for Marsh, Williston had written several condemning letters that came back to haunt him.

Cope was a devious man, who by 1890 found himself frustrated at almost every turn. He had exhausted his moderate fortune, partly through unwise mining investments. Though he importuned everywhere, he could find no source of funds for publishing his long manuscript on Miocene and Pliocene vertebrates after the Hayden survey ended; and he was unable, in spite of an energetic campaign, to prevent Marsh from becoming re-elected to the presidency of the young but influential National Academy of Sciences.

When the Secretary of the Interior demanded, in December 1889, that Cope place in the U. S. National Museum all specimens he had collected for the Hayden survey, Cope was furious, and he blamed Marsh. He had put a great deal of his own money into fossil collecting, and he would not give up fossils he considered his own. So he attacked on another front.

In a news story on January 12, 1890, written by William Hosca Ballou for the New York *Herald,* Cope accused Marsh and John Wesley Powell, director of the U.S. Geological Survey, of "plagiarism and of gross ignorance and incompetence in the performance of the important public duties intrusted to their care." He contended that Marsh and Powell controlled the National Academy of Sciences, that Marsh kept government collections at Yale under lock and key, that Marsh instructed collecting parties to destroy specimens in the field beyond those of interest to himself, that Marsh retained the salaries of Geological Survey employees working under him, that Marsh—incompetent to do the work himself, Cope said—published the writings of his capable assistants as his own and plagiarized the work of others, that Marsh pre-empted land where Cope was exploring for fossils, that Powell's geology was inaccurate, that Powell duplicated the work of state geological surveys in the U.S. Geological Survey, that Powell hired congressmen's sons and journalists to curry favor.

The remarkable feature of Cope's accusation was that he obviously had been accumulating detailed evidence against Marsh for years. In fact, he had once bragged to Henry Fairfield Osborn of his "accumulated store of Marshiana . . . which at some future time I may be tempted to publish."[1]

He also announced delightedly to his wife in 1886: "I got a courageous letter from Dr. Williston for ten years in Marsh's employ. This will do great execution if it becomes necessary to use it. It shows M's modus operandi perfectly."[2]

What kind of personality would collect items of this kind as joyously as he collected new fossils?

Among the various items supporting Cope's charges, and printed that day in the *Herald*, were two undated letters to Cope from Williston:

"I wait with patience the light that will surely be shed over Professor Marsh and his work. Is it possible for a man whom all his colleagues call a liar to retain a general reputation for veracity! * * * I do not worry about his ultimate position in science. He will find his level, possibly fall below it. There is one thing I have always felt was a burning disgrace—that such a man should be chosen to the highest position in science as the president of the National Academy of Science while men of the deepest erudition and unspotted reputation are passed by unnoticed. Professor Marsh did once indirectly request me to destroy Kansas fossils rather than let them fall into your hands. It is necessary for me to say that I only despised him for it."

[1] Osborn, *Cope*, 585.
[2] *Ibid.*, 363.

And:

"The assertion of Professor Marsh that he devotes his entire time to the preparation of his reports is so supremely absurd, or rather so supremely untrue, that it can only produce an audible smile from his most devoted admirers. I have known him intimately for ten years. During most of the time while in his employ I never knew him to do two consecutive, honest days' work in science, nor am I exaggerating when I say that he has not averaged more that [sic] one hour's work per day. He is absent from the Museum fully half of the time, and when in New Haven he rarely appears at the museum till two o'clock or later and stays but an hour or two, devoting his time chiefly to the most absurd details and old maid crotchets. The larger part of the papers published since my connection with him in 1878 have been either the work or the actual language of his assistants. At least I can positively assert that papers have been published on Dinosaurs which were chiefly written by me. * * *

"Professor Marsh's reputation for veracity among his colleagues is very slight. In fact he has none. * * * Those who know him best say—and I concur in the opinion—that he has never been known to tell the truth when a falsehood would serve the purpose as well. Those are strong statements to make of one holding such a position as he does, but I state them the more freely from the fact that everybody here (Yale College) concurs in them. He has no friends here save those who do not know him well."

These were certainly strong and bitter statements from Williston.

The newspaper article had been in preparation long enough for word to have preceded it through scientific circles, as the *Herald* itself said:

"Next Professor Williston was mysteriously moved and wrote to the HERALD that his letters concerning Professor Marsh were mostly written some years ago, under exasperating circumstances, before he had become connected with Yale College [as a professor of anatomy]."

Williston's letter to Marsh of January 2, 1890, was also quoted:

"I have given no one authority to use my name in connection

with charges against you or any of your work. On the contrary, I within one week, positively refused to have anything to do with the subject.

"The whole subject no longer concerns me, and is distasteful. What I said before was, I thought, in justice to another. I have no personal grievances."

Shortly after Williston's employment by Marsh had ended, Oscar Harger, an assistant to Marsh since 1870, had died at the age of forty-four from cerebral hemorrhage. This apparently affected Williston deeply. Family letters indicate that Mrs. Harger was a close friend. Williston had left Marsh's employ in anger, and Harger's death may have brought back that mood. He wrote a memorial to Harger for *American Naturalist,* a scientific journal that Cope had bought chiefly to ensure quick publication of his discoveries. In his memorial Williston said of Harger:

"Born with unsound physique, his life has been a constant struggle with difficulties that a man with a less indomitable will would have found unconquerable. . . . His life for twenty years has been wholly that of a student and investigator, but the published works by which he is known to the scientific world are not numerous or extended, though important. . . . The real work of his life . . . will never be appreciated save by those who knew him well. A patient and accurate observer, possessed of truly remarkable logical powers, and a man of very extensive and most accurate knowledge, the results of his eighteen years' work in vertebrate palaeontology have been of great value, notwithstanding the fact that none of them have been published by him. . . . To my personal knowledge, nearly or quite all the descriptive portion of Professor Marsh's work on the Dinocerata was written by him, and was published without change, save verbal ones. The descriptive portion of the Odontornithes was likewise his work, but this I cannot say from personal knowledge."[3]

Probably Williston's letters to Cope, publicized in the *Herald,* were written about this same time.

In the course of the week-long news stories (which Williston

[3] "Oscar Harger," *American Naturalist,* Vol. XXI (1887), 1133–34.

clipped and mounted in a scrapbook—unfortunately without marginal comment), Marsh provided answers to Cope's charges and aimed several of his own—especially theft of specimens and damaging of borrowed specimens by Cope, and predating publications so that Cope's named specimens preceded Marsh's. Cope and Marsh each offered a reason for the long-standing feud between themselves, each different naturally.

Cope contended that, soon after he had shown Marsh the New Jersey dinosaur localities, in 1868, "I found everything closed to me and pledged to Marsh for money considerations. . . . I left him, and since then have suffered a steady persecution for twenty years."[4]

Marsh maintained that, in 1870, when he proved that Cope's first specimen of the long-necked plesiosaur *Elasmosaurus* had been mounted with the head at the wrong end, Cope's "wounded vanity received a shock from which it has never recovered, and he has since been my bitter enemy."[5]

In his long reply to Cope on January 19, Marsh gave his views toward his assistants:

"Nearly all of these assistants have been faithful to their duties and faithful friends to me. Some of these were men of rare ability, and I could only retain their services for a limited time, as wider fields were before them and I rejoiced at their success. . . .

"My other assistants, who remained with me for a shorter time and then passed on to other scenes, were nearly all employed in mechanical and clerical work alone, as most of them were not sufficiently versed in scientific work to make their services of special value to me. Of these some left of their own accord. The work of others was not satisfactory and I could not retain them.

"For the latter Professor Cope promptly expressed great sympathy and friendship, and most of his ammunition in the present attack is derived from them alone. In his fertile imagination men whom I had employed simply to clean fossils or measure them became at once profound anatomists, whose opinions on the most

[4] New York *Herald*, January 13, 1890.
[5] *Ibid.*, January 19, 1890.

difficult problems of paleontology were conclusive. A touch of Professor Cope's magic wand, and again the same men became authors, who kindly wrote the works that I had for years in preparation."

Williston bristled and replied in an interview (probably January 20; the clipping is undated):

"Professor Marsh made definite contracts with me to do certain definite work for a stipulated salary. He treated me in that respect as he agreed to do. I never asked credit for work, never expected it and do not now. I have no right to say that he has treated me unfairly in his published scientific work. I received what he agreed to give, a money value for services.

"Will Professor Marsh deny that at the close of my connection with him he was one to recommend me to the chairman of the faculty of Yale College for the degree of doctor of philosophy? Do they give this degree at Yale for excellency in clerical and manual labor? I have been misrepresented in many ways. I can only trust that the truth will at last appear."

Williston was only one of many scientists inadvertently drawn into the unfortunate public washing of dirty linen, and many of the others were older and wiser than he. Surely he had never expected that his private letters to Cope would become ammunition in a public fray. Others of Marsh's assistants had also been quoted with adverse remarks of their employer, and George Baur resigned from the Yale laboratory during the week. As is discussed in Schuchert and LeVene's biography of Marsh, most of the assistants in the Yale laboratory shared and contributed to each other's opinions of Marsh. They resented not being allowed to publish independently, and they chafed at the irregularity of salary payments that Marsh was prone to make.

The biographers pointed out the irony of the feud:

"The pity of it is that the long pent-up bitterness which found release in this ill-judged newspaper polemic was so unnecessary. Practically all Marsh's assistants had successful careers in Paleontology or Geology, despite his refusal to allow most of them to start independent work while on his payroll. And who shall say that the abundant fossil material with which they worked at Yale, and the training they received therefrom, was any handicap to them in later years?"[6]

Williston certainly learned field and laboratory paleontology well, and he lost his awe of writers of books.

[6] *O. C. Marsh*, 312.

PART TWO

1890 to 1902

CHAPTER 8

Back to Kansas

IT IS VERY LIKELY that the unpleasantness of the newspaper fracas influenced Williston's decision to leave New Haven. At least his position as professor of anatomy was not sufficient to hold him there when he received two offers from Kansas in 1890. The first was from Kansas Agricultural College, his alma mater, offering him a professorship in biology. This he declined, still bitter at their earlier treatment of his favorite professor, Benjamin F. Mudge.

The second letter was from a friend, Francis Huntington Snow, inviting Williston to the University of Kansas at Lawrence as a professor of geology. This he readily accepted, for September of 1890.

Snow was one of the many transplanted New Englanders in Kansas.[1] Born in Fitchburg, Massachusetts, in 1840, he was in high school there when the abolitionists began talking of keeping Kansas part of the "North," a cause that Snow's father (a manufacturer of paper) fully approved. The young man attended and made a distinguished record at Williams College, where Mark Hopkins presided. Though strongly pro-Northern during the Civil War, Snow disapproved of fighting so joined the Christian Commission, a volunteer group that provided comforts to the troops. After the war he completed his education at the Theological Seminary in Andover, intending to become a Congregational minister. He began preaching but had often wanted to teach. Several of his friends had moved to Kansas throughout the years, and when an offer came from one of them in 1865 to teach at the new university in Lawrence, Snow accepted for the following year.

He had expected the professorship of languages, but "in order

---

[1] For an account of Snow's life, see Clyde Kenneth Hyder, *Snow of Kansas.*

to keep the control of the institution out of the hands of any one denomination, it was understood that two professors should not be chosen from the same denomination until all the leading denominations should have at least one representative in the faculty."[2] The Methodists and Baptists had pre-empted the first two choices, and the Congregationalists barely won their choice over the Presbyterians for the remaining professorship, that of mathematics and natural history.

Snow's teaching of natural history was not so wide of the mark as it may seem, for at Williams College he had received a broad education, and had been president of the Lyceum of Natural History, an active collecting and discussion group. At Kansas he began with a keen interest in ornithology but soon turned to entomology, particularly its application to farming. Many of his publications were on destructive insects, though papers on the birds of Kansas, on meteorology, and on many natural history observations appeared as well.

The University of Kansas opened only twelve years after the founding of the town itself. Forty miles west of Kansas City (Missouri), Lawrence had begun in 1854 on the slopes rising from the Kansas River (locally called the "Kaw") up to the high ridge known as Mount Oread. Like Williston's childhood home, Manhattan, it was a product of the New England Emigrant Aid Society and was named for Amos A. Lawrence, a Boston businessman who was one of the society's most active founders.

From its beginning the citizens of Lawrence had chosen the heights of Mount Oread for a college, and in 1856 Amos Lawrence provided the first endowment of $10,000. Troubles plagued the birth of the college: shortage of funds, though several prominent Lawrence people donated money; rivalry among the several church denominations for the sponsorship of a college; the bitterness of the entry of Kansas as a state, and the Civil War; a battle with Emporia for the state university after statehood; and even Quantrill's bushwhacker raid, which destroyed much of Lawrence

[2] Wilson Sterling, "Historical Sketch of the University of Kansas," in Wilson Sterling (ed.), *Quarter-Centennial History of the University of Kansas, 1866–1891,* 84.

in 1863 while the town was trying to meet its promise to the legislature of $5,000 to begin the university.

The determination of the city's prominent citizens was strong throughout the setbacks. According to Wilson Sterling: "The city of Lawrence had long been regarded as the literary metropolis of Kansas, by her own citizens, at least, and when the question of location of state institutions came up for consideration, the people of Lawrence preferred to secure the State University to any other institution, even the capital."[3]

By 1863 the state university was established high on Mount Oread. Quantrill's raid turned out to be a blessing in disguise for the infant university, as relief funds for the victims of the raid were diverted to the early building fund.

The first building, North College, opened in 1866 to "twenty-six young ladies and twenty-nine young gentlemen" under three professors: E. J. Rice, professor of belles lettres and mental and moral science; D. H. Robinson, professor of languages; and F. H. Snow, professor of mathematics and natural science. The Reverend R. W. Oliver was the first chancellor.

The three professors took their teaching duties seriously, and immediately Snow was recognized as an outstanding teacher by students and faculty alike. Said a student later:

"He was friendly, he was kind, he was patient, he was honest, he was lucid and forceful in speech, he was enthusiastic; and above all and under all was his manliness and fearlessness. These characteristics won for him the respect, the admiration, and the affection of hundreds of students who came under his tutelage. In after years we loved to recall, not so much that we had studied botany and zoology at the University, as that we had studied them under Professor Snow."[4]

In the spring of 1890 Snow became the fifth Chancellor of the University of Kansas. He and Williston were old friends. Their acquaintance had begun during Williston's student days at the Agricultural College in the 1870's, undoubtedly through Benjamin

[3] Sterling, *loc. cit.*, 63–64.
[4] W. C. Stevens, quoted in Hyder, *Snow of Kansas,* 116.

F. Mudge, who had worked with Snow and J. D. Parker of Topeka in 1868 to found the Kansas Academy of Science. How well Snow and Williston had continued their acquaintance during Williston's New Haven days we do not know, but presumably each was familiar with the other's entomological publications from their very earliest meeting when both were interested in the elusive *Amblycheila cylindriformis*. Snow's offer to Williston in 1890 indicates his admiration:

"W. J. Baumgartner reports that he heard Snow say that he had consented to become Chancellor only if Williston should join the faculty. The minutes of the Board of Regents suggest this possibility, recording that on April 10, 1890, Williston was elected Associate Professor of Geology and Paleontology. Snow, who as President of the Faculty had doubtless had some voice in making appointments, accepted the Chancellorship on the following day."[5]

And Williston said, in a tribute to Snow: "When, in 1890, I accepted his invitation to become a member of his faculty in the University of Kansas, it was chiefly because he was the Chancellor."[6]

On April 21, 1890, Snow wrote Williston: "I rejoice that you have accepted the professorship. . . . We receive many [inquiries] in reference to coal, oil, natural gas, and other valuable Kansas products, and their satisfactory answer will tend to strengthen the institution before the public. Your training has been so broad, you are so very able a man, that I shall feel safe in leaving to your charge many things in the museum as well as in the general work of instruction.

"Do not fail to bring the [collection] of flies; and I trust you may find time to continue to act as the standard authority upon this subject after your removal to Kansas."[7]

In spite of having accepted the professorship, Williston almost changed his mind at the last minute. He went to Kansas in August,

[5] Hyder, *Snow of Kansas*, 282.

[6] "Francis H. Snow, the Man and Scientist," University of Kansas *Graduate Magazine*, Vol. VII (January, 1909), 128.

[7] Copy of a letter sent to the author by Laura Neiswanger of the library of the University of Kansas.

and naturally stopped to see his father in Manhattan first. Faculty members of the Kansas Agricultural College still tried to persuade him to teach there instead and made tempting offers. A few days later he visited Lawrence, arriving unfortunately while Snow was absent, and he was very annoyed at his reception, as he wrote Annie:

"Candidly, so far, I am disappointed, and disgusted. Scarcely any one has paid any attention to me. Prof. Sayre very kindly took me about last evening to some members of the Faculty, and it was 'Prof. Wilkinson,' 'You are from Connecticut I believe.' I am disgusted, and I understand the reason—a supplementary catalogue has been published, in which I am put at the tag end of the Faculty as 'Samuel Wendell Williston, M.D., Associate Professor of Geology.' I am placed in a position that I resent. Those who do not know me take me to be some unknown man that they are receiving on *trial*, with name and reputation to make! I shall tell Prof. Snow frankly tonight [he was due back that day] that they must either give me an equal rank and pay with the rest or I shall accept the Manhattan place. . . .

"I don't like the idea of being at the last end of the faculty here. 'S. W. Williston, M. D.'—bah.' "[8]

Snow's return improved the situation immediately:

"He [Snow] has promised me," Williston wrote four days later, "that I shall be put on the same rank with the rest of the Faculty, and so far as he is concerned he has done all he could to have my salary made higher. He could not have done any more last spring. He guarantees the full salary next spring, and will endeavor to have it brought about before that time—and *because* the [Agricultural] college has offered me what they did, he thinks he will be successful. Had I not accepted the offer, as it was made, it is quite certain that I should not have had the chance to come at all—I have decided to remain. . . .

"I could not possibly ask for better facilities in my own work. I am practically to have *all* my time to do just about as I please. This year I shall have only one class a day for one half a term.

[8] Letter of August 23, 1890.

I shall have four rooms in the Museum, a laboratory, work-room, class-room and private room—the last the pleasantest room in the building. . . .

"The regents are talking about organizing the Medical department this year; if so they will ask me to be its dean.—I don't think I want the place."

Snow was able to carry out his promise for Williston was advanced to full professor on September 24.

He began teaching meteorology and geology with great confidence:

"I have only the seniors and all exercises in the senior year are optional, so that it largely depends upon the popularity of the teacher how many students he has, and those professors who draw large classes in optionals soon get the reputation of being 'strong men' and are estimated accordingly. I am not afraid but what I shall have my share! Seniors are required to prepare for a graduation a thesis of 10,000 words, the work ranking as one study. Will Snow, the professor's eldest son, has elected an entomological subject under me, and I have already set him to work."[9] No wonder the chancellor had told Williston to bring with him his collection of flies.

Williston's early confidence was soon confirmed. By the spring of 1892 he was pleased to learn that the students called him "one of the best teachers in the university."[10]

Lawrence, Kansas, in 1890 was a town of 12,000 people. The townspeople had brought with them from New England their social graces and their culture. Although dependent upon the farmers of the surrounding plains, they considered themselves a cut above these people, and the presence of the state university increased their pride. Annie told her parents: "This is a one-horse town & the University is the horse."[11]

The streets were unpaved and turned to mud when winter snows melted:

[9] Letter of September 15, 1890, to Annie, still in New Haven.
[10] Letter from Annie to her mother, April 20, 1892.
[11] Letter of September 29, 1892.

"The walking is wretched again," wrote Annie to her parents.[12] "It took me nearly an hour to clean my dress after I got home [from church]. You dont [sic] have to go to the theater here to see a leg show. All you have to do is to take a walk on Massachusetts St. on a muddy day or stand at the crossings. Some of the women hold their dresses up in the back nearly to their knees."

Kansas has always been famous for its weather, and Lawrence shared the reputation, except that it was considered tornado-free. As Annie said: "There is more weather to the square inch in Kansas than any place I know of."[13] Letters to her parents recorded summer temperatures up to 100° (baking had to be done early in the morning), winter temperatures down to 14° below zero that froze pipes, spring wind gusts up to 84 miles an hour that took off roofs and scattered fences, summer thunderstorms with nearby lightning strikes followed by downpours of rain and often hail, tornadoes not very far away, snowstorms leaving several inches of snow, followed by slush and mud for weeks, and leading almost to floods along the nearby river. Muddy roads sometimes kept the farmers from getting into town with supplies.

A good winter storm brought out the skaters and coasters: "The boys start at the top of the University hill & slide down for three blocks—on the side walk—if anyone is in the way they must get out of it or take the consequences."[14] One professor's wife knew the consequences: she rode five blocks to the bottom of the hill perched on the back of a small boy who had tried to steer between her legs as he sped "belly-buster" down the snowy sidewalk.

Not all the weather was bad; spring especially could be very pleasant. But the weather was always unpredictable.

Sidewalks were of planks, often with "a good many holes in them," or of cinders from the winter's ash barrel. Elm and maple trees shaded the streets, but lawns were almost unknown, as blue grass would not grow well in the extremes of Kansas weather. Water was stored in cisterns for each house, and sewer lines were

12 Letter of February 21, 1891.
13 Letter to her parents, August 18, 1895.
14 Letter from Annie to Genie, January 11, 1892.

133

not installed until the mid-1890's. The town had few telephones; the Willistons' connection to downtown was not put in until 1899, though five families had a shared connection to the university before then.

But there was space. Annie wrote: "The houses in the town all have plenty of room around them, there are about two houses on a block and every block has a back alley running through the middle of it, so that people can get to their barns without going through the dooryard."[15]

Lawrence was well supplied with transportation, for both the Union Pacific and the Santa Fe passed through it, occasionally carrying distinguished visitors and touring entertainers. Educational facilities they had as well; besides the university there were four grammar schools and a high school. But the university library was still small and incomplete, in both fiction and scientific books. For children the usual source of reading was the well-stocked library of the Sunday Schools. Of these there were plenty, for Lawrence had fifteen churches. According to Williston: "The Congregational Church [of which they became members] is, I believe, the only church that has a large organ,—it is *the* aristocratic church of the town!"[16]

Annie felt that dress goods, furniture, and all household supplies were inferior to those of the East and more expensive, and she was quite disappointed in the Christmas displays in the stores. Williston ordered his stationery supplies from New Haven, as he could not find what he wanted in Lawrence. Many items were available in Kansas City, and shopping trips there by train were customary for many of the university people.

The campus setting was choice, as Williston's sister-in-law Genie, while working for him in 1892, wrote to her parents:

"There are bob-whites in this country for I heard one the other day on the other side of the hill. The paper says the whip-poor-wills can be heard even in the center of the town but I haven't heard them; but every night I am sung to sleep by the peepers. . . . There

[15] Letter to her parents, October 26, 1890.
[16] Letter to Annie, September 7, 1890.

are hosts of birds, and the flowers are coming out, the strawberry blossoms are everywhere and they say the berries are large and thick. I have spotted several places where they are especially thick on the campus. The students by the way don't hang around the campus at all, so it is like the country the other side of Snow Hall. Trees have been set out in spots, and it is there I find flowers. The top of the hill was a ledge and rock enough was taken out to build the Main building, a very large structure.

"As I sit cleaning old bones several thousand years old, I can look out of the window at the green fields & hills stretching away for miles. That view is the best thing about Lawrence."[17]

But housing was more difficult, for "the houses for rent are a ragged looking lot," wrote Genie. For the first few years in Lawrence the Willistons were hard pressed to find good places to live, especially with the growing family. Ruth was eight years old when the family moved to Lawrence, and the second daughter Hyla was sixteen months old. Dorothy was born in 1891 and Eugenie in 1893. By then the family was ready to build a house, for Williston had come by a financial windfall. He and J. T. Willard of Kansas Agricultural College had together found a meteorite in Phillips County, Kansas, which they bought from the landowner for $60 and sold to George Frederick Kunz for $2,500.[18] It was an impressive one, in 3,050 pieces, the largest about 250 pounds, and the total of all pieces was 1,230 pounds.[19]

Williston promptly bought a house lot at the corner of Lee and Louisiana streets with his half of the meteorite money, scraped together all the money he could find, and had a house built from plans Annie got in New Haven. He directed the house construction in every small detail, watching his costs and changes in construction carefully, while Annie stayed in the East for the arrival of their fourth daughter.

[17] Letter of May 18, 1892.

[18] Kunz was a renowned gemologist, then working for Tiffany's, and also a special agent of the Geological Survey. This meteorite is probably the one identified by G. T. Prior (*Catalogue of Meteorites*) as the Long Island, Phillips County, Kansas, find. The larger pieces are now at the Field Museum of Natural History, Chicago.

[19] Letter from Annie to her parents, October 24, 1892.

Williston proudly described the house as "the most commodious and handsomest of any owned by the faculty," an opinion that Annie shared when she returned. It was finished immediately after the chancellor's new house, by the same contractor, and at the other end of the block that came to be known as faculty row. The last child, Samuel Hathaway Williston, was born in this house on the wintry night of January 28, 1899.

CHAPTER 9

On with Bugs and Bones

Paleontology in His Own Right

Williston's appointment as professor of geology brought him back to the paleontology he had abandoned after leaving Marsh's employ. Through him the University of Kansas joined the ranks of the excellent in vertebrate fossils.

Snow's enthusiasm for collecting in his professorial days had begun the fossil collection, although in his early years in Kansas he had refrained from usurping the material from his good friend Mudge of the Agricultural College. "Mudge and Snow had agreed to divide between them the kingdoms of the living and the dead— Mudge to study the fossil forms and Snow the living forms of life in Kansas. (Theirs was the boldness of the early gods.)"[1]

Snow did collect fossils on one trip with his students and with Mudge in 1877 or 1878, near Hackberry Creek in Gove County, Kansas (the stamping grounds of Williston for Marsh and Stern-berg for Cope about the same time). "Snow found twenty-eight fishes and saurians and Mudge twenty-two in one day. In less than three weeks the party collected 41 saurians, 117 fishes, and 6 pterodactyls. The most valuable find (Mudge pronounced this discovery worth all the others) was Snow's—a fossil saurian with the snakelike scales clearly preserved, still the only known specimen of the sort. During a period of forty years a large museum in New York attempted to buy it, but it remains in the museum in Lawrence."[2]

Another collector for the university before Williston was Judge E. P. West (1820–92), a lawyer who became interested in geology and fossils when past fifty. During the 1880's he was employed by the University of Kansas as a collector and as curator of fossils.

[1] Hyder, *Snow of Kansas,* 123.
[2] Hyder, *Snow of Kansas,* 154.

Judge West was justly, but jealously, proud of his collection and, already an old man when Williston moved to Lawrence, he was rather a thorn in the latter's side. Yet Williston understood him: "Personally Mr. West was, in many respects, a man of remarkable character, with a tireless energy and an indomitable will. At an age when most men are content to lean upon others, he still asserted, in an undiminished degree, the self-reliance and independence which had always characterized him. When past 70 years of age, he spent a season in the fossil fields of western Kansas, camping out alone, under the blazing sun and severe storms. . . . To him, more than to any one else, is due the credit of the building up of the collection of fossils of the State in the museum of the University, a collection unequaled elsewhere, and one of which the State may be justly proud."[3]

The intensive collecting of natural history specimens by Snow and his students (chiefly of birds and insects) and by West had more than filled the university's storage facilities by the early 1880's. The legislature approved a request of $50,000 for a special building for the department, and in 1886 the "Snow Hall of Natural History" was dedicated, to the delight of the enthusiastic students. E. D. Cope gave the principal address.

To that building went Williston in 1890, to study and augment the fossil collection. The field in Kansas was all his now, for Mudge had died eleven years before. It was a field he knew, too, from his early days of collecting for Marsh.

He began that first year with a plesiosaur just found by Judge West. Getting back to paleontology apparently rekindled his youthful enthusiasm, for Annie wrote her parents: "Wendell was writing up his fossil yesterday and got so excited about it and the tea that he drank that he didn't get to sleep till about four o'clock."[4]

His first field trip of the new job was in May, 1891, with E. C. Case,[5] Charles Sternberg, still a free-lance collector, and briefly

---

[3] "E. P. West," *Transactions of the Kansas Academy of Science,* Vol. XIII (1893), 68–69.

[4] Letter of October 26, 1890.

Professor Vernon L. Kellogg (of zoology). The group began at Rush Center, a little west of central Kansas, where they found Tertiary mammal bones, chiefly rhinoceros. They moved on to the Smoky Hill River, near Elkader, where after commencement E. E. Slosson joined them.[6] The trip was the first funded by the newly founded Geological Survey of Kansas, intended to survey the mineral resources of the state, a project long desired by Snow.

Williston enjoyed getting into the field again: "The trip has done me a great deal of good. I can walk ten or fifteen miles and not feel tired. Or use a pick and shovel for hours. My hands and face are tanned about the color of mahogany." He reported a good appetite, even for "bread, coffee, bacon, beans, when we can get water to cook them, and canned corn."[7] The only fresh meat was an occasional rabbit. The collecting was good:

"Did I tell you that I have made twenty-five *splendid* lantern views of scenery in Western Kansas, having the chalk cliffs, fossil grounds, etc? I got them with the direct intention of using some of them in a magazine article that I have planned and begun. We got some of the most perfect specimens ever obtained in Kansas or any wheres else. Judge West is at work upon them, and as fast as possible I shall make photographs and restorations of them so by spring I shall have magnificent material for a popular illustrated article that I am *bound* to have published in one of the lead-

[5] Ermine Cowles Case (1871–1953), whose name appears often in these pages, was Williston's first student in paleontology, and one who went on to an outstanding career. Born in Kansas City, Missouri, he entered the University of Kansas in 1889 and received his B.A. and M.A. in 1893. His Ph.D. was from the University of Chicago in 1896, where he worked with George Baur, a former assistant to Marsh, on Permian reptiles and amphibians. He returned to Kansas to marry one of Chancellor Snow's daughters. Case taught for ten years at Wisconsin State Normal School, and in 1907 went to the University of Michigan for the remainder of his teaching career. His collecting specialty was Triassic amphibians and reptiles, and he published extensively on fossil vertebrates. He was director of the University of Michigan Museum of Paleontology from 1921 to 1941 and chairman of the department of geology from 1934 to 1941. Students found his courses fascinating.

[6] Edwin Emery Slosson had graduated from the University of Kansas the previous year and was to become a professor of chemistry at the University of Wyoming for some years. In 1903 he turned to journalism, became an editor, and published several books.

[7] Letter to Annie, June 26, 1891.

ing magazines. Here in Kansas they have great respect for a person who writes anything for a leading magazine, and I shall fix my standing better by doing so—besides there is a hundred or two dollars in it.

"I have all the material for a restoration of a pterodactyl, that has never before been made, and a mosasaur besides the plesiosaur and one or two big fishes. I have begun the restoration of the Pterodactyl—it will require a sheet of paper 18 feet long and four feet wide! I shall make the drawing life-sized and then photograph it.

"The saurian I got is a wonderfully complete specimen—*every* bone in the skeleton complete and in order—ten feet long. I was horribly tempted to wish that I had found it under my own expenses; it is worth $500."[8]

The collectors found "about 80 saurians, 35 pterodactyls, 25 turtles, 4 birds, and several rare fishes. The saurians include two of the best ever taken from Kansas. . . . In addition a splendid lot of shells, baculites, barites, and selenite crystals."[9]

From the summer's collection came a series of papers by Williston, but not yet for a popular magazine; most appeared in the *Kansas University Quarterly.*

In 1892 and 1893 he collected and prepared an exhibit of Kansas rock and building stones for the Chicago World's Columbian Exposition of 1893, which celebrated the quadricentennial of the discovery of America. Simultaneously Erasmus Haworth,[10] the new professor of geology, prepared an exhibit on mining, and Lewis L. Dyche, professor of natural history, prepared an impressive display of animals, including Comanche, the horse that had survived Custer's 1876 battle at Big Horn, Montana, and that had died at Fort Riley, Kansas, in 1891.

Williston spent more than a year gathering building stones throughout the state from some fifty quarries, sometimes com-

[8] Letter to Annie, August 16, 1891.

[9] University of Kansas *University Courier*, August 1, 1892.

[10] Erasmus Haworth (1855–1932) was an economic geologist who taught at the University of Kansas from 1892 to 1920. He organized the state geological survey in 1894, and served from then to 1915 as state geologist.

bining his travels for these with lectures and fossil inspections. He was not fascinated with the project, but he scorned a request from the new University of Chicago that the exhibit be given to them after the fair, knowing that the samples would be valuable to the University of Kansas museum. The clays and stones of this collection were cut into six-inch-square blocks, polished on one side. Pieces of each were analyzed chemically and tested for strength. After the Chicago fair the collection was housed at the University of Kansas museum as a reference for builders, architects, and engineers.

In 1894, anxious to use six hundred dollars of field trip funds (that could not be used for other purposes), Williston arranged a trip to the South Dakota Badlands for about a month with his laboratory assistant T. R. Overton and several students: E. C. Case, B. M. Dickinson, E. S. Riggs,[11] Barnum Brown,[12] Irving Hill, Ralph C. Gowell, and George Jewett, plus entomologists Hugo Kahl and Will Snow. A collecting party from the University of Nebraska under Erwin H. Barbour[13] was nearby and it provided a rivalry in collecting—not in the tradition of Cope and Marsh, however. Brown and Riggs did annoy Barbour by pinning labels on prairie dog holes identifying them as *Daemonelix*; the prairie dog was one of Barbour's specialties. Barnum Brown recently recalled that 1894 trip:

"Dr. Williston was always cheerful and usually covered with flour paste which we used with burlap strips to bandage specimens. He would start to work on a specimen and then turn it over to me and say, 'Brown, you take it out. I am so anxious to see the speci-

[11] Elmer S. Riggs (1869–1963), born in Indiana, raised in Kansas, received his B.A. and M.A. from the University of Kansas. His professional career was with the Field Museum of Natural History from 1898 until 1942, where he became curator of paleontology. He collected fossils throughout the West and in South America.

[12] Barnum Brown (1873–1963), then a freshman at the University of Kansas, later became a paleontologist at the American Museum of Natural History in New York for 66 years. His collecting of dinosaurs for the museum began at Como Bluff, Wyoming, in 1897, and continued throughout the world until he had collected more dinosaurs than anyone else. He also made extensive collections of other natural history specimens.

[13] Barbour had worked in Marsh's laboratory with Williston, was professor of geology at the University of Nebraska from 1891 to 1938.

men when it is out that I am afraid I will injure it in excavation.' "[14]

The collecting was enlivened by one of the notoriously fierce hailstorms of the Western plains, which Annie recounted to Genie: "The hail was six inches deep & made a hole in the stovepipe big enough to put your two fingers through. They were all in the field when they saw it coming and W[endell] & Case ran for the camp. The tent went over like a piece of paper, Case's hat was found a half a mile away—one rubber blanket lost entirely. W & Case held the tent down over their heads & their arms & legs were black & blue for days, the driver was under the wagon sheet & the hail went through it & cut a gash in his head an inch long. They call Barbours party the 'Dudes' with their leggins & fixings but they are all bent on beating them on getting fossils. The boys work well. They had to dig a well the first thing & so have good water."[15]

Among the large collection of fossil mammals and marine reptiles gathered that summer were a new species of mosasaur, a Titanotherium skull, and two skeletons of a new sabre-tooth cat. Williston said proudly of the first that it was "what I believe to be the most perfect skull of a Mosasaur yet known in any museum. The specimen, which includes nearly the entire skull, the larger part of a front paddle and about forty vertebrae, has been mounted in the University Museum."[16]

In 1895 Williston's field trip fund was increased to $1,500, and on June 13 (to the dismay of one superstitious mother) another student expedition left Lawrence for fossils, this time to Wyoming. They were accompanied by one of the university regents, James P. Sams.[17]

After two weeks of unsuccessful prospecting, they were guided by W. C. Knight[18] to "a place they could work on for two years"

[14] Letter to Williston's daughter, December 21, 1962.

[15] Letter of June 28, 1894.

[16] "New or Little Known Extinct Vertebrates," *Kansas University Quarterly*, Vol. III, No. 3 (January, 1895), 166.

[17] James P. Sams, described in the Lawrence *Daily Journal* (February 27, 1893) as a "prominent farmer from near Seneca," was a regent from 1893 to 1901, through a difficult political time in the university's history (see Chapter 12). He was always interested in and partial to the work of the university.

[18] Wilbur Clinton Knight (1858–1904), born in Illinois, raised in Nebraska, and

north of Lusk, Wyoming, and the eager Kansas collectors cleaned out the fossils in three days. Williston was hunting a Triceratops, and—surprisingly—the group found an entire skull of one, 2,400 pounds. Shades of early collecting days: Indians were on the warpath in western Wyoming, to Annie's alarm, but the collectors were farther east.

For three years Williston had no major collecting trip, but throughout his years in Lawrence he frequently made short fossil forays, when word of a new specimen reached the university by letter or news story. One reported large reptile turned out to be a petrified tree. Annie grew philosophical about having her husband gone, though she certainly missed him: "He cant [sic] stand it long to stay in one place—Well, the university pays his expenses while he is gone & it is that much cheaper for us at home."[19]

In the summer of 1898 Williston took three students to home ground in western Kansas, near Scott City, on Ladder Creek, a tributary of the productive Smoky Hill River. Another nearly complete mosasaur was brought in from this trip, with the skin and the stomach contents well preserved.

In July, 1899, Wyoming had almost as many paleontologists as fossils, for a geological expedition of about a hundred men was guided there by W. C. Knight on a trip sponsored by the Union Pacific Railroad to study the geology of Wyoming.[20]

From Laramie on July 19 the expedition traveled for thirty-nine days by wagons, in groups of three wagons for each ten men, each group forming its own cooking and sleeping unit. The participants collected vertebrate and invertebrate fossils enthusiastically at many places. Como was a popular stop, as were the Freezeout Hills; all admired the Grand Canyon of the Platte River, and some scaled Laramie Peak.

Williston was only partly committed to this large expedition, for he and E. H. S. Bailey (professor of chemistry at the Univer-

a graduate of the University of Nebraska, was professor of geology and mining at the young University of Wyoming from 1893 until his early death.

[19] Letter to her mother, August 8, 1897.

[20] Wilbur C. Knight, "The Wyoming Fossil Fields Expedition of July, 1899," *National Geographic Magazine*, Vol. XI, No. 12 (December, 1900), 449–65.

sity of Kansas and a close friend of Williston) joined the group only for two days in Laramie and then struck out on their own for dinosaur fossils in the Freezeout Hills, west of the Laramie Mountains and just north of Medicine Bow, Wyoming. Other groups did similarly, for Williston found collecting parties from the American Museum of Natural History, from the Carnegie Museum, from the University of Wyoming (separate from Knight's large expedition), and one from the Chicago Field Museum, led by his former student E. S. Riggs. Williston's own party was small, consisting only of himself, Bailey, W. T. Lee, J. W. Beebe, W. N. Logan, and H. T. Martin (E. C. Case joined them from Chicago toward the end). But they shared camp with the University of Wyoming collectors, and two of the other parties were close enough to drop in for visits and to share antelope meat.

In five days the Kansas group had extracted a ton of dinosaur bones: *Morosaurus, Diplodocus, Stegosaurus,* and *Creosaurus.* Williston reported the picking and shovelling hard work. But he always enjoyed the scenery and wildlife of his camps, and he carried home seeds and bulbs for his garden.

For two days the Kansas collectors were interrupted by the large expedition, whose stop in the Freezeout Hills Knight described:

"Here the geologist and paleontologist found unbounded opportunities. The various bands forming the great fold in the Freezeout Hills were all uncovered, so that it was possible to study the entire section in minutia. . . . This being a comparatively new field and the dinosaur beds being exposed for a distance of 10 miles on each side of the camp, dinosaur hunting was the order of the day. Long before sunset on this never-to-be-forgotten 29th of July, men were returning to camp from every direction loaded down with bones; others were seeking teams to haul their heavier loads to camp, and though they worked diligently, it was nearly 10 o'clock before the last load of fossils was brought in. The next day's work unearthed a still larger quantity, the entire shipment from this point amounting to several tons."[21]

[21] Knight, *loc. cit.*, 457.

While at Kansas, Williston had no funds for a fossil-preparing group like Marsh's, but he had a series of assistants. After the death of E. P. West in 1892, Annie's sister, Genie, worked for Williston. Her duties, defined by Williston before she came, were "cleaning specimens with awl and tooth-brush, making and mounting microscopical specimens, preparing type-written MSS for publication, cataloguing specimens, writing letters, etc. etc."[22] Genie was versatile and handled the work well, but she returned to New Haven, where she had left her son with her parents, in the late summer of 1893.

Mary H. Wellman worked in the laboratory for a time; she later became assistant in entomology at Stanford. Grace Kirtland worked for Williston from the spring of 1894 until the summer of 1895. At the same time Williston had another assistant, T. R. Overton, who accompanied him on collecting trips in the summers of 1894 and 1895; Overton left in 1896 to "go to preaching." He was probably a preparator while Miss Kirtland presumably handled office details. She was also working on encyclopedia articles that Williston was writing at the time.

During 1894, Handel T. Martin began working in Dyche Museum as the curator, and proved to be excellent. Martin was an English-born early settler in western Kansas who began collecting fossils in the Cretaceous chalk near his farm. He sold fossils widely before working on the staff of the Smithsonian Institution, the American Museum of Natural History, the Yale Peabody Museum, and finally the University of Kansas. He made violins in his spare time.

From his paleontological studies at the University of Kansas Williston published about sixty papers on fossils, of which only three were for the popular market he had once considered so necessary to fame. Among his most valuable contributions were a series of papers for the newly established Geological Survey of Kansas in 1897 and 1898, on the Kansas Niobrara Cretaceous formation, the Kansas Pleistocene, fossil birds, dinosaurs, crocodiles, mosasaurs, and turtles. Williston summarized all the known discov-

[22] Letter of December 22, 1891.

eries of each group and let fly some barbs at Marsh's work, while always speaking kindly of Mudge. Osborn said that Williston's "work on the Kansas Cretaceous fauna, following the very disjointed contributions of Leidy, Marsh, and Cope based on inferior material, marks the turning-point in this field to the new order of description and generalization based upon complete material, including even the skin impressions of several great mosasaurs. In his observations on the mosasaurs, plesiosaurs, pterodactyls and marine turtles, and the birds with teeth, Odontornithes, he placed the osteology of these several animals on a much more secure basis. . . ."[23]

Of special value while he was in Kansas was his work on the fierce marine mosasaurs, presented in several short papers and a significant monograph (1898), that summarized the previous work on the group, presented excellent anatomical descriptions, and described the animals' habits. Lull summarized:

"[Williston] speaks of the creatures as marine lizards of moderate size, ranging from 10 to perhaps 37 or 38 feet, living in shallow waters, although some of the larger of them ventured far out to sea. Their feeding habits, as evidenced from the very peculiar lower jaw which had a joint in its mid-length, are discussed, but Williston felt that the rigidity of the breast girdle precluded any very remarkable feats in the way of swallowing bulky prey. He believed that the food consisted of the numerous small fishes which swarmed the seas with them—possibly an occasional young mosasaur such as, curiously enough, is almost unknown as a fossil. He believes, further, that the mosasaurs rarely came ashore, although they must have done so for egg laying, as there is no evidence that they were viviparous, but the body is not sufficiently serpentine, nor the limbs sufficiently strong, for terrestrial locomotion. They were very pugnacious, as numerous exostoses on the skeleton show. The body was covered with a scaly skin, the scales closely resembling those of a large monitor in size and shape. This knowledge is

[23] H. F. Osborn, "Samuel Wendell Williston, 1852–1918," *Journal of Geology*, Vol. XXVI, No. 8 (November–December, 1918), 683–84.

Clarence E. McClung, the distinguished student at Kansas who followed Williston into paleontology and medicine.

Meteorite found in Phillips County, Kansas, by Williston and J. T. Willard (presumably posing here) in 1892. The sale of this meteorite provided Williston with the money for his house lot in Lawrence.

The Williston family, about 1900.

The stagecoach from Lander to Rawlins, Wyoming, in 1904.
The hundred-mile trip took thirty hours.

Roy Moodie quarrying during the 1905 Wyoming expedition.

Fossil diggings near Baldwin Creek, Wyoming, in 1904.

Williston called this "A Fossil Camp." Chicago expedition of 1904.

Roy Moodie and Bartholomew excavating a plesiosaur,
near Willow Creek, Wyoming, in 1905.

Opening into underground cavern of Popo Agie River, Wyoming, as photographed by Williston in 1905.

Williston at the collectors' camp in New Mexico in 1911.

Fossil camp on Paleo Creek near Arroyo de Agua, New Mexico, in 1911.

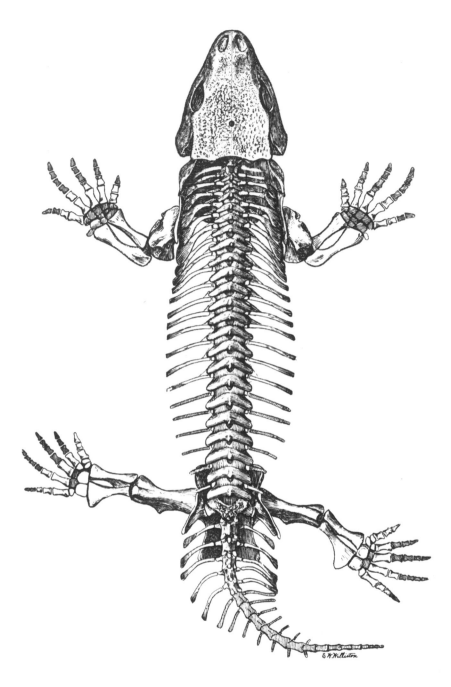

Skeletal restoration of the problematical *Seymouria baylorensis* from Texas.

Restoration of *Seymouria baylorensis* as drawn by Williston.

Carapace of dinosaur found on the 1905 Wyoming expedition.

The Williston home in Lawrence, at the corner of Lee and Louisiana streets, soon after its completion in 1893.

The outstanding collector and preparator, Paul C. Miller, in the field, probably in New Mexico in 1911.

based upon a specimen of Tylosaurus in which the carbonized scales are present on the anterior part of the body. Not only are the skeletal restorations of the three principal genera given, but a restoration in the flesh of *Clidastes velox*, with the associated *Uintacrinus* and *Ornithostoma (Pteranodon) ingens*.

"The publication of this memoir, supplemented by the researches of [Louis] Dollo of Belgium, gives us a body of information concerning the mosasaurs as authoritative as it is complete, and one which has served as a basis for all subsequent research upon the group."[24]

Entomology

For relaxation Williston turned to the study of flies whenever possible. One of his disciples wrote: "He loved the flies, primarily because he felt free when he worked on them; but also because they are abundant and rich in forms, can be collected and studied everywhere, and furnish numberless illustrations of evolutionary principles. Late in life he said to me, 'The happiest hours of my life were those spent on the Diptera.' "[25]

By 1891 in Kansas he had completed an article of one hundred quarto pages on the Diptera of Mexico for a British publisher. Its receipt in England led to another offer:

"I have just received a letter from the Trustees of the British Museum, asking me to undertake the diptera volume for a new work on the West Indies, and offering to pay for the work, though intimating that the remuneration will not be great. I am in a great quandary over it, not knowing what to do. If the pay will be sufficient, I think I will undertake it.—It will run through three or four years, and make a quarto volume of 400–500 pages with 15–20 colored plates. The other contributors are among the most eminent zoologists of the world.

"The MS that I sent has been thought to be of sufficient im-

---

[24] Richard Swann Lull, "Samuel Wendell Williston," *Memoirs of the National Academy of Sciences,* Vol. XVII, 5th Memoir (1924), 122–23.

[25] Aldrich, "Samuel Wendell Williston," *Sigma Xi Quarterly,* Vol. VII, No. 1 (March, 1919), 21.

portance to make a separate volume, and will be published during the year."[26]

This offer was for the monumental *Biologia Centrali-Americana*, supported by Frederick DuCane Godman and Osbert Salvin, who devoted forty years to the gathering of specimens and the editing of the detailed studies on Central American biology, for which each animal group was handed over to an expert in that field to describe.

Williston did, of course, agree to take over the Diptera part of this work, which was published in 1896 after many evenings of work. The project helped him through a long separation from his family in 1893, when his wife awaited in New Haven the building of their house, and the "remuneration" was welcome on the house expenses.

Even before completing the West Indies work, Williston began revising his manual on North American Diptera. His reason to his publisher father-in-law was simple: "If we do not do this pretty soon some one else will undertake it."[27] Optimistically in May of 1894 he estimated that the revision could be finished by that September, but it was not completed and published until 1896. The second edition was twice as large as his original eighty-four-page pamphlet.

In addition to these major works in entomology, Williston published almost forty shorter papers on insects while at Kansas, so that some issues of the *Kansas University Quarterly* contained his papers on both fossils and flies. Although he taught no classes in entomology, students in that field came to him for research projects, beginning with the chancellor's son Will Snow, and continuing through a number of others. He contributed many specimens to the University museum, so that by 1896 it was estimated to have more than 4,000 species of Diptera, many of them type specimens, and 20,000 specimens.

All Williston's work on flies was done at home, usually in the evenings and during school vacations, and Annie generally found this satisfactory. Occasionally she bemoaned the condition of his

26 Letter to Annie in New Haven, May 14, 1891.
27 Letter of May 16, 1894.

study—littered with specimens, papers, dust, and tobacco—and she could only clean it thoroughly when he was on a field trip. She commented once to her sister that Wendell always felt malaria when he worked on flies.

Williston's paleontology students were interested and amused at his hobby, and commented on his constant interest in flies, which he always collected as enthusiastically as fossils on expeditions. He sometimes paused in a classroom lecture to snatch a gnat from the air for quick identification.

His choice of a subject for study while he chafed under Marsh had proven wise. The then-unstudied Diptera provided him an outlet for unspent energy, and he always enjoyed the prominence he gained thereby. The respect he earned was well deserved. Aldrich summarized:

"In the nineties Williston busied himself mostly with tropical flies, the published results being mainly found in *Biologia Centrali-Americana*. As in his entomological beginnings he had no rivals, and he had some ten years the start of all who came after him, he easily maintained through most of his life the position of chief authority in the order; and his wide knowledge of genera and great ability made him recognized in Europe as one of three or four world authorities.

"His chief interest was in genera and the higher categories, and this was increasingly true in his later years. He was a student of evolution in a large way, searching for generalizations. In this respect his entomological career blends into complete harmony with his other biological labors."[28]

Williston himself once wrote to C. E. McClung: "Much of the best work I have ever done or shall do in science, was in entomology, but I suppose my reputation, whatever it is, will rest chiefly upon my paleontological work."[29]

His reputation rests securely on both fields, occasionally to the surprise of a present scientist who knows Williston's name in only one of his two professions.

[28] Aldrich, "Samuel Wendell Williston," *Sigma Xi Quarterly,* Vol. VII, No. 1 (March, 1919), 21.

[29] C. E. McClung, "Samuel Wendell Williston," *Sigma Xi Quarterly,* Vol. VII, No. 1 (March, 1919), 17.

CHAPTER 10

The Other Professions

The Doctor

WILLISTON continued his boyhood interest in medicine, and although his first appointment at Kansas was as professor of geology, his final one was also as dean of the school of medicine. His medical interest had been less in direct practice than in public health, and so he labored to improve the practice of medicine in Kansas.

The University of Kansas had wanted a medical school even before 1890, and Williston was active in the promotion of it as soon as he arrived there, as he promptly wrote to his father-in-law:

"I meet the Board of Regents tonight to talk of plans for the organization of a medical department. They will in all probability organize the school next year, and I will be made Dean, and as the deans of the departments are paid higher salaries than the rest, it will be of direct benefit to me."[1]

This hope—and the increased salary was to remain imminent for eight more years. A push was given in 1894 when Dr. Simeon Bell offered to the university cash and land in Rosedale (near Kansas City) for a hospital site. Chancellor Snow wanted a four-year medical course, with the proposed gift as the nucleus of the school, but the regents were not favorably inclined. Williston joined the battle, often conferring with the regents and occasionally speaking to medical groups. It was an uphill fight, against resistance by state boards of health, by other colleges, and by members of the university faculty and regents. The compromise in 1897 was the establishment of a two-year plan of medical courses.[2] In a later history of the medical course, Williston wrote:

[1] Letter of September 24, 1890.

[2] The four-year medical school in Kansas City was finally established in 1912 on the land donated by Dr. Bell.

"The scientific departments were extended and so modified as to furnish facilities for instruction of a medical character; the department of physiology was greatly extended and given facilities for high grade laboratory work; and for the first time in an American University not granting the degree of Doctor of Medicine, the department of human anatomy was founded and provided with the best facilities."[3]

The battle was not over, for recognition by medical schools still had to be obtained for the two years of study. As Williston said, he himself in June, 1899:

". . . presented the claims of the school to recognition before the Association of American Medical Colleges, which had hitherto refused such recognition. The fight here resulted in victory, afterward consummated at the meeting of the Association at Atlantic City. It was supposed that this would be the end of the matter, but unfortunately the Illinois State Board of Health, one of the most influential of the country at that time, still refused recognition; preventing the acceptance by the Chicago Colleges of Medicine of students from the University for advanced standing. Inasmuch as this refusal set a very pernicious standard, it became necessary that it should be reversed. By personal interviews with the president of that Board, and with the assistance of President Harper of the University of Chicago, this recognition was finally won; and the telegram acknowledging that fact a little later gave the greatest encouragement to the faculty of the University of Kansas School of Medicine. Finally in the spring of 1902 like recognition was granted by the Regents of the University of New York; and the Kansas University School of Medicine was finally established as a 'reputable school of medicine,' though giving only the first two years' work of the course and not granting the degree of Doctor of Medicine. Since that time, various like courses have been established in other Universities of America, receiving recognition as a matter of course; but the University of Kansas was the pioneer that made the way easy."[4]

[3] "The Origin of the University of Kansas School of Medicine," *Journal of the Kansas Medical Society,* Vol. IX, No. 6 (1909), 212.

[4] *Ibid.,* 214.

In addition to his paleontology classes, beginning in 1892 Williston taught physiology and histology. From that time he added medical courses steadily as the medical school finally became a reality. In the fall of 1899 the two-year medical course opened with thirty students, "quite as many as I wish to see the first year," said Williston.[5] He was keenly interested in the medical students and liked to entertain them at home.

Although a determined and self-assured man, Williston was essentially modest, and honors startled him. His daughter Ruth reported one incident:

"Last night the senior class of the medical school got up a surprise on papa. He was upstairs putting the baby [Samuel] to sleep when they came, and didn't suspect a thing till he went down and found them all spread out in the parlor. They presented him with a beautiful big oak [leather-covered rocking] chair which must have cost them fifteen or twenty dollars & papa was just staggered. He wouldn't say a word! & the boys thought it was great, because they said he had often had them in that fix but they never had got him before. Well he was mightily tickled and surprised! He thought at first that they had come to talk about quizes [sic] and had some bone to pick. They brought along a lot of ice cream and acres of cake and that surprised him some more and he asked mama where she got all that stuff."[6]

Williston also found time to serve on the Kansas Board of Health, a controversial organization that had finally been established by the state legislature in 1885. Among the problems behind the board's establishment was a quarter-century-old controversy between regular physicians and eclectic[7] and homeopathic physicians. Kansas had more eclectics than the other middle western states, and they maintained a strong antagonism to licensing requirements for medical practitioners. Legislators refused to pass laws on licensing that did not include eclectics and homeopaths,

---

[5] Letter to Annie, visiting in New Haven, September 14, 1899.
[6] Letter to her cousin Harold, May 24, 1901.
[7] Eclectics use plant remedies especially.

and regular physicians refused to include them. The result was, according to a contemporary Kansas doctor, that Kansas "had become, almost unawares, the dumping ground for the professional refuse from nearly every state and country on the planet. We had not only our quota of educated and reputable physicians, but we had everybody else's quota of disreputable and disqualified mortals calling themselves physicians."[8]

Williston said much the same thing long before he served on the board of health; he was addressing the Kansas Pharmaceutical Association:

"I say, and I believe those of my own profession will bear out my statement, that the profession of medicine in our state is crowded with ill-prepared practitioners. By no means would I say that we have no able men among our physicians here; on the contrary, Kansas need not blush for its better physicians,—men who have made themselves learned and able in spite of the fact that they have had little encouragement."[9]

He continued with his philosophy on licensing:

"It is pretty apt to be the case with all of us that we are not unwilling to see the way made more difficult to a diploma or license after we have attained that end ourselves; the requirements can then be increased, forgetting that if we had had to conform to those requirements ourselves we might yet be hoeing potatoes or herding cattle. Nevertheless, we have a perfect right to require conditions which we could not have met ourselves; because the conditions under which we labored were made for us by our father, and we are the ones who must make the conditions for our sons. Our experience teaches wherein we might have done better, and that experience should be harvested for our sons' benefit.

"But, the only requirements that we have any right to ask are honesty and competency. We may have become competent through the rough school of experience, but at what expense? A famous oculist once said that he had acquired his skill by spoiling a hatful

---

[8] G. F. Johnston, "Medical Registration," *Journal of the Kansas Medical Society* (1902), reprinted in Centennial Issue of the *Journal*, Vol. LX, No. 5 (May, 1959), 83.
[9] Address to the Kansas Pharmaceutical Association, May 18, 1892.

of eyes; let us require our sons to get that experience without the loss of a hatful of eyes."

The first break for good medical practice came with the establishment of the board of health. "Under the law of 1885, the Board was to make and enforce rules for public health, keep all vital statistics records [none had been kept in Kansas before], concern itself with sanitation and contagious diseases, and work with local health officers, all on a budget of from two to five thousand dollars annually."[10]

Opposition continued. For some years bills were introduced regularly into the legislature to abolish the board. Williston commented on the attitude of the people of the state in 1899:

"The trouble is that there are too many who are yet imbued with the idea that when a person dies it is fate, but that when a hog enters the unreturnable bourne, save in the appointed way, that it is carelessness. An epizootic of hog cholera causes consternation, but an epidemic of scarlet fever is a dispensation of providence! The one is stamped out with all possible vigor, and the aid of the highest experts is called for; but the other is dealt with in a very feeble way, if at all."[11]

The young board of health survived. Gradually the antagonism died between regular physicians and the eclectics and homeopaths, many of which latter practitioners were well trained and expert doctors. It may be that Williston's childhood interest in homeopathy helped bring the groups together; at least upon his appointment to the board of health in 1901, "he showed his enthusiasm for work in behalf of the health of the community and his ability to get things done by injecting new life into this body."[12]

A seven-man board of examination and registration was promptly established, consisting of two eclectics, two homeopaths, and three regular physicians (one of whom was mostly a paleontologist!). They obviously began their licensing with themselves, for

[10] Thomas N. Bonner, *The Kansas Doctor*, 82.

[11] "Relations of the State Board of Health to the Public," address dated 1899.

[12] E. H. S. Bailey, "Doctor Samuel Wendell Williston," University of Kansas *Graduate Magazine*, Vol. XVII, No. 2 (November, 1918), 36.

Williston's Certificate of Authority to Practice Medicine and Surgery in Kansas was number 7.

From that stormy and slow beginning, Kansas went on to become one of the foremost states in public health early in the twentieth century. Williston's role was important but brief, and he soon left the state to teach at the University of Chicago. The most powerful board of health figure in the next decade was Samuel J. Crumbine, who gained nationwide fame with his hard-fought battles against houseflies, public drinking cups, and germs in public places.

During Williston's years in Kansas he did not practice medicine often. Occasionally a faculty neighbor called on him for treatment, and he did vaccinate a number of people during a smallpox threat. He accompanied Snow, as both friend and medical adviser, on a relaxing trip to Arkansas in 1900 after the chancellor's nervous collapse. He contributed to malariology by providing to Kansas student Marshall Barber his first "visual acquaintance with malaria parasites," a sample of his own long-infected blood.[13] Barber went on to become a world expert on malaria.

Williston inspired students in all the fields he taught. Among his foremost in medicine was Clarence E. McClung,[14] who became acting dean of the medical school when Williston left. "McClung's studies of the chromosomes which determine sex attracted worldwide attention and are said to have stimulated more scientific research than any other discovery made in Old Snow Hall."[15]

But Williston's major contributions to medicine were in establishing a first-rate medical school, teaching many of its courses, and setting up high-quality licensing of Kansas doctors. When he left the state in 1902, he left medicine behind.

[13] Hyder, *Snow of Kansas*, 264.

[14] C. E. McClung (1870–1946) was born in California and attended the University of Kansas, where he received a Ph.G. (1892), A.B. (1896), A.M. (1898), and Ph.D. (1902). An associate professor in 1900, he became head of the department and curator of the vertebrate paleontology collection in 1902 when Williston left, as well as acting dean of the medical school. In 1906 McClung went to the University of Pennsylvania as a professor of biology. He published many articles on heredity and some on the Cretaceous fishes of Kansas.

[15] Hyder, *Snow of Kansas*, 262.

The Educator

From a boyhood awe of professors Williston had progressed to becoming the idol of his own students in Kansas. He carried a very heavy teaching load, in geology, vertebrate paleontology, comparative anatomy, physiology, histology, and hygiene, to students ranging from freshmen to Ph.D. candidates. He also taught evening extension classes in evolution, and he frequently gave public lectures, an outside commitment that was first approved as a public service but later forbidden by the regents. When it was allowed, Williston readily gave talks throughout the state, sometimes combining the trips with a bit of fossil collecting. The extra income from the lectures was always welcome.

The traveling conditions in most of Kansas just before the turn of the century did not make it easy to give lectures in small towns. Annie told of one of her husband's expeditions:

"He doesn't think much of 'one night stands' and said he wasn't going to do it any more. Waiting around in little one horse stations, a half or whole day for a train to go to the next town, & irregular meals & sleep if any is rather tiresome to say nothing of wearing. Wendell was the only passenger going & coming on one portion of the road & he had a pass. The conductor told him he ought to feel honored to have a special train—& when he was coming back he told him he might go back & forth past the windows so that folks outside might see that there were some passengers on board."[16]

From his vast experience in teaching, Williston assessed the educational system of the 1890's and found it wanting. This was not his first revolt against traditional education, for, as he said: "When I received my bachelor degree . . . my commencement speech was a diatribe on Latin and Greek, which had exacted a full half of all my college work."[17]

Several of his addresses declared his views strongly on the issue in education of the 1890's. Most colleges then had a fixed four-year course for all students, with very few optionals, but Stanford Uni-

[16] Letter to her parents, February 21, 1892.
[17] "The Future of the Sigma Xi," *Science*, Vol. XLVI, No. 1181 (1917), 147–48.

versity and Harvard University allowed almost unlimited choice to the student. Williston preferred the middle road of choice with guidance that is now the custom. Many of his comments are still pertinent today, and all show his deep concern for the student.

In his presidential address, "Science in Education,"[18] to the annual meeting of the Kansas Academy of Science on October 28, 1897, Williston said, in part:

"The system of optional has gone quite far enough in some directions, not far enough in others. The average student, who has not yet made up his mind what he will do with himself, is bewildered and confused by the multiplicity of studies opened up before him .... Throughout all his preliminary course in the high school, as well as in his freshman and sophomore years, the study of language and mathematics has been strongly emphasized and he has had hardly a glimpse of any other branch of knowledge. In the name of common sense, then, how can he be expected to have acquired any taste whatever for unrelated and dissimilar studies, or to have any conception of their relative importance? His advisers have been chiefly linguists and mathematicians, whose ignorance of the natural sciences is often equaled only by their prejudice against them. It is a fact that the larger proportion of those who have become students of the natural sciences have had their inclination formed despite of rather than by means of the university. The university seldom intimates to them that science studies ought to form an important part of their general training. . . .

"I believe, therefore, that the principle, now so largely adopted, which permits the student to browse about at his own will, with a nibble here and a bite there, is wrong. He should be permitted and required, early in his life, to gaze upon the broad field of knowledge and at least to taste some of its enjoyments, in order that he may find out what his best and easiest path will be towards success. Away with the medieval idea that a course in arts fits a man for anything. It does not and never will, unless it changes very much from what it yet is. . . . Why, then, does the latter [a course in arts]

18 *Science*, new series, Vol. VI (1897), 863–72. Also in *Transactions of the Kansas Academy of Science*, Vol. XVI (1899), 16–24.

assume such transcendent importance in education? Solely upon claim of culture. How many are the sins that are committed in thy name! The classical student, who has devoted five or six of the best years of his life to the study of the ancient languages, with little or no attention given to the modern sciences, is dwarfed and narrowed in his conceptions of life, even as the scientific student would be with no knowledge of the languages. . . . I by no means wish to deprecate the study of language and of philology. They are among the noblest that the student may undertake, and well worthy of the ardent pursuit of the specialist. So, too, are the professions of law and medicine; but no one will presume to say that everybody should be a lawyer or a physician in order to be cultured. . . .

"Twenty-five years ago the classical course was the almost invariable one in our colleges; but even in those times I was required to learn the rudiments at least of physics, chemistry, botany, zoology, and geology. Now modern education has liberalized the course by making the larger part of the language studies compulsory, and all, or nearly all, the natural sciences optional! . . .

"In thus claiming some recognition for natural sciences in the course of liberal arts I shall doubtless be accused of narrowness. I trust, however, if I am, that it will not be imputed to ignorance of the classical course. I studied, when a youth, Latin and Greek for the prescribed time of six years each, and have since learned to speak or read three or four of the modern languages.

"But I do more than claim recognition for the sciences. I claim broadly and emphatically that the natural sciences, any or all of them, are as valuable and as necessary as pure cultural studies as are the languages; that intelligent and successful study of them will do as much, if not more, in making the student a broad man, a successful man, as will the study of Latin or Greek. And they will do more in making him an honest man. Nowhere in all the broad field of knowledge will he learn better to think exactly than in the natural sciences. Nowhere will he be more impressed with the importance of truth for truth's sake. . . .

"In fact, the strictly classical course . . . is perfectly adapted for but one class of people—gentlemen of leisure, who are not dependent upon their daily toil for their bread. . . .

"Were I, then, to say what the universities and colleges ought to do, it would be this: Make all the ancient language requirements for admission optional, and demand as much preparation in the physical and biological sciences as in the foreign languages. The preparation in English should be made far more rigorous and thorough. In the college course, if anything besides English is required, and I think there should be, I would have the natural sciences as necessary a part of the education as language and mathematics. I would not have it possible for a student to graduate from the college without having studied, and thoroughly studied, mathematics as far as trigonometry, at least one foreign language, and at least one physical and one biological science. And I do not mean a few weeks of study in any of these branches, but exhaustive, careful, critical study."

Williston felt that a university owed a wide education to a variety of students, an advanced concept for his day. In an address entitled "Higher Education in Kansas" to the Kansas chapter of Sigma Xi in June, 1902, he said in part:

"The college and the university must remember, and they will remember, better in the future than they have in the past, that they exist for the people and not that the people exist for them. The kind of education that the people demand must be given to them, and not what we in our pedantry think they ought to have. To bar the doors of higher education to those who desire to learn to be better merchants or architects or plumbers or wheelwrights, by insisting that they must spend five years in the study of foreign languages before they are fitted to study English literature, or political economy, or botany, or chemistry, is illogical, is wrong. . . . The common test of a candidate for admission is not what he can do, but what he has done, and if he has not done certain things we say that he is unfit to do anything well. I care less for the kind of preparation a student has had than for his capacity to do those things well which he undertakes to do. Greater latitude should be given to the candidate for admission, and more should be demanded of him in his college work. But colleges usually are too particular in admitting him and too easy in graduating him. It is a common experience among educators in science to find that the college graduate in the humanities makes a no better student in the laboratories than does the high school graduate of equal natural capacity. The knowledge of the humanities he has thus acquired broadens out his life, perhaps, and benefits him in the end, but it is gained at too great a cost."

Williston's concern over the length of time necessary to complete a professional course, still a problem in education, was evident in an address to the Women's Medical College of Kansas City in May, 1899, entitled "Medical Education":

"The time required to attain the medical degree is already long enough, and the cost is great enough. I have spent many years of my life in teaching young men and women in the medical college and in the university, but I have not become so much imbued with the scholastic idea as to believe that college education is all or even the best part of the preparation for one's life work. There is danger of over education for the real duties of living. There is the danger of becoming pedants and scholars, narrow and intolerant, where living, breathing pulsating men and women are needed. The man or woman who spends his or her life until he is thirty years in the college and university has lost much of the very best education that the world can give, the education of men and women, of human nature. I cannot and never will believe that scholastic education should be prolonged beyond the twenty-fifth year for the average man. What is desired is not so much the education of teachers as the ability to educate one's self—the ability to think for one's self and to profit by errors. Education should be prolonged only so far as it will give the recipient best control over himself; far enough to minimize the errors he will make. The details of the knowledge you get in the college course is far more fleeting than the young person usually thinks. . . ."

Also in the address to the Kansas chapter of the Sigma Xi in June, 1902, Williston summarized the character of the college professor—with a plea for higher salary which went unheeded in his lifetime:

"The time has been when the college professor was placed upon a pedestal to be approached with that mental obeisance which was supposed to be the due of the preacher in olden times—a man away and apart from the world, who could not drive a nail without wounding his fingers; who worked for love and went where the Lord called him. Thirty years ago he was apt to be some broken-down preacher or decrepit pedagogue, bespectacled, absent-minded and unpractical; chosen not so much for what he knew himself as for what he could tell of other people's knowledge. But the modern professor is, or should be, very much flesh and blood—a man in touch with men, meeting his pupils as friends, and not as a musty folio tome; alive to all that interests men, and also fully aware of his own rights and privileges. He has lost none of his dignity, but other callings in life have dignified theirs until they stand by his side. There is no longer the gap there was between the professor, preacher, doctor and lawyer on the one side, and the banker, merchant and business man on the other. Like many other men he finds his greatest pleasure in a useful life. He is not, or should not be, greatly in love with money, nor does he often seek to lay up those things which moths do corrupt. He wants a competence and the means to do his work well, because like other true men he values his reputation more than vain-glorious display. A salary of ten thousand a year would ordinarily make no better a teacher of him than one of three or four thousand—he must work for the love of his work, or his usefulness is very slight and he cannot afford to waste time in mere money-getting. But so long as the world generally measures a man's capacity and usefulness by the income he receives, he will value money for the recognition it gives him and the power it gives him to do better work. He has frailties like other men, and the desire for recognition, if it be a frailty, is one of them. But few professions, however, have members who are less envious or less quarrelsome. Indeed he too often is distrustful of his own merits."

CHAPTER 11

Williston in His Prime

Habits

Wꜰᴀᴛ was this man like in his prime period from thirty-nine to fifty-one years of age?

Professor S. W. Williston was a robust man striding across the university campus, ruddy complexioned, broad shouldered, five feet, ten inches tall, and weighing about 185 pounds. "In his office and lecture room he often wore a coat that seemed to be a bit too small, the sleeves being noticeably too short."[1]

In dress he was quite careless most of the time, but special occasions brought out his best clothes, neatly cared for, and then he looked very distinguished. He was usually bearded, but he removed his beard when his young daughters tugged too persistently at it and occasionally when summer heat set in.

A hearty eater, he gained weight until he went into the field where strenuous exercise and scanty fare slimmed him down. After each field trip he would buy several pounds of dime-store candy and nibble on it in the evenings. On Sunday evenings he always popped corn for the family.

Williston had little sense of organization. His study at home was always untidy and his wife despaired of cleaning it. Boxes of flies were scattered across the desk, and were at times invaded by the children when they were small. Tailor-made cigarettes were forbidden in Kansas then, so Williston rolled his own of Bull Durham or smoked a pipe, and tobacco littered the floor. Infrequently he gave up smoking (and sometimes tea and coffee as well), but he soon returned to it. McClung said:

"At home, in the evenings, he would throw himself into a study of his collection of flies. With a constant succession of cigarettes he would delve into the anatomy of one fly after the other until

[1] Letter from former student Arthur W. Hixson, April 30, 1963.

he had completed a group upon which he was, at the moment, interested, meanwhile scattering ashes all over the neighboring territory."[2]

Williston's lack of organization has come down through the years, in the form of a series of notebooks. Each of these has minutely written detailed descriptions of individual Diptera, some copied from the works of others for reference, some of new species. But each notebook began as another project—the by-laws of the medical society at Yale, an early school notebook of Ruth's with several pages in the middle of a younger sister's scrawls, and household finances.

Evenings at home, when not devoted to flies, were often given to drawing illustrations for his paleontology papers. Williston never had a hired illustrator working for him, but, thanks to his own background in anatomy and competence in drawing, he could do all his own illustrations. Photography was one of his hobbies too, and after his summer's fossil collecting in 1895 he developed in the kitchen at home the 250 photographs he had taken.

But there were many relaxed family evenings too, when he played light music on his guitar or read to his family. One of his favorite authors was Charles Dickens, as in his youth, but he sometimes read one of the new novels of the day. He concerned himself with his children's progress in school, offering rewards for high grades and urging high-quality work. He offered prizes, too, for the best cake, bread, and pie made by one of the girls. Over the years he became more remote from his children's concerns, and, though he showed great interest in their early schooling, he later told his oldest daughter that educating women was a waste of time as they just got married. (Ruth took the advice to enter botany that she overheard him give to a young man—and she never married.)

Williston wanted his wife to cultivate outside interests and for a while he urged her to continue the painting she had done before marriage. He helped her with papers for her weekly literary club, Friends in Counsel. He must only rarely have commented on his

[2] "Samuel Wendell Williston," *Bios*, Vol. XIV, No. 1 (March, 1943), 36.

wife's dress, for he caught her by surprise once when he said he would like to see her in something a little gayer. But he was as pleased as his daughters when they learned that Annie had been called "the prettiest of the professors wives" and "the belle of the Faculty."

House projects occupied Williston from time to time—enclosing the balcony for plants (with the help of Barnum Brown), putting in a goldfish pond, revarnishing floors and painting periodically, and when his wife was visiting in New Haven he was prone to renovating the master bedroom for her. Annie deferred to him on house furnishings as she found his choice good and that he didn't want "any cheap things around." He made a carriage robe of cat skins for one of his young daughters, and occasionally he made root beer and wine (leaving heaps of grape skins to be cleaned up by others). He was a very good, but untidy, cook.

Ever a student himself, he learned Spanish during his years in Kansas, simply by buying copies of *Don Quixote* in Spanish and in English. Annie read the English aloud while he followed the text in Spanish.

Williston enjoyed occasional fishing trips to a lake near Lawrence with other professors, and for several years a group of faculty families held Memorial Day picnics there. Another favorite family outing was an all-day trip to the farm of Joseph Savage, three miles from Lawrence. The Willistons reveled in the fresh cider and baskets of apples there and enjoyed looking at the collection of "curiosities, fossils, indian arrowheads, agates, quartz, and lots of other allied things, enough to stock a museum."[3] Savage did contribute specimens to the university museum; he and his wife were both members of the Kansas Academy of Science and were the parents of one of the university's first students.

Sunday afternoon walks were another family pastime, led by Williston. A favorite destination was the old mill, the remains of one built sturdily by Swedish workmen years before. In the spring the family hunted for early flowers and dandelion greens on Mount Oread.

[3] Letter from Annie to her parents, October 26, 1890.

By far the greatest share of Williston's daylight time at home went to his garden and plant room. Each morning while waiting for breakfast and as soon as he reached home, he was among his plants, checking their growth, counting buds, and tending them. Growing plants in the uncertain climate of Kansas has never been easy, but Williston approached the problems with his customary thoroughness. Each fall he took up large numbers of plants and stored them over the winter in the basement and throughout the house. Tulips were a special favorite. Some plants were put into a Wardian case in the dining room window, and over the years both the upstairs balcony and the downstairs porch were glassed for more plants. After sending a package to his wife's family, Williston described his own successes:

"You will probably have received before you do this a package of plants from Good & Reese. The Apios is a hardy climbing vine like Wisteria, the orange, Hibiscus and Abutilon are winter blooming perenial [sic] shrubs. Pot them in five or six inch pots and sink the pots in the ground. [Our] Orange has been in bloom for three weeks and will continue for the next month. It is only about ten inches high. I think that it is the most satisfactory house plant that grows. I dont [sic] know but I have grown cranky on plants and have wasted lots of time on them, but I never found anything that gives me so much pleasure. You like plants so well perhaps you will like to know what we have now growing outside and in. I cant [sic] remember them all! but the most of them are 60 kinds of roses, 14 kinds of Fuchsia, 12 of [Abutilons], 5 Hibiscus, 2 of Hydrangea, 1 Viburnum, 9 of [Ipomoeas] (Moon flowers), 8 of lilies (two easter lilies will be in bloom in a few days, they are nearly three feet high and have eight buds each), 5 kinds of Callas, 10 kinds of Cactus; 5 kinds of Cannas, 1 Jessamine, 1 Olea, 1 menna, 1 Night blooming Jessamine, 1 Solanum, 1 Ficus two feet high, 1 Strobilanthes, 1 Clerodendron, 1 Pleroma, 1 Achanae, 1 Grevillea, 2 kinds of Agave, 2 kinds of Euphorbia, 1 Agapanthus that will be in bloom soon, 1 Water Hyacinth, 2 kinds of Amaryllis, 1 Hyancinthus candicans, 1 Spider [lily], 1 Crinum, 1 Thalia (a plant that grew seven feet high last summer) 2 kinds of Caladiums,

1 Colocasia (like a Caladium, but larger), Honey suckles, Wisterias, Clematis, Apios, Bitter-sweets, Ampelopsis, three Washington Palms, 3 Otaheite oranges, 1 Passion vine, second yr., 6 kinds of Begonia, Geraniums ad libitum, a bulb bed ten feet square crowded, an Althea, Brugmansia, etc. etc., including 12 kinds of Gladiolus, etc.

"You see I have run daft, but the twenty dollars they have all cost give me more concentrated pleasure, and Annie equally, than any twenty dollars I have ever spent in my life. I planted some large elms along La [Louisiana] street, and have in the back yard, three of the crab apples of the college campus, some grape vines, currants, and June berries. Besides I have a large bed planted of Rocky Mt. wild flowers [brought from fossil trips] and have about twenty kinds of annuals to plant out in the spring. It is my ambition to make our yard conspicuous for its shrubbery and plants. The only thing that worries me is the time that I give to them from my other work, but as I dont [sic] cycle or play tennis, I guess I can stand it."[4]

Williston often gave plants and cuttings to visiting friends and neighbors, and he acquired others from them as well as on his field trips. Annie once commented in mock despair: "When Wendell heard about the moccasin flowers [in Connecticut], he immediately said 'I wonder if they cant [sic] send me some "roots." ' I never saw such a man. He wants every kind of a plant he sees or even heard of."[5] Annie obviously enjoyed them very much herself, often listing in letters to her family the many flowers blossoming throughout the year. She used flowers for centerpieces and decorations whenever she entertained.

When Williston left Kansas, he left his gardening behind, except for an immense Crinum that occupied the sunny windows of his house in Chicago for years.

Through Annie's family Williston retained ties with the East, for Annie and the children spent several summers there with her parents and he made shorter visits. The Hathaways had a share in

[4] Letter to Genie, February 10, 1896.
[5] Letter to her mother, July 3, 1898.

a summer property at Haddam (Little City), Connecticut, and this became a second home to the Willistons. The land had been bought from the Indians by an ancestor of Mrs. Hathaway's and by the 1890's it had been placed in trust by that generation's owner to be used by all members of the family for twenty years whenever convenient during the summers. Each spring a local man was hired to dig up and plant the vegetable garden, a necessity for there were no stores nearby. The house was old and the kitchen facilities primitive, but all the family loved it. Here they rambled in the fields, picked huckleberries and earned pocket money by selling them, raised gardens, and renewed family ties.

Social Life

Most of the family social activities revolved around the university: concerts, commencement exercises, receptions at Chancellor Snow's, parties among the faculty, and sporting events (Williston was once on the faculty basketball team). He hated to miss the annual science club party, known as "It," at which were parodies of the faculty and general hilarity. One year he was appointed the "Liar" at this function. "Dyche was the one last year," reported Annie, "but Wendell's big outlandish animals gave him the precedence."[6]

At least once Williston led the forty members of the Biological Club on an overnight, coeducational field trip by wagon twenty miles from Lawrence to study biology first hand. The students dubbed the location Camp Williston and thoroughly enjoyed themselves.

After a few years in Lawrence, the Willistons began entertaining groups of students, first those in paleontology and later the medical students. Annie was harrassed at first over how to feed and entertain the groups, but she soon learned to set out great quantities of cake and ice cream. At the Willistons the group visited, played cards, looked at photographs, and sometimes danced to their professor's guitar playing.

[6] Letter to her mother, January 28, 1894.

Williston also entertained distinguished out-of-town geologists, for as Annie noted: "All of the way up geologists in U.S. or most all have been here to see Wendell's collection & his fossils have done more to make K. U. noted than anything else."[7]

Cope was among the first, in June of 1892, but he stayed at a hotel and Annie refused to feed him. Apparently this was because the weather was very hot; it was Annie's first experience with Kansas summer heat.

Old friends from Marsh's laboratory came to visit, often to or from collecting: John Bell Hatcher, then at Princeton, stopped by in February of 1895; George Baur, then at the University of Chicago, visited on his way home from collecting in Wyoming in September of 1895; and Erwin H. Barbour, then at the University of Nebraska, visited in December of 1900.

To Annie the most distinguished of all was Henry Fairfield Osborn, of Columbia University and the American Museum of Natural History, who stayed at the Willistons in May, 1897. The visit was on a Sunday, and Williston showed Osborn his collections. Annie remarked: "Osborne [sic] never works on Sunday but today he said he was very wicked but he could not let the opportunity pass. I told him I was afraid we had a good many wicked ones here then."[8] Annie, obviously in awe of Osborn's wealth, found him very pleasant and fond of children.

Osborn was again in Lawrence in May, 1901, to meet Prof. Eberhard Fraas of Germany there. The Willistons entertained the two distinguished paleontologists, who then continued west to meet their special car at Cañon City for a tour of the fossil fields. Fraas later exchanged European fossils for some of the Kansas ones from the university museum.

Williston had been a member of the Kansas Academy of Science for many years, and he attended its meetings whenever possible. Annie went with him to Atchison in 1892, and was one of the few women there. With true wifely pride she concluded that her husband's talks "were the most interesting of the lot. They were more

[7] Letter to her mother, October 14, 1900.
[8] Letter to her mother, May 16, 1897.

in a popular style than the others."[9] In 1897 Williston was president of the Kansas Academy of Science, and the following year he was elected a life member.

The social organization of greatest importance to Williston in Lawrence was the Old and New Club, founded in 1874 and still in existence.

"No other club is like it, and it was patterned after none. It is composed of congenial souls who meet for pleasure, intellectual pleasure. It has no officers, never had, has never taken a vote on any subject, keeps no records of any kind, except those of pleasant memories, has no fees or dues, never had a member even try to place a motion before the house, is composed entirely of men members and always has been, and yet has functioned in a lively way for more than half a century.

"Certain men of Lawrence just came together because they wanted to, because they were congenial spirits, because they felt it would be well for them to associate together and exchange ideas and views, and because everyone of them had a longing to increase and make better his knowledge, his culture and his views of humanity. A simple beginning this was, but it was prompted by the highest and best feelings of some of the best citizens Lawrence has ever claimed. . . .

"The host usually reads the paper of the evening. . . .

"The best part of the program is the conversation which follows the paper. Those poorly informed on the subject presented ask many questions, and the entire membership indulges in discussion, no preparation in advance having been made. No one more than any other one is supposed to speak first, either by education or length of time he may have been a member of the club. These discussions generally are confined to subjects brought out by the paper. In fact, it is looked upon as a sort of honor for a sufficiently favorable subject to be chosen and so brought out that it may hold the center of attention for hours. Such conversations necessarily must be of a high order, and it may well be doubted if at any other place, or at any other time has a group of men banded

[9] Letter to her parents, October 16, 1892. Williston presented three papers.

themselves together for such high purposes and kept going for more than half a century."[10]

Chancellor Snow, one of the original members, brought to Williston the news of his election to the Old and New Club in December, 1894, just before the banquet celebrating the twenty-first anniversary of the club. Williston took the honor seriously, according to Annie:

"I have not seen Wendell so interested in getting his clothes ready for the occasion for a long time. He got out his dress coat and brushed and sunned it, got some white ties and patent leather shoes. He was the only one there in a dress suit, but he said he did not care for it was the proper thing."[11]

The club then had fourteen members, about half from the university. Annie mentioned Professors Sayre, Carruth, Canfield, Robinson, and Chancellor Snow. The distinguished town members included Judge Solon O. Thacher (state senator and district judge); druggist B. W. Woodward ("probably the best connoisseur of art and literature Lawrence has ever had"[12]); Col. O. E. Leonard, owner and editor of the Lawrence *Journal*; and others.

Although Williston looked forward keenly to the monthly club meetings, his wife dreaded the approach, in rotation, of each meeting at her house. Through the years the dinners had become more elaborate, so that Annie found that a six-course dinner was expected. The hostess did not appear during the evening, but directed traffic in the kitchen as the courses were served and removed by high-school daughters of the members. During the paper and conversation, the wife was expected to keep young children quiet upstairs. Borrowing of plates, silver, and high-school daughters was prevalent. Mrs. Sayre owned a set of oyster plates, which were used for the first course at almost every dinner. The Willistons varied this once by serving oysters on fossil oyster shells he had collected in Kansas.

Annie's accounts to her parents of the club dinners at her house

[10] Kansas City *Star*, July 10, 1927.
[11] Letter to Genie, December 23, 1894.
[12] Kansas City *Star*, July 10, 1927.

naturally tell more of menus than of the evening's conversation. To her great relief, before her first dinner, she heard about the most important "member" of the club, Lucy Brown, "a colored woman who makes a business of getting up suppers . . . & usually helps at all the suppers or most of them for this club." Lucy knew the likes and dislikes of the members as well as their digestive idiosyncracies. It was she who carefully slipped some other food into the oyster plate of one member and who reminded the hostess of certain foods that were to be carefully omitted.

The first club dinner at the Willistons was a success:

"Well, the great club supper is over and we are still alive. Lucy Brown . . . arrived about half past one & did nearly everything. First she fixed her potatoes & left them soaking—we had Mrs. Sayre's potatoe[*sic*] slicer. Then she fixed the oranges, bananas & pineapple for the fruit salad—& set it in the snow—then she fixed the chicken to fry—we had three young ones & they cost a dollar for the three—by that time I had fixed several new lamp wicks & the burners to the other lamps & got dressed—& so we set the table. The fringed cloth was not long enough so I used one of my best ones & pieced out with another—& my fringed napkins as far as they went & my best ones. There were just thirteen places as we had word that the fourteenth man would not be here—five on a side two at one end & one at the other—Judge Thacher always sits alone at one end. My jardiniere with a pretty foliage plant made a center piece. Miss K[irtland, Williston's laboratory helper and their boarder] lent me her spoons—& the souvenir ones we used & with the oyster fork, other fork & a knife & two spoons at each place made the table look real pretty. I had my little doilies scattered around the table with pepper & salt on two, olives on another & pickles & two sugar & creamers. Of course oysters was the first course, & they were all in the holes in the plates when the men came in & two long salt crackers on the side of the plate. Gene Sayre & Ruth [Williston] and Lucy did the waiting—I thought Ruth might as well begin and learn. Next they had their fried chicken & french peas & the Saratoga potatoes [potato chips] were passed—also graham bread & hot biscuits. I bought the bread. (no

I made a mistake) the soup came next—it was made of tomatoes & milk & was called 'mock bisque.' Wendell said it was about the best soup he ever ate—then came the chicken course, & after that the fruit salad & my poor loaf cake. I sat up till after 12 the night before to bake it & then it wasn't quite done & fell a little—but it tasted good. Lucy said they ate up everything clean—& Judge Thacher took up his bones and just cleaned them—only two oysters were left & those were so big that Woodward could not eat them. Ruth finished them in the kitchen. Wendell had a gallon of cider he has had sealed up & kept for this occasion but that makes only 16 glasses & Mrs. Sayre had instructed Prof. Sayre & Prof. Canfield they mustn't ask for any more (a la the Ruggles family). Mrs. Sayre was in the kitchen & helped get one course ready while the other was being served. Wendell said it was more of a supper than they have had at any meeting he has been to. . . . Lucy staid till every thing was put to rights & for all her time & skill asked seventy five cents which you may know was gladly paid. She cooked everything & it was delicious & it was served & looked beautifully. She is a prize. . . .

"Lucy said all the ladies who had the 'Old & New Club' felt very much relieved when they had got through with their part for the year."[13]

The wives continued to vie for first place in elegance of dinners until Annie remarked that "they are so elaborate now that Wendell stays awake half the night after them."[14] She intended to serve a simpler repast, but she couldn't bring herself to. When she presented the guests one night with oysters, consommé, deviled crabs, roast turkey, tomato salad, fruit gelatine, and cake (plus side dishes), "the doctor in the crowd besides Wendell passed around pepsin pills afterward to those who had delicate stomachs."[15]

One marvels that the men were able to converse at all after such banquets. But converse they did, and Williston, when host, contributed a wide variety of subjects: irrigation, the mental supe-

[13] Letter from Annie to her mother, February 10, 1895.

[14] Letter to Genie, February 17, 1898.

[15] Letter from Annie to her mother, February 2, 1902.

riority of men over women (of which Annie said: "I told him he needn't expect any more fine suppers if that is the way he is going to do. The women will all be down on him."[16]), the value of modern fiction, arsenic poisoning, and phrenology.

The Adviser

Glimpses of this man in comments by others tell us something about his impact on his students. McClung recalled his first meeting with Williston:

"The dark room adjoined a laboratory of the chemistry building in which I worked. One day I saw a large, energetic and somewhat unkempt gentleman busily engaged with a camera making lantern slides. From day to day he returned to his task and I was tempted to make enquiries regarding his work, but, being a humble Freshman in the Pharmacy School, I could not muster up courage to speak. What I dared not do he however made easy for me by approaching my desk to enquire what engaged my attention under the microscope. With this simple enquiry began a friendship whose influence upon my life can not be measured. Soon I had learned about the making of lantern slides and also what the particular ones were for upon which he labored. There was to be a series of public lectures upon evolution, inaugurated by the redoubtable champion of Darwin, Chancellor Snow, some of which were to be given by the diligent maker of lantern slides. My interest in the photographic processes and their manipulator grew and I marveled at his successful efforts and equally at his failures. The means did not concern him—only the end. My tidy and orderly instincts were shocked at the frank and unconcerned admission that he expected to spoil every other plate, and it was beyond my comprehension how his methods produced such good results. I never did learn how, in his disregard for detail, he accomplished such accurate work. [Williston usually extinguished his cigarettes in the developer, which certainly didn't guarantee good results.]

"Later I went to the lectures on evolution and had a new and

16 Letter to her mother, March 6, 1898.

surprising view of my photographic friend. Instead of the genial and unconventional laboratory worker there stood an earnest and imposing gentleman in frock coat, who, in high pitched voice and rapid utterance, talked for an hour upon a subject which my freshman, pharmaceutical mind followed most limpingly. Although it is a quarter of a century ago I can recall in detail the voice and gestures of this astonishing man who, upon one day, could be so simple and common, and upon the next the inspired prophet, in public exposition, of philosophies which profoundly moved his large and critical audience."[17]

McClung illustrated Williston's major contribution to the University of Kansas: all who were to go on into scientific research, in whatever branch, came under Williston's influence there. Students flocked to him and left with their own names known in print:

"An insight into the fairness and justice of Dr. Williston's character in all work of this kind is shown by his care to acknowledge the services of those who have helped to make it a success. He very frequently suggested and outlined work for the younger men which he was glad to have them publish in their own names. They, of course, acknowledged the assistance he had given them."[18]

He was a father to the students as well, as Aldrich testified:

"In January, 1893, I went to the University of Kansas to study, drawn entirely by his presence there. He received me with open arms, and helped me in every way possible until I left in July to take up my work in Idaho. . . . In Kansas he lent me money; he wanted me to live in his house; he could not do enough to further my scientific aspirations."[19]

In correspondence with McClung over students whom they both knew, his paternal concern recurs:

"Year after year there are questions and advice about the students passing between our laboratories. Of one he [Williston]

[17] "Samuel Wendell Williston," *Sigma Xi Quarterly*, Vol. VII, No. 1 (March, 1919), 10.

[18] E. H. S. Bailey, "Samuel Wendell Williston," *Sigma Xi Quarterly*, Vol. VII, No. 1 (March, 1919), 27.

[19] "Samuel Wendell Williston," *Entomological News*, Vol. XXIX (November, 1918), 327.

speaks as of a son, over whose scientific faults he has spent sleepless nights; of another as a source of continued satisfaction because of his solid progress. His appreciation of the proper method of securing success appears in the discussion of another student 'If he would only go to work with all his energy to accomplish some special and useful work, the things would come to him in the end, which he now seeks to obtain by "influence" and "pull." ' Perhaps nowhere better than in advising me does he show in these letters his real attitude toward scientific work. Among numerous passages I find the following typical statements: 'Have patience and WORK.' 'Keep at it, eternally doing research work.' How characteristic of his own habit are these admonitions!"[20]

Others confirmed this:

"[Williston] came to us in his prime, a largish man irradiating good will. His great soul took us all under its wing. He wanted us youngsters to keep hitting on all cylinders. 'You young men should write a hundred pages every year,' he said to Hugo Kahl, our Swedish assistant curator of insects. . . . But Williston did caution us to put under a carpet anything we wrote for publication and leave it there for a year; then if it still seemed OK to send it out. Did he always follow that advice himself, I wonder, when with typewriter going at top speed and the boiler of his eager enthusiasm at the point of explosion, the momentum of his thesis was hardly restrainable before it brought up against the printing press?"[21]

In his dealings with enthusiastic students Williston sometimes tried to turn them away from his own profession. One was McClung, who recalled:

"With characteristic fairness, he repeatedly pointed out that there was no money in such a following, and that unless I were willing to live as he did I should choose another and more lucrative calling. When I had once decided upon my course, however, he

---

[20] McClung, "Samuel Wendell Williston," *Sigma Xi Quarterly*, Vol. VII, No. 1 (March, 1919), 14.

[21] W. C. Stevens, "Reminiscences," *The Fiftieth Anniversary of the Founding of the Kansas Chapter of the Society of the Sigma Xi*, Lawrence, University of Kansas (1941), 29.

made every effort to aid me, and in this endeavor he never slackened his purpose so long as he lived."[22]

Williston's advice to Charles N. Gould, a young schoolteacher[23] who was showing him a new fossil location, was similar:

"During the various talks we had while out in the hills together, I told him something of my hopes and aspirations and that I was seriously considering becoming a geologist. He endeavored to dissuade me. Among other things he said: 'It's a dog's life, Gould, and there is nothing in it. A geologist never makes any money, he works hard all his days, he is called a fool and a crank by nine-tenths of the people he meets, and he lives and usually dies unappreciated. I would advise you to try something easy, like law or medicine or selling shoes, or stick to school teaching. There is more eating in those jobs than there is in geology.'

"But after I had convinced him that it was geology or nothing for me, he began to give me oceans of good advice. Among other things, he said:

" 'Whatever you do or do not do, Gould, begin early to publish. I have watched scientists for twenty years, and it is my experience that it is the scientific damnation of any young person starting out in a scientific career to go five years without publishing. The world does not know, nor does it care that you are alive, and the world is not going to give you the glad hand. It is up to you to take the world by the throat and make it recognize you . . . .'

" 'The essential thing is to break into print, get your thoughts into type, get them on paper. Write about these bones we have been collecting, or go out in the Flint Hills east of Winfield, your home, make some cross sections of the rocks, collect some fossils, write a paper, and get it published. It does not make so much difference what you print, as long as you get into type.' "[24]

[22] "Samuel Wendell Williston," *Sigma Xi Quarterly*, Vol. VII, No. 1 (March, 1919), 11.
[23] Gould (1868–1949) was to become an excellent geologist. He organized the department of geology at the University of Oklahoma and founded the state's geological survey.
[24] Charles N. Gould, *Covered Wagon Geologist*, 47–48.

Thus was Samuel Wendell Williston in Kansas—working steadily himself, encouraging others to work also, but never too busy to give advice to those who asked.

CHAPTER 12

Problems of Kansas

WILLISTON'S years at the University of Kansas were the happiest of his life. Kansas was home to him. He had the freedom of a professorship, with no one to tell him what he had to do. He could do research on subjects of his own choosing, knowing that he could do it well. He worked hard at the University of Kansas—lecturing, collecting, studying, writing, establishing the medical school.

His position was one of eminence locally and became one of eminence elsewhere as the numbers of fossils and of scientific papers grew. He was on close terms with the president of his college and respected by the regents. Fellow faculty members respected and liked him; students respected and loved him.

Why, then, did he go to the University of Chicago in 1902? The first and simplest reason was: more money. All the years at Lawrence, Williston had deplored the small salaries paid by the University of Kansas. He needed a larger salary for his growing family.

State politics was part of the university's financial problem in the 1890's, as the Republicans and the Populists alternated control of the state legislature, and hence the regents.

The Populist movement had begun in the 1880's among middle western and southern small farmers as a response to the steadily declining prices they were receiving. The Farmers' Alliance, which began as a nonpolitical social group, gathered tremendous numbers and by 1890 entered the political arena. It advocated lower railroad rates, lower interest rates, breaking up of large land holdings of the railroads especially, and the issuance of more silver or paper money. The first People's party ticket in the nation was in 1890, in Kansas, where the Populists gained control of the state's house of representatives. In 1892 they won the Kansas governorship and

had a fossil skull in his hand and chatted to me about it. As we approached the door he slipped it into his pocket, saying 'I'd better put this away or the Museum people will think I'm stealing it.' . . .

"Once or twice he invited the class to his apartment in the evening. With the refreshments he regaled us with stories of fossil hunting on the Plains."[10]

Charles Behre recalled that Williston's classroom manner "was most informal and might well be described as rather fatherly. In fact, his relation to all of his students was much like that. I remember that he used to come to the graduate student residence fraternity called Gamma Alpha, and pick up quite a number of the 'boys' and take them to a movie as his guests. I also recall that he set up examinations and frequently asked us, 'Is this examination too long, or is it too short, and if it is too short, what additional questions should I ask?' "[11]

Augusta Hasslock Kemp recalled her course on amphibians and reptiles from Williston: "It met afternoons on the third floor of Walker [Museum]. When Dr. Williston found me sitting on the stairs awaiting his arrival, he showed me where he hung the key, so I could get in as early as I pleased. [The nearby-hanging key was a self-defense measure of Williston's after an early day at Chicago when he lost his key and had to cancel a class.] Most of the small class worked all afternoon, except two pre-medics, who considered it a dangerous precedent. All of us helping, we finally put the loose bones of a crocodile skull in place, but how disgusted Dr. Williston was when he found one bone in backwards and upside down. Once the question, 'What is the difference between a dinosaur and a crocodile?' went entirely around the class. He finally answered it himself and then gravely said, 'Exactly right.' "[12]

The four students who received Ph.D.'s at Chicago under Williston's direction were E. B. Branson (1905), Roy L. Moodie (1908), Maurice Mehl (1914), and Herman Douthitt (1916).

[10] Letter to the author, April 7, 1962.
[11] Letter to the author, April 19, 1963.
[12] Fisher, *The Seventy Years*, 24.

CHAPTER 14

Into the Permian

IN his new position, Williston began with Kansas bones by completing a memoir on North American plesiosaurs, published by the Field Columbian Museum in 1903. According to Lull:

"The monographic studies on the group [plesiosaurs], undertaken by Williston, were for the purpose of clearing up the confusion which then existed concerning these animals, but he deemed it wise, as there was still much to be done, to publish his detailed researches on the three species *Dolichorhynchops osborni*, *Brachauchenius lucasii* and *Cimoliasaurus snowii*, rather than wait for the completion of the entire work, and it was fortunate that he did so, in view of the fact that the second part did not appear."[1]

He was in the field again in the summer of 1903, back in Wyoming where he intended to meet W. C. Knight again, but Knight died suddenly at that time. The field party got to Logan County, Kansas, where E. B. Branson[2] found "an extraordinarily complete specimen" of a mosasaur—twenty feet long and "with nearly every bone in its proper position."[3]

Wyoming was again the site of interest in the summer of 1904. The collecting area was fourteen miles from Lander, on Willow Creek, and the party included E. B. Branson, Roy L. Moodie,[4]

[1] Lull, "Samuel Wendell Williston," *Memoirs of the National Academy of Sciences*, Vol. XVII, 5th Memoir (1924), 124.

[2] Edwin Bayer Branson (1877–1950) went on to a distinguished career in geology. Born in Kansas, he received his A.B. and A.M. at the University of Kansas in 1900, and then followed Williston to Chicago where he got his Ph.D. in 1905. He taught first at Oberlin College, Ohio, and in 1910 went to the University of Missouri as professor and chairman of the department of geology. He emphasized the importance of field work to geologists and took a keen interest in his students.

[3] S. W. Williston, "The Relationships and Habits of the Mosasaurs," *Journal of Geology*, Vol. XII (1904), 43.

[4] Roy Lee Moodie (1880–1934) received his A.B. at the University of Kansas in 1905 and his Ph.D. under Williston at the University of Chicago in 1908. He joined

E. E. Ball, and N. H. Brown, the county surveyor of Fremont County. Brown had discovered the fossil beds, which Williston called the Popo Agie for the nearby rushing river. Williston was less than enthusiastic about back country travel (thirty hours on the stage coach), but he was delighted to find that he could "stand more climbing and tramping, or as much as these young fellows."[5] The hard ground couldn't keep him from sleeping and he reported eating like a horse. "The Mosquitoes were fierce out there," Ruth wrote her grandfather about her father's trip, "but . . . couldn't hold a candle to the wood ticks!"

The group turned up four new reptile species that summer. Coming back from the fossil site Williston stayed overnight in Rawlins, Wyoming, with E. Kennedy, "an old acquaintance who assisted me in collecting in 1878."[6] He then stopped in Laramie to examine and photograph specimens in the museum of the University of Wyoming. When he learned that William H. Reed, also of 1878 dinosaur-digging days at Como, was in collecting camp for the University of Wyoming, he decided to ride out the fifty miles with Reed's team driver to visit his old friend. The two explored the Triassic red sandstones together, and undoubtedly reminisced.

Again in the summer of 1905 Williston headed for the productive Wyoming fields. A brief note to Annie announced the major find: "We have made a most remarkable discovery of a new kind of dinosaur covered over with a carapace like that of a turtle, and our summer's work will be a great success after all. . . . We are 8 miles from Lander. . . . Am feeling first rate and most jubilant over our discoveries."[7]

The new creature, one half the size of its armored relative *Stegosaurus*, was christened *Stegopelta landerensis*. The collectors were working in dark blue shales and found several species of

the staff of the College of Medicine at the University of Illinois in 1909 and contributed to studies of skeletal development, the history of anatomy, and fossil amphibians. He was an undisputed expert in paleopathology.

[5] Letter to his family, June, 1904.

[6] Letter from Williston to Annie, July 7, 1904.

[7] Letter of August 24, 1905.

plesiosaurs, several crocodiles, and an assemblage of freshwater (or brackish) mollusks along with the dinosaur.

From 1904 to 1906 Williston visited museums throughout the United States to make comparisons on plesiosaur skeletons. Among other places, this took him back to Yale, where he had a fresh look at collections he himself had made for Marsh long before.

By 1908 his paleontologic interests were changing toward the branch in which he was to make his greatest contribution—the Paleozoic amphibians and reptiles. Before 1908 he had published just a few descriptions of Paleozoic vertebrates but from that year on he worked and published very extensively on them.

In the Pennsylvanian period of geologic history, some 250,000,000 years ago, the area that is now midcontinental United States was generally a warm, lush swampland. Variations in topography and climate certainly existed and the ocean covered some inland places, but over vast areas great tropical plants flourished and died, forming thick coal beds. Modern deciduous trees and conifers had not yet appeared, but the ferns, the rushes, and the scale trees grew to thirty and fifty feet tall. Insects were enormous. In this moist habitat the primitive salamanders flourished—small ones a few inches long and large ones up to ten feet long. The far future Age of Reptiles was scarcely to be guessed at from the few tiny reptiles that had developed in the Pennsylvanian period.

A major climate change in the next period, the Permian, may have contributed to the evolution of the terrestrial vertebrates. Deserts covered some areas and the climate turned colder—neither proper environments for unprotected salamanders. These survived along stream courses, developing into armored, thick-bodied, sluggish animals. The reptiles diversified, producing a great variety of forms, some agile and others quite slow. They were not large—only up to ten feet long—and only one kind, the finback, was unusually decorated. The reptiles were evolving from the amphibians at this time, and some of the forms are borderline cases in the evolution of the vertebrates.

It may be that Williston's interest in the early vertebrates began in the museum, for in 1908 he said:

"Recently, in the examination of the Texas Permian material in the Chicago University collection [collected earlier by E. C. Case], I was so fortunate to find a skull of *Lysorophus* in connection with vertebrae, which, upon preparation proves to be wonderfully perfect and complete. . . . *Lysorophus* was a slender, well-ribbed, serpentiform, legless, probably blind, and mud-burrowing amphibian, with long, one-headed ribs attached neurocentrally, and with notochordal vertebrae, strangely resembling, though genetically very distinct from, the modern Caecilia."[8]

Undoubtedly inspired by the museum specimens, Williston made his first trip to Texas. "I renew my youth each time that I chase down the fossils in their native lairs,"[9] he wrote at the time to McClung. In September, 1908, he was near Seymour, Texas, where to his delight Paul Miller, the preparator, found great quantities of the small *Lysorophus*, among other fossils. It was a new and different kind of locality that he wrote home about:

"The whole country is in one great big cattle ranch belonging to a man by the name of Waggoner and compassing nearly 3000 square miles! It is fenced with barbed wire which we have to crawl through or drive over. The country is very broken and every thing is very *red*. The water we drink is about the color of paint, and our bread is pink! but it is not unwholesome. Everything grows big here!

"A few days ago while lying under a tree at noonday—Miller off taking a wash and the cook away I heard a tremendous squalling, which I imagined as that of a frog caught by a snake. Just in front of the tent a big blue racer (a snake very much like a black snake but light blue in color) had a tremendous frog in his mouth. I watched him and photographed him till the frogs legs were going down his mouth, which took about 5 minutes, and then as he turned to go I dropped the axe on him and cut him in two, for I wanted his skull. Mr. frog continued to travel on down, and when he got to the chopped off end he came out and jumped off lively for the

[8] "A New Group of Permian Amphibians," *Science*, Vol. XXVIII, No. 714 (1908), 317.

[9] McClung, "Samuel Wendell Williston," *Sigma Xi Quarterly*, Vol. VII, No. 1 (March, 1919), 15.

water! It so amused Miller, who came up, that he laughed for ten minutes. The snake measured 6½ feet long, the largest I ever saw. Tarantula spiders (black) with a body about an inch and a half long are everywhere, and Miller worked out of his blankets this morning a centipede six inches long. He had never seen one before —and he was astonished! Miller is making a collection of lizards and has about 20 in a box of five different kinds. As I am writing Miller has just jumped out of his blankets and says there is something alive in them!"[10]

Williston intended to go to Abilene, Texas, also to see Permian fossil footprints of a salamander-like animal. Some of these had been sent to him earlier that year by an Abilene high-school teacher, Augusta Hasslock.[11] But his old problem, malaria, reappeared and he did not get to Abilene.

Possibly this was the time that Paul Miller later told of, when Williston left field camp in midweek because of illness and drove into town where Miller was to join him Saturday. "When Paul arrived Professor Williston complained about having suddenly put on weight and was indignant when Paul pointed out that the trouble arose not from overweight but from the fact the Professor was wearing Paul's suit, not his own as he had supposed."[12] And, to Miller's dismay, Williston had spilled gravy all down the vest!

Alfred S. Romer described the Texas Permian red beds and their significance:

"Few, if any, fossil beds give a broader picture of vertebrate evolution than the continental deposits of the Lower Permian (and perhaps uppermost Carboniferous) of north central Texas. The period of their deposition is important in the history of reptiles, for at that time the early radiation of that group was under way. . . . The abundant Texas Permian material is preserved in clays and is three dimensional, facilitating morphological study. . . .

[10] Letter to Annie, September, 1908.

[11] Miss Hasslock had taken a course from Williston in the summer of 1907. She got a M.S. from the University of Chicago in 1910 and later married John F. Kemp, a school superintendent. She taught high school science, studied invertebrate fossils (mainly cephalopods), and wrote essays and poems until her death in 1963.

[12] Letter to the author from William D. Johnston, Jr., May 18, 1962.

"Although the region is reputed to be 'rich' in fossils, fossiliferous areas are far from being evenly distributed and are difficult
for the uninitiated to discover; much of any collecting trip con-
sists in wearing out shoe leather, covering barren break after barren break. Fossils seldom occur in isolated fashion, but are, rather,
found in 'pockets' which appear to represent deltaic lagoons or
eddies in stream channels where washed-down cadavers settled.
Usually a number of specimens (even if fragmentary) are present
in a pocket, but seldom are deposits rich or extensive enough to
warrant quarrying or to merit the term 'bonebed.' Only three major
bonebeds have ever been discovered. . . ."[13]

One of these was the Craddock bonebed six miles northwest of
Seymour found by Lawrence Baker of Williston's group in 1909.

That trip began in July, and included Williston, his ten-year-old
son Sam, Baker, and Paul Miller. Williston named a new species of
fossil salamander for the unconquerable preparator (*Trematops
milleri*). The Craddock bonebed yielded a number of specimens
of *Dimetrodon*, a small, long-spined carnivorous reptile. Williston
himself found a nearly complete skull of *Diplocaulus*, probably an
aquatic amphibian, first described by Cope years before.

Baker recently recalled that trip: "Our collecting expedition in
north Texas was the first of four years of the Big Drought. We
drank any water that a thirsty cow would. However, we had one
of those cloudbursts that are the bane of Texas. The Little Wichita
River went on a rampage and we couldn't get to town when we
ran out of provisions. For a week or more we had to subsist on
jackrabbits and bullfrogs. One night Williston insisted on saying
a grace which was:

'Jackrabbits hot, jackrabbits cold,
Jackrabbits young, jackrabbits old,
Jackrabbits tender, jackrabbits tough.
Thank the good Lord we've had enough.' "[14]

[13] "The Texas Permian Redbeds and Their Vertebrate Fauna," in T. S. Westoll
(ed.), *Studies on Fossil Vertebrates*, 157–60.
[14] Letter to the author from C. L. Baker, November 10, 1962.

Williston himself liked to tell of a roadside cafe sign he once saw in Texas during his collecting days there:

MEAL	25c
SQUARE MEAL	50c
HELL OF A GORGE	75c

Paul Miller continued to collect in the Texas Permian for a number of years for the University of Chicago. Miller was a Danish emigrant to the United States. Born in 1876, he came to this country at the age of twenty and chose to live in the wide-open plains near Medicine Bow, Wyoming. He joined the 1890 collecting group from the American Museum of Natural History at nearby Como Bluff, and soon became a preparator at the museum in New York. Williston hired Miller for the University of Chicago in 1904, and he later became the Curator of Vertebrates. "Almost single handed he brought the vertebrate collections of Walker Museum in the course of time to rank among the finest in the nation."[15]

Williston's daughter Dorothy recalls Miller as a pleasant, quiet man, often a visitor at their house. He named his only son Wendell Williston Miller. The preparator "had endless stories about the Professor's absent-mindedness. How Mrs. Williston asked Paul to check on the Professor's dress each day to see if he had forgotten his collar or tie—and had provided Paul with spares of any clothing that was likely to have been forgotten."[16]

In his thirty-nine years of employment at the University of Chicago, until his death in 1945, Miller collected extensively in the Permian red beds of Texas, in the Oligocene and Miocene of western Nebraska, in the Karroo Basin of South Africa (with Romer in 1928–1929), and in the Pliocene of Honduras. His preparation work on fossils was outstanding.

One of Paul Miller's idiosyncracies was that he could not abide rattlesnakes. Williston's favorite story of his preparator was when the latter was hunting fossils in Texas and, unprepared, came

[15] Everett C. Olson, untitled memorial to Paul C. Miller, *Society of Vertebrate Paleontologists News Bulletin* (December 31, 1945), 21.

[16] Letter to the author from William D. Johnston, Jr., May 18, 1962.

across a particularly large rattler. Not a stick nor a stone was in sight. So Miller pulled off one of his field boots and heaved it at the snake—which curled up around the boot and continued to rattle. Off came the other boot, to be hurled at the snake. Now the rattler had two boots—and Miller had none, in cactus country. Painfully he made his way back to camp in his socks, then in another pair of shoes and armed with both gun and axe, he marched back to retrieve his field boots and his prey. He spent the evening picking cactus spines out of his feet and socks by lantern light.

Among Miller's valuable paleontological discoveries was a pocket of fossils in Texas about six miles from the Craddock bonebed which he found in 1909. Williston named it the Cacops bed for the numerous remains of one animal. *Cacops*, "among the oddities of vertebrate paleontology," was an aquatic froglike creature of "absurd appearance"; it had a large head, no neck, a stubby tail, and a turtle-like partial carapace.[17]

"The numerous skeletons contained in the deposit lay upon each other through a thickness of about two feet or a little more; those near the top were more isolated, those lower down packed more closely together and more disturbed in their relations. As a rule the various skeletons are more or less united, but frequently legs, tails, and even single bones are found isolated. The material in which the remains occur is the dark red clay forming the greater part of the exposures of the Texas Permian deposits, but the bones themselves are incrusted with a thin, more or less adherent, hard matrix, sometimes removable with difficulty. The bones of the upper layers have a less thick incrustation, but in the lower ones the skeletons lie more closely packed together, the skeletons or parts of skeletons often being cemented together in masses of considerable size. Because of this it is often difficult to separate any one skeleton without disturbing the others. The remains lay in a space some six or seven feet in width by ten or twelve in length. . . . The material was brought to the laboratory in bandaged blocks of various sizes from fifty to four hundred pounds in weight, as it was found most

[17] S. W. Williston, "Cacops, Desmospondylus: New Genera of Permian Vertebrates," *Bulletin of the Geological Society of America*, Vol. XXI (1910), 250.

convenient in the field to divide them. . . . Among the skeletons and parts of skeletons so far worked out, in part or wholly, there are at least a dozen skeletons of *Varanosaurus,* as many or more of *Cacops,* including eight or ten good skulls, five or six of *Casea,* the skeleton of *Captorhinus* . . . and a few bones of *Seymouria.*"[18]

Miller's discovery was truly remarkable, considering the erratic nature of the Texas fossil fields, for "with the exception of a few ounces of bone fragments a half mile away, not another indication of a fossil was discovered in the adjacent exposures covering several hundred acres."[19]

While excavating the Cacops bed in 1910 Miller found a "remarkably complete specimen" of *Seymouria baylorensis,* the problematical vertebrate that straddles the anatomy of amphibians and reptiles. Augusta H. Kemp long afterward recalled "being in the lab when they [probably Williston and Miller] were taking a picture of Seymouria baylorensis. . . . You would have thought it was the 'heir apparent.' "[20] It was, of course, actually a "missing link."

Williston summarized the results of the extensive Permian collections in his first paleontologic book, *American Permian Vertebrates,* in 1911. The study took him again to specimens at Yale, collected for Marsh by David A. Baldwin in New Mexico many years before. Some of the specimens were still in packing cartons, which was not too surprising as Baldwin was working in New Mexico for Marsh during the hectic race of 1877 for bigger and better dinosaurs. Baldwin's specimens were too small to be of interest that year.

The Yale material turned his field interests to what Williston called the Baldwin beds in New Mexico, so in the summer of 1911 a field party including Williston, his son Sam, E. C. Case (then at the University of Michigan), and Paul Miller headed for Abiquiu, New Mexico, after getting information from Charles Schuchert at Yale on Baldwin's collecting area. Friedrich von Huene of the University of Tubingen, Germany,[21] joined them for three weeks.

[18] S. W. Williston, *American Permian Vertebrates,* 4–5.
[19] Williston, "Cacops, Desmospondylus: New Genera of Permian Vertebrates," *Bulletin of the Geological Society of America,* Vol. XXI (1910), 250.
[20] Letter to the author, September 2, 1962.

Williston's arrival in New Mexico was typical for him in those days. As the story was recounted later: "Case and Williston came by train. Miller met them when they got off the Santa Fe sleeper at Lamy. As they met him, Case said to Miller, 'Pssst! Take a look at Williston's shoes.' Williston was wearing one black shoe (his own) and one brown shoe. Apparently, when he got up early in the morning on the sleeper, he had put on the first two shoes that came handy, and one of them happened to belong to the gentleman in the upper berth who was no doubt surprised and irritated when he discovered the swap later in the day. When they left the field for civilization Williston refused to buy a new pair of shoes. However, they stopped at Kansas State on the way, where Mrs. Williston met them, and since he had to give a lecture there she insisted that he buy a new pair of shoes for the occasion."[22]

Abiquiu, Williston said, "is the second oldest town in North America! a church was built here a few years after the settlement of Santa Fe, and before the settlement of San Augustine—Parts of the church are still standing, but it has of course been nearly rebuilt many times. And the total population of the City is about 100! —one store, three saloons, and a dozen or twenty adobes."[23]

From Abiquiu they entered the red beds through El Cobre Canyon, to "the most dreary and forsaken region I think I was ever in," wrote Williston. "We spent a whole day in hunting water, subsisting meanwhile on rain water in pools in the rocks. We had packed up to go back to Abiquiu, when we met a hermit, who lives here and he showed us where to find water we can drink, though it has a considerable alkali in it."[24]

The collectors gathered a wide variety of fossils—invertebrate, vertebrate, and plant—from the Pennsylvanian brachiopod *Spirifer*, through Permian labyrinthodonts, to Triassic phytosaurs and the primitive dinosaur *Coelophysis*.

[21] Then on his way to becoming an outstanding authority on dinosaurs. See Edwin H. Colbert, *Men and Dinosaurs*.

[22] Letter to the author from Alfred S. Romer, April 17, 1967. The incident may not have applied to this particular trip but it seems the most likely.

[23] Letter to Annie, July 6, 1911.

[24] Letter to his family, July 9, 1911.

Williston spent part of the summer of 1912 studying specimens again in the Yale Museum. In late August, accompanied by Paul Miller, he headed for old familiar ground: Cañon City, Colorado. After a brief stop there, they went on to Durango on the spectacular route:

"From Salida here has been nearly all through the mountains on the narrow guage [*sic*] R. R., and passenger trains run only in the day time. From Salida we climbed to Marshall Pass, 19,850 feet, the R. R. constantly curving and doubling on itself. In the afternoon we went through the Black Cañon, with walls a thousand feet high and nearly perpendicular. Telluride is a mining town elevation 9,000 feet, and coming from there we again climbed above the 10,000, almost to the snow line, turning and doubling along the steep mountain sides, in many places so steep that if the cars had left the track they would have fallen five hundred feet. Indeed not long ago two cars did fall that distance. It is only 160 miles from Telluride, but it has taken us ten hours to cover it."[25] The narrow-gauge railroad still covers this fantastic route, as does an even more precipitous highway.

The collectors hunted fossils near Trimble, Colorado, but "practically without results." Williston was philosophical: "But I don't care—we can't always get a bonanza like we have the past two years."[26] They gathered fossil shells for Stuart Weller and returned to Chicago.

The 1912 field trip was practically Williston's last. He was aware that his fossil-finding ability was declining. In the summer of 1915, while the family was all in Socorro, New Mexico, he took Sam for a few weeks to the Baldwin bonebeds in Rio Arriba County again. In the spring of 1918 he spent a month in Texas with Miller.

He was never at a loss for new material to study, however, for the indefatigable Paul Miller and students (Herman Douthitt and Maurice Mehl[27]) collected each year in the Texas beds, and Miller steadily worked out the crumpled fossils from clay nodules.

[25] Letter to Annie, September 8, 1912.

[26] Letter to Annie, September 14, 1912.

[27] Maurice G. Mehl (1887–1966) became a worthy member of the geologic profession. He received his B.S. (1911) and his Ph.D. (1914) at the University of

In 1905, when William R. Harper died, Harry Pratt Judson replaced him as president of the University of Chicago. Williston continued to get along well with the new administration. According to one of his students, much later: "He was an expert on managing with very little funds [on field trips]. Harry Pratt Judson . . . always felt he had to give him several times what he asked for."[28] The habit of having been economical for many years could not be broken quickly.

Williston's paleontological publications continued, becoming summaries in the later years of amphibian and reptile classification. One of his most readable publications, for the layman, is *Water Reptiles of the Past and Present*.

As a partial summary of the unusual fossils from the Permocarboniferous time, Williston published some restorations in 1914.[29] Many of these detailed drawings were done in 1912, in long evenings at home at his cluttered desk. With both modesty and honesty he summarized: "Whatever may be the merits of these restorations as works of art, they have been drawn with most scrupulous accuracy so far as form and proportions are concerned, the musculature derived from the study of living reptiles." He would no doubt be pleased at the frequent reappearance of a number of his restorations in later paleontologic articles.

For one of his final projects in 1917, Dorothy provided him with a comfortable working area at home:

"Father has brought his typewriter and all his drawing apparatus home, and I moved all the furniture that he wanted to use into the parlor . . . and now he plants himself in the middle of the corner that I have separated off like a barroom counter, and reaches in all directions. He is surrounded on three sides by work places, and on the fourth by a window. . . .

Chicago. In 1919 he joined the staff of the University of Missouri and taught there until his retirement, after which he was on the staff of the Missouri Geological Survey. In the tradition of Williston, Mehl was noted for his personal interest in every student and for his vivid reconstructions of extinct animals. His research was chiefly in vertebrate paleontology, conodonts, compaction of sediments, and accumulation of petroleum.

[28] Letter to the author from C. L. Baker, November 10, 1962.

[29] "Restorations of Some American Permocarboniferous Amphibians and Reptiles," *Journal of Geology*, Vol. XXII, No. 1 (1914), 57–70.

"We took all the rugs out from under him, furnished him with a wastebasket, an ash tray and a drop light and let him go after it. He is so taken with his corner that he has stayed up until half past ten tonight, an unusual thing for him."[30]

While at the University of Chicago, Williston published about seventy-five papers and books on paleontology, a great many of the papers in the *Journal of Geology*, which—as one of Harper's innovations in the form of department journals published by the university press—had begun publishing in 1893. Like O. C. Marsh, Williston did not live to complete the monographs he intended, but he did publish copiously in lesser papers.

As he developed his views on the relationships and classification of the vertebrates, as usual he did not hesitate to criticize the opinions of his fellow paleontologists. But his tone and his attitude were much different from the vicious remarks of Cope and Marsh. His willingness to admit to having been wrong at times, his readiness to credit the work of others, and his always genial personality usually prevented others from taking offense. One exception was Robert Broom[31] of South Africa but that was resolved in the final year of Williston's life when Broom wrote:

"It was quite a pleasure to hear from you again after a few years of separation due to an unfortunate misunderstanding. Your little paper on the classification of reptiles duly reached me and has pleased me much. It is the best classification we have yet had...."[32]

Lull effectively summarized Williston's later contributions to paleontology:

"... To him we also owe a very large part of our exact knowledge of the Paleozoic air-breathers, for his indefatigable work in the field and laboratory, aided by a few, very devoted co-laborers, has brought to light a fauna amazing in its extent and degree of perfection—entire skeletons of forms many of which were either new to science or known in very fragmentary condition. Williston not only gave a very clear understanding of the osseous morpholo-

[30] Letter from Dorothy to Hathaway, July 4, 1917.

[31] Broom (1866–1951) was the first to describe and study the important Karroo Permian fossils of South Africa.

[32] Letter of April 22, 1918.

gy of the forms under consideration, throwing much light upon such vexatious problems as the homologies of the cranial elements, of the individual vertebrae, and of the amniotic sternum, but by careful comparative study of existing forms was enabled to restore his creatures in the flesh in a way that, anatomically at least, is thus far above criticism. He discussed at some length the life conditions, feeding and other habits, prowess, and evolutionary adaptations of the forms which he studied, and his knowledge was such that he could generally recognize such resemblances as were the result of convergence and such as actually implied a like heritage. His ideas concerning the phylogenies of the amphibian and reptilian groups developed somewhat slowly, due to his desire that such should be founded upon a considerable body of attested fact. In his final paper on phylogenies, in 1917, he acknowledges, as the best that we have, those broader groupings of such men as [Henry Fairfield] Osborn, whose work he was inclined to criticize most emphatically when it first appeared 15 years before.

"Williston laid a broad and fundamental foundation for the fabric of our knowledge concerning the cold-blooded air-breathers, building solidly and securely much of the superstructure as well. It is doubtful whether later students of the reptiles particularly will find much that is amiss, especially when the last work of the master shall have been published posthumously. On the other hand, it is the writer's belief that they can build thereon fearlessly, knowing that that which has been done is secure."[33]

What made these accomplishments possible?

Primarily, Williston was an excellent observer. In the field he quickly learned to distinguish each geologic horizon, and within the fossil-bearing beds he could spot the projecting fragment. Others could do that, too—Charles Sternberg was an excellent fossil finder.

But Williston's power of observation carried him a step farther. Because of his excellent knowledge of anatomy, he could visualize the characteristics and distinctions of each animal group. No new

[33] Lull, "Samuel Wendell Williston," *Memoirs of the National Academy of Sciences,* Vol. XVII, 5th Memoir (1924), 134–35.

fossil was an anomaly to him; it was related to and distinguished from the known forms immediately in his mind.

Williston was an evolutionist. In his opinion the only purpose of classification was to further knowledge of evolution. He himself said:

"Perhaps the most encouraging sign of advancement in our science [vertebrate paleontology] during the past ten years has been the recognition of certain methods or factors of evolution that permit us to orient ourselves better, to discern more clearly the true lines of evolution, and of these I refer more especially to parallel evolution. We have been deceived in the past, time without end, in almost every branch of animal and vegetable life, by adaptive characters, characters evolved in response to like environmental conditions, so often imputed to real heredity. . . .

"Especially has our knowledge of the early reptiles acquired in the past few years thrown a flood of light on the evolution of the class, at least in the revelation of earlier errors. . . . The connecting chain between the most generalized of reptiles, as represented by *Seymouria*, to the most generalized of mammals is now almost complete; nowhere are there differences that in themselves are of more than family value, perhaps not even that. . . . Classification will have attained its highest perfection when nothing more than specific differences are the final distinction between families, orders, and classes. . . .

"In no other class of animal or vegetable life has classification —that is, real phylogeny—reached the high plane that it has in the Mammalia; nowhere does taxonomy, that bugbear of the microscopist, approximate so near the final truth, and this happy result has been due chiefly to the paleontologist. To him has been and always will be the last word in taxonomy—that is, evolution."[34]

The young man who pored over Darwin's books at a small college in Kansas in 1866 became a distinguished contributor to the details of evolution himself.

---

[34] "Evolutionary Evidences," in Symposium on Ten Years' Progress in Vertebrate Paleontology, *Bulletin of the Geological Society of America*, Vol. XXIII (1912), 257–62.

control of the state senate, but, after a riotous contest in which both Republicans and Populists convened in separate sessions, they lost control of the house. The senate continued its majority in 1894, while the house continued Republican. A fusion ticket of Populists and Democrats was successful in 1896, but the national party collapsed quickly after the defeat of the combined Populist and free-silver advocates in 1896, so two years later the Republicans again had control in Kansas. The decade of political instability was a continual problem for the state university.

Chancellor Snow had repeated clashes with state politicians over his insistence that the appointment of regents must be based on competence, not on political patronage. He almost lost his own post in 1897 in retaliatory action by the legislature. The Populists were not popular among the university faculty, who watched with dismay the disruption of the Agricultural College in Manhattan under a Populist-controlled board of regents. (At that college more than half the faculty were summarily dismissed on June 30, 1897, without stated reason.) Nor was the university faculty pleased with the legislator in 1893 who protested building the new library on the basis that Lincoln had gotten along without one.

Williston's part in the political see-sawing was indirect, except as a victim and as a close associate of Chancellor Snow. The latter spoke freely to him of the problems and asked his help on escorting inquiring (and often obstructive) legislators on tours of the museum and laboratories. Populist regent James P. Sams was sympathetic toward the university; he was often entertained at the Willistons and accompanied the fossil expedition to Wyoming in 1895.

The political bickering was most evident in university finances. Williston began there at a salary of $1,500 in 1890. A year later professors' salaries were increased to $1,800, and the next fall to $2,000. The financial situation was reasonably comfortable in 1895, when the establishment of the medical school was first under serious consideration. Field trip money was liberal that year also for Williston: he had $1,500 to use for collecting and was able to outfit and support two separate trips. But economy-minded voters were increasing their influence. Leaves of absence and vacations were curtailed, as were trips to give paid lectures. But the major dissension arose because of inequities by the regents: when salary changes were announced, a special few received a little extra, with no differences in their duties (deanships carried a higher salary, but uniformly).

A fiscal crisis in university funds in November, 1896, resulted in no pay to university employees for one month—at a particularly unfortunate time of year. Many of the faculty had to borrow where they could. By the following March the legislature had completed their cuts and Annie reported:

"At last the legislature are through and gone home, and I hope they will stay there & bag their heads and never get back to Topeka again. The salaries are cut to 1750 for most of the professors but Wendell & Prof. Haworth [of geology] get 1800 nobody knows why—but they will get more than $50 worth of ill will from the rest. [Four others] get $2000. . . . Most of the professors feel that they have been insulted I think. Snow is cut to 4000 but the bill to depose him from the regency was killed as it should have been. Everybody has lost heart and I dont believe they will work so hard as they have hitherto."[1]

Some of the faculty relaxed at a poverty party in April, at which they wore patched clothes and supped on ice water and mush and played blind man's buff, and then returned to their reduced circumstances. The cuts affected the science professors in their laboratories as well, of course, and this was disheartening. Occasionally Williston could sell a specimen from the museum collection to another institution, and this money could be used for field or laboratory expenses.

Finally in 1899 salaries were raised. By then Williston was dean of the medical school, in which position he received again $2,000 while professors received $1,900. In 1901 another $100 was added to Williston's salary.

His views on the pay of professors were expressed in an address to the Kansas chapter of the Sigma Xi in June 1902:

[1] Letter to Genie, March 13, 1897.

196

"But what are the realities? After many years of preparation he [a professor] finds at last a place which pays the salary of a fairly good clerk, perhaps a thousand dollars a year. It is only exceptionally that he is fitted to begin his life work much under thirty years of age, for more is required of him in preparation than of members of other professions, if he is to rise to the highest usefulness. If he is a true man he gives the very best that is in him, that he may accomplish that which will finally bring him the recognition which his older colleague receives. By the time he is forty, and when the highest period of usefulness has been reached, he is receiving the highest salary he can ordinarily ever expect. All that is necessary now for him is to keep his position. If he is an exceptionally able man perhaps he is then receiving the income of a second-class physician or lawyer of equal age. Who would willingly trust his life in a difficult surgical operation to a surgeon who could not command a greater income than two thousand dollars a year? Why do we expect to get good men and women for teachers with less than half the salary of a physician or lawyer? Someone may answer, 'Because the professor's life is an easy one, with little to do and no anxieties.'

"What would you think of a parish that expected its pastor to deliver three sermons a day, five days in a week and forty weeks in the year? You would shortly expect to find such a preacher in the insane asylum. The earnest and useful professor works as hard as do the members of any other profession, and the best can be got from him only when he is not driven. . . .

"The university professor is unfortunate in having his tastes educated above his income, but he lives in reasonable contentment, nevertheless, provided he can work and properly care for those whom he loves."

To care for those whom he loved Williston devised ways to augment his income. The fortuitous meteorite find of 1892 enabled him to build his house. His continual outside work on Diptera brought some income, especially the study of West Indies flies and Mexican flies, plus the rather small proceeds from his *Manual of*

Diptera. He gave lectures, he consulted on water problems for the city of Lawrence, he sold some of his books and journals to the university library, he made lantern slides for other professors for a short time, he sold a few popular articles to magazines, he wrote encyclopedia articles, and he appeared as expert witness in some legal cases. Some of these things he would have done anyway, but, as indicated in family letters, more often pressure for money made him take the time for them.

Annie contributed also to the budget. She was an exemplary manager of money who did not yearn for luxuries for herself. Her discouragement over money came at Christmas and when she felt that the children required new clothes, not herself; she made clothes for all the family except her husband. She entertained always as a duty, not as a recreation for herself. Her luxuries were items for the house—for serving the Old and New Club or making the house presentable for guests. She had household help—a laundress once a week and a succession of girls for cleaning (except in the leanest days), but these were appropriate to her era, her station, and, just barely, to her finances. In addition she kept one spare bedroom for a boarder, and a series of Williston's students and employees occupied the room: W. H. Brown, who later married one of Snow's daughters and settled in Rhodesia; Grace Kirtland, Williston's assistant; Hugo Kahl, an unobtrusive Swedish entomologist, loved by the children, who worked for Will Snow; Barnum Brown, who went on to a distinguished career in paleontology; and the brilliant C. E. McClung.

The regents' arbitrariness in salary and other university affairs contributed to a decline in Chancellor Snow's health, and he suffered a nervous collapse in June, 1900, eight months after the tragic loss of his oldest son.[2] Restored but unwilling to continue as chancellor, Snow resigned in September, 1901. His relinquishing

[2] Will Snow began as an entomologist (working under Williston), but he turned to journalism. While covering the story of the return of the 20th Kansas Regiment to San Francisco from the Spanish American War, on October 10, 1899, he fell from a tugboat in San Francisco Bay and was drowned. The body was never recovered.

of the chancellorship must have contributed to Williston's decision to leave the University of Kansas. He had come at Snow's request originally.

The jealousy created by salary inequities left all the faculty bitter. McClung, who knew Williston well, felt that faculty squabbling led to his departure:

"Despite his absolute fairness and unselfish disposition it was inevitable that in a school of this size there should be jealousies aroused by the prominence of one of its men. That this should be so in his case was always a source of wonder and regret to Doctor Williston. The time came eventually when the consciousness of this adverse feeling became so strong with him that he could no longer endure the thought of it and, when opportunely an offer came to him from Chicago, which promised new and unfettered conditions for work, he reluctantly accepted it. With no bitterness but with a sense of shame and hurt he left the institution where he had planned to complete his life work. The feeling of regret which this step occasioned him he never lost, and frequently in his later letters I find expressions of longing to be back in Kansas. A hope that something would take him back never entirely left him, and the home he had built near the University he retained in this hope. Sometimes he even ventured to express this compelling desire. Thus I find in a letter of March, 1908 the following: 'I am looking forward to retiring in a few years and then going back to Lawrence to devote the remainder of my life purely to research—entomology or paleontology, it matters little.' Whether pleasure or disappointment came in his new surroundings this longing for Kansas was always with him and frequently, in later letters, I find expressed the wish that we might be there together again, with another friend who was also called to work elsewhere. This constant homesickness could not fail to react upon his health. In 1912 he wrote: 'After ten years' absence I long as much as ever for Kansas—am still homesick.' "[3]

[3] "Samuel Wendell Williston," *Sigma Xi Quarterly*, Vol. VII, No. 1 (March, 1919), 13–14.

Williston presented what may be considered his valedictory to Kansas as he bowed out as president of the Kansas chapter of the Sigma Xi in June, 1902. In part he said:

"In the twelve years that I have been a member of this University, I have seen it increase in size from about four hundred University students, to more than twelve hundred. I have seen a new library building, a new physics building, a new chemistry building, new shops, a new chancellor's residence, and a new museum building. I have seen its museums built up until they have obtained a world-wide reputation. I have seen the engineering school become an entity and achieve notable distinction, and the law school increased in its course and in its requirements, a school of medicine well begun and widely recognized, and the pharmacy school strengthened and improved. I have seen the University broaden out much and still doing most excellent work.

"I have also seen the cost of education everywhere increased by reason of the greater demand for improved facilities.

"But I have not seen the salaries of its teachers increased in ten years past. I have not seen a proportional increase in the number of its teachers—there were then forty-four and now eighty—there should be a hundred and twenty. The annual income has scarcely doubled and it should have been increased three fold. It costs less in this University to educate its students than in any institution of equal or even approximately equal rank; its professors are paid less. Is this economy? Is it even good business prudence on the part of the State? . . .

"Through forty-five long years I have known Kansas. I have watched it leap upward from the bloody travail into vigorous youth, buoyant in that self-confidence which its strong sinews gave it. I have seen it stricken with drouth and scourges, bowed down by want and famine, to recover as does the bent bow. I have known it to be ridiculed for its vagaries, but always respected for its sturdiness of character. I have known it to be forgetful at times, lapsing from the straight-forward path of good sense, but I have never known it when education was not its watchword. I believe that the state which I love so well, where my boyhood was spent and the best of my manhood has been given, will not be recreant to those higher principles which have made it what it is. Through difficulties to the heights has been its motto in the past. It will be in the future. It will not, it must not, it shall not fall behind in the march for higher civilization. Its star of progress leads onward still."

The low salary, Snow's resignation, and problems with the rest of the faculty probably all contributed to Williston's willingness to leave Kansas, plus a long-lingering desire to be at a major university. He may well have also been eager to reduce his commitments, after the establishing of the medical school. Ever optimistic, he looked forward to devoting his remaining years only to paleontology. Many productive years were ahead of him, but in many ways the move to Chicago was a mistake and may well have shortened his life. It is said that he wept when he decided to leave Kansas.

PART THREE

1902 to 1918

CHAPTER 13

At Harper's University

WILLIAM RAINEY HARPER wrote Williston on May 13, 1902:
"I am happy to write you that at the meeting of the Board of
Trustees held last Tuesday, you were elected Professor of Paleontology in the University of Chicago. It is understood that you will
receive a salary of $2,000., and that you are also to have official
connection with the Field Columbian Museum with an additional
salary of $1,500. for such service. I assure you that we appre-
ciate the meaning of your coming. . . ."

And so in September Williston joined a distinguished roster at
Harper's ten-year-old experiment in education, the outcome of
some years of planning by energetic and careful Baptists.[1] In the
1880's Thomas W. Goodspeed and Frederick T. Gates persuaded
the not unwilling John D. Rockefeller of the need for a major
university in Chicago. William Rainey Harper was Rockefeller's
choice as president because of his realistic but grandiose dream of
a great new university which would revolutionize education. The
quarterly teaching system, heavy emphasis on research with a light
teaching load, extension courses for large numbers of people, and
a university press were some of the innovations of the enthusiastic
Harper. These and a rapid expansion imposed a heavy financial
load on the fledgling university, which was only spared bankruptcy
by frequent aid from Rockefeller.

Among the earliest appointments to the new university was
Thomas C. Chamberlin as chairman of the department of geology.
Chamberlin had been president of the University of Wisconsin but
apparently the combination of student problems there, a desire to
do less administration, and a higher salary at Chicago induced him

[1] For a detailed account of the founding of the University of Chicago, see Richard
J. Storr, *Harper's University*.

to take the new position. (As president of the University of Wisconsin he had received $5,000 a year; Chicago's offer as department chairman was $7,000.) From Wisconsin also came Chamberlin's close friend, Rollin D. Salisbury. These two men dominated the department of geology for thirty years, Chamberlin as department head until he became emeritus in 1918, and Salisbury as close assistant to Chamberlin and then department head from 1918 until his death in 1922. T. C. Chamberlin was a distinguished man of broad vision, highly respected by his fellow faculty members at the University of Chicago. He was "in constant co-operation with President Harper, who relied much on his broad knowledge and his experience in university administration."[2] He was, of course, a major contributor to our knowledge of the origin of the universe.

Charles O. Whitman was another of the early Chicago appointments by Harper, as chairman of the zoology department. He was one of almost half the faculty of Clark University who accepted positions at the University of Chicago. Whitman, an excellent researcher in embryology, evolution, and animal behavior, was also the founder of the Marine Biological Laboratory at Woods Hole, Massachusetts, which he directed during the summers for twenty years.

Vertebrate paleontology was a science between geology and zoology, and it became an early argument between those two departments. "The matter of where it should be was the cause of a rather acrimonious struggle between Chamberlin and Whitman . . . early in 1894. Both wrote several strong letters to President Harper; finally, the three thrashed it out (a nine-sheet stenographer's report recorded the proceedings), with the predictable result that it had to be set up as a unit by itself."[3]

George Baur, an associate of Williston's earlier in Marsh's laboratory, taught paleontology until his death in 1898. Whitman then made a tentative offer to Williston at Chicago, and Williston agreed

[2] R. A. F. Penrose, Jr., "The Early Days of the Department of Geology at the University of Chicago," *Journal of Geology*, Vol. XXXVII (1929), 324.

[3] D. Jerome Fisher, *The Seventy Years of the Department of Geology, University of Chicago*, 7.

to take it,[4] but the offer did not become final. Chamberlin must have been deeply involved in the 1898 decision, for in a letter of June 28 of that year he told Harper:

"After pondering over the subject raised by the letter recommending Professor Williston, the feeling has been growing strongly upon me that if he is to be selected some readjustment of department relations to secure the conditions prerequisite for success in building up his courses should be reached before an engagement is concluded. This should be done in justice to him as well as to the University. In his present situation he depends upon his geological course to feed his paleontological classes. When here a year or so ago he indicated something of the success of his paleontological classes, and so I was prompted to inquire what percentage of his paleontological students came to be interested in the subject from their course in zoology. He gave me a look of surprise and answered—'Why, none at all', and he proceeded to explain that in his course in general geology he brought the students into contact with the fossils and they thus became interested in them and were led on to paleontological studies. . . ."

The debate for ownership of paleontology was not resolved then, and in 1902 Williston became professor of paleontology— and the only member of the department. There was no indication, however, that he was expected to enlarge the department. Nor was he offered the $7,000 salary of a chairman.

Williston's reply to Harper's letter on his appointment told of his hopes and sorrows:

"Your letter received. I have asked the Recorder to send me copies of the University Register and other matters relating to the scientific departments. After I have studied therein a few days, and have become better acquainted with the methods of the University—so different from our own—I will send to Professors Chamberlin and Whitman the courses I desire to give for their suggestions, to be then incorporated in their announcements.

"I am looking forward with many hopes and expectations to the work at Chicago. It will be a relief to me to be freed from so much

[4] Letter from Annie to her mother, May 1, 1898.

that has borne heavily upon me in the past few years. But, the past week has been a very trying one to me. It has been hard to make the people here comprehend that the decision is already made—and harder still to part with my collections and my friends. I see, however, such great possibilities and probabilities in the new work, and so many new friends, there, that I anticipate a happy life, and, I hope, a useful one."

The first year at Chicago was a prosperous one for the family from Kansas, but disheartening too. Some of the higher salary disappeared in the even higher costs of the big city and especially in a series of colds and grippes and dismal illnesses. Also, Annie's mother was critically ill in New Haven, and Annie worried. Except for Williston himself, the family never did feel comfortably established in Chicago and at the university. The first severe blow fell at the end of the first academic year, when Williston learned that his appointment at the Field Columbian Museum had been for one year only. His salary then was abruptly reduced to what he had been receiving in Kansas—and in a city of higher costs. Annie and the children moved to New Haven for the following year, both to save cost and to care for Mrs. Hathaway. The enforced separation did not endear Chicago to them, even after their return.

The unhappy professor wrote to Harper in November of 1903:

"Will you pardon me for expressing my anxiety to learn whether anything further has been decided regarding my work? . . . The sudden dimunition in my salary is causing much distress in my family and anxiety to myself. We are doing what we can with our summer's [paleontological] material, so that I am not idle.

"The plan for the reorganization of this paleontological department which will be presented to you by Prof. Chamberlin is one which I earnestly hope may be carried through, if nothing else more feasible presents itself. In the teaching especially I believe that my work may be made much more effective thereby—in making paleontology a more elementary and integral part of both zoology and geology. It is very pleasant to teach graduate students only—my class now numbers seven—but paleontology is zoology and geology.

"The plan is in great measure not experimental with myself. I have tried it in past years successfully. I shall be personally glad to do anything whereby these two departments in our university may be strengthened—rather than to try to build up a department for experts only."[5]

Harper was sympathetic, but even then a university president could not do everything he desired to do immediately. It was another year before he could announce to Williston:

"It is arranged, and ordered, in connection with the budget which begins July 1, 1905, that you are to have the full work of a professor and receive the salary of $3,000. I tried to get this to $3500, but was unable to do so. When I tell you that this was arranged in spite of the fact that we have cut out $83,000 on the whole, you will appreciate the difficulty involved. I understand that you will consult with Professor Whitman and arrange for certain work in connection with his department. I am particularly anxious that you should get your hands on the undergraduate students for work in zoology. I appreciate the fact that this does not help you out for the present year, but I am hoping that even yet we may be able to bring things into better shape for this year. I thought that the permanent was the most important."[6]

The budget cut referred to by Harper was the result of founder Rockefeller having insisted on a balanced budget for the year—or he would make no further contribution. It is obvious that Harper must have made a very special effort to improve Williston's situation that year in spite of the university's budget problems. However, extra work went along with the salary increase, an appointment at the affiliated Rush Medical School teaching comparative anatomy.

Williston's office, on his arrival at Chicago, was established on the third floor of Walker Museum, one of the earliest buildings. It had been pledged by George C. Walker before the university opened and was dedicated in October of 1893. Walker had intended it as a natural history museum and hoped it would acquire many

[5] Letter of November 13, 1903.
[6] Letter of February 17, 1905.

exhibits from the 1893 Columbian Exposition, probably including Williston's exhibit of Kansas building stones. R. A. F. Penrose, Jr. did succeed in getting some of the exhibits for Walker Museum, but the new Field Columbian Museum acquired much of the material. So the museum was occupied by the geology department, supposedly temporarily, plus miscellaneous collections.[7]

As had been so in Kansas, Williston was a popular professor at Chicago, though his classes were smaller. He no longer had the university-wide influence that he had known in Kansas, and his impact on outstanding students in all scientific disciplines was much less. The geology graduate students, however, soon considered his paleontology courses mandatory.

His chief classroom characteristic was informality, much appreciated by the students without loss of respect. They referred to him as the "Doctor." "I never knew Williston to use notes when teaching or lecturing,"[8] wrote C. L. Baker. To his professional material he added anecdotes of his field days with Mudge and for Marsh, and "very decided views concerning his contemporary vertebrate paleontologists."[9]

Olof Larsell recalled his course of the summer of 1913: "The class met in a rather cluttered small laboratory in Walker Museum. Dr. Williston would lecture very informally but in a manner that made those fossils live. Frequently while lecturing he would reach for some object in the air in front of him, invisible to the class, and examine the gnat or small fly with the lens he kept pinned to his [watch chain].... Once a week we went to the Field Museum of Natural History, then located in Jackson Park, where he would introduce us to the fossilized skeletons as well as to their stuffed and mounted descendants. One morning I sat down on a park bench to await the hour of opening of the Museum. Presently Dr. Williston came along, also a little early, and sat down beside me. He

[7] Walker protested the occupancy of his museum by a single department in 1902, but geology had nowhere else to go. Rosenwald Hall was finally built for geology in 1915 adjacent to Walker Museum. The new building acknowledged paleontology in its decor, including two Permian reptiles as corner gargoyles.

[8] Letter to the author, April 7, 1962.

[9] Letter to the author from Margaret Fuller Boos, July 29, 1962.

Williston's bookplate, drawn by his daughter Dorothy and symbolic of his paleontological and medical interests. The landscape is Permian; the row of books and pen indicate his many writings; and the caduccus is the symbol of a physician.

Restoration of *Diplodocus*, the dinosaur that may have led Marsh to give his watch to Williston, in a drawing by Charles R. Knight.

Williston's rendering of a landscape in Permocarboniferous times with two *Eryops* in foreground.

Restoration of *Araeoscelis gracilis* Williston, a two-foot-long Paleozoic reptile from near Seymour, Texas, in a drawing by Williston.

Williston's sketch of a beetle. Caption reads *"Pasamachus Elongatus* (Say) (A terrible name for so small a beast) July 1, 75 Found by 'Brous.' "

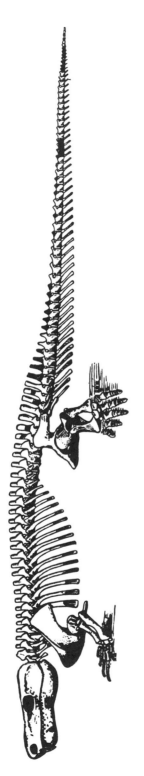

Skeletal restoration of the primitive reptile *Limnoscelis paludis* Williston, from New Mexico, as drawn by Williston.

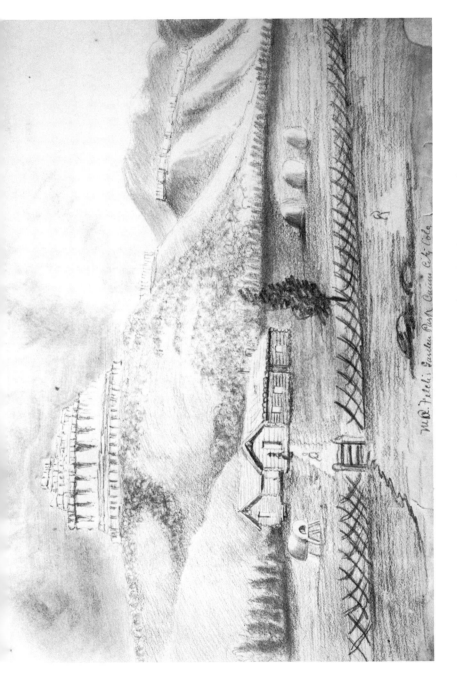

Sketch by Williston of the dinosaur locality at Garden Park, Cañon City, Colorado, as it appeared in 1877.

Williston at work in his study.

CHAPTER 15

Sidelights

More Flies

A GLANCE at Williston's bibliography misleadingly indicates that he did very little work on his avocation of Diptera after going to Chicago, for only five entomological works are listed after 1901. Actually he completed there his most significant work in the field: the third edition of the *Manual of North American Diptera.*

Probably the idea of revising the manual began during Williston's discouragement over money during the second and third years at Chicago, for he had often turned to his fly collection to console himself ever since he began the study to avoid problems under O. C. Marsh. He expected the book to bring "considerable money" to him, but he was overly optimistic.

By the beginning of 1906 he was well under way on the revision and corresponding on its details with his father-in-law publisher. He was soon almost regretting his decision:

"I am afraid that I should never have undertaken the revision of the Manual, if I had known what I was getting into. . . . The figures of course will be scattered through the text, and, altogether, there will be about four hundred separate drawings. As each one takes me from fifteen minutes to half an hour to make, you can see what a task it is."[1]

The first two manuals had no illustrations. The third included 800 drawings and photographs by Williston and 200 more from other entomologists, some of whom had also written separate chapters. This magnum opus described 1,200 genera in 405 pages.

It covered a broad field, one of major significance, although to Williston it was only a relaxing hobby. The Diptera and man have been at odds for years. This insect order is readily distinguished by having only one pair of wings; the second pair customary to most

[1] Letter to J. T. Hathaway, March 20, 1906.

other insects is reduced to a pair of knobs commonly called balancers or halteres. Included are names familiar to all: house flies and horse flies, mosquitoes, gnats and midges (including blackflies and no-see-ums), bot flies and horse bot flies, fruit flies, crane flies, soldier flies, tse-tse flies, tachinid flies, shore flies, bee flies, assassin flies, flower flies, leaf miners, and more.

The manual was finally done. Williston's daughter Dorothy reported that, on its completion, her father dropped the manuscript on his desk with relief and commented, "Well, that's finished. When it is revised again, it will be by someone else." He was correct. Years later C. H. Curran tackled the group again, and he reused many of the original plates which were provided to him by Mrs. Williston.[2]

When the manual appeared in 1908, it was widely praised by entomologists. John B. Smith wrote from New Jersey:

"You have gone back and indicated where we must start in with the conception of insect development, and also the method of development within the limits of an order. . . . You have done a good deal more than simply write a book. You have brought an order, of which nothing was known when I wrote you for the first synoptic tables for the Brooklyn Bulletin, into one that is better known than any other with the possible exception of the Coleoptera. . . .

"It is really worth living and working at a thing for twenty five years if you finally land as complete a product as you have succeeded in doing."[3]

After this major accomplishment, Williston practically turned his back on flies. He had sold a major part of his own valuable collection to the University of Illinois during the early years at Chicago. Of the many specimens he had named, Aldrich said:

"The types of Williston's new species are much scattered. His Syrphidae were acquired by the National Museum; the rest of his earlier collections by the University of Kansas; his Biologia

[2] *North American Diptera.* Curran emphasized his debt to Williston in the complete classification and dedicated the volume to him.

[3] Letter to Williston, October 19, 1908.

[Central America] material and that from St. Vincent went to London, and I understand were finally deposited in the British Museum; the American Museum of Natural History obtained his later collections, including some duplicates of type series from St. Vincent and perhaps Mexico. Williston did not believe in designating a single type specimen, hence in some cases his types of the same species are in two museums. He had no collection of Diptera in his last years, although he still retained his fine library in the order."[4]

After his death, for some years, a number of requests came to the family asking to buy the entomological library, but it was kept intact for many years and finally given to the American Museum of Natural History.

Only the rare biologist can become an expert on two animal groups as diverse as primitive vertebrates and modern flies. But Williston found in them a common denominator—evolution. In this passage, was the paleontologist or the entomologist speaking?

"One must learn the values of characters in classification before he can be successful in instructing others, or in making his discoveries known. And this knowledge can only be acquired by long and faithful study of living things and due reflection thereon. . . . There are no principles too deep, no speculations too lofty to find application in such creatures as flies. . . ."

The words are from the introduction to the *Manual of North American Diptera*. It was the universal naturalist speaking.

Society of the Sigma Xi

The organization to which Williston devoted the most time was the honorary science society, Sigma Xi. To a man of his temperament, it is possible that the appeal of the Sigma Xi was that it began as a revolt. Although he joined it himself later, he was familiar with its founding:

"Some students of Cornell University, feeling the injustice of the

<hr/>

[4] "Samuel Wendell Williston," *Entomological News*, Vol. XXIX (November, 1918), 325.

old-fashioned kind of education that gave all its honors, all its encouragement to the students of the liberal arts, planned an honor society in the sciences. They thought, as most of us now think, that not all of good was confined to Latin and Greek, that there was also merit in the natural sciences, that the student of geology or of engineering was as deserving of honors and of encouragement as the student of the classics. As they walked home from the commencement where the honors of Phi Beta Kappa had been liberally bestowed, they conceived a society that would recognize in an equal way the merits of the bachelor of science. And the Sigma Xi was born."[5]

Williston became a member in 1893 of the University of Kansas chapter, which had been founded only three years after the organization's birth in 1886. Twice, for two-year terms, he was the Kansas chapter representative, and he annually entertained the local members at his home in Lawrence. In 1899 he became vice-president of the national society and presided at a meeting in Denver, Colorado, in the summer of 1901, when the founder and first president of the society, Henry Shaler Williams, was ill.

At this meeting Williston became president and continued through 1904, spanning his transfer to Chicago. Henry B. Ward, a possibly biased officer of the society commented that "No one came in contact with Doctor Williston without hearing of Sigma Xi; he was so full of the subject that it came out on every occasion."[6]

Williston's contributions to the society were several. He especially urged the founding of new chapters at various universities, in a zeal to encourage scientific research and to bring together the workers in the many branches of science for mutual benefit. Beginning at home, he helped with the establishment of the University of Chicago chapter within his first year there and was invited to preside at its first meeting.

As society president Williston's major concern was with the

[5] S. W. Williston, "The Future of the Sigma Xi," *Science*, Vol. XLVI, No. 1181 (1917), 147.

[6] "Samuel Wendell Williston," *Sigma Xi Quarterly*, Vol. VII, No. 1 (March, 1919), 29.

quality of membership. The part of his presidential address of 1902 that dealt with the future of the society was considered of sufficient importance that it was voted to become an appendix of the constitution. In his address of 1904 he faced the problem of the eligibility of undergraduate students for membership:

"Perhaps the most imminent danger which confronts the Society is a too great liberality in dispensing its honors. While, as I have elsewhere urged, the Society should not and must not exist for the purpose of distributing honors, yet it must be very careful to whom its honors are given, that it may retain its high ideals and high standards."[7]

During 1904 he tried to combine the societies of Sigma Xi and Tau Beta Pi (honorary engineering society), apparently in an effort to bring together pure research and applied research scientists.[8]

Williston stepped down from the presidency in 1904 because he felt that "no one man can see all sides or appreciate all that is best for the Society."[9] But he continued to help it along the lines he had started, and eventually a membership eligibility was established. This period was summarized by a later president, Julius Stieglitz:

"The Society faced the continuing vital need of contact with the young undergraduate student at as early a time in his development as the aims of the Society made possible and at the same time it was confronted with the fact that unless it put greater emphasis on achievement versus promise in this time of thriving graduate schools and research institutions, it would be threatened by a loss of caste and prestige among those who realize what achievement means in science. The solution to the attainment of these two vital objects of the Society was seen in the revision of the Constitution which permits chapters to limit full membership to graduate students and faculty members who have already carried out research work and to grant associate membership to undergraduate

7 *Ibid.*, 31.
8 Letter to Williston from W. G. Macgruder, Ohio State University, April 20, 1904.
9 Ward, *loc. cit.*

students of special promise and attainments which make for research. Dr. Williston was a staunch advocate of this change in the constitution and those familiar with the evolution of this instrument will recognize in the forceful passages emphasizing research *achievement* his influence, indeed his actual wording."[10]

In addition to aiding in the revision of the constitution Williston for years advocated a society journal. He finally accomplished this goal, as others hesitated over the work involved, by liberally offering to be managing editor himself. He wrote to the society secretary, H. B. Ward, a week later:

"In fact I got a little anxious, after I had, rather impulsively, made the proposition at Cleveland [to be managing editor], since I have a book on my hands that I have promised the publisher by next June [*Water Reptiles of the Past and Present*], and I have nearly all the illustrations to get ready. I have seen the procrastinating spirit of conventions, and especially our conventions for so long, that I thought if something definite was not proposed the whole thing would go over indefinitely. And, I believe, to keep up the higher rank of the Society, which will undoubtedly now be attempted, something of the sort will be absolutely necessary. ALL THAT I AM INTERESTED IN IS TO SEE THE THING STARTED."[11]

Thus began *Sigma Xi Quarterly*, now *American Scientist*, a noteworthy publication representing the best of science.

In the last year of his life Williston was still planning for the Sigma Xi. On December 3, 1917, he wrote to secretary Ward:

"I shall certainly be at Pittsburgh if I am able to consume my daily rations, and my appetite is good now!

"I only fear that if I get to talking at the Sigma Xi I may speak rather vigorously. It seems to me that there is a great future before the Society if we will only recognize it, and I get impatient with those who would stifle it and make it a toy society."[12]

[10] "Samuel Wendell Williston," *Sigma Xi Quarterly*, Vol. VII, No. 1 (March, 1919), 23–24.
[11] Letter of January 8, 1913, quoted in H. B. Ward, "Samuel Wendell Williston," *Sigma Xi Quarterly*, Vol. VII, No. 1 (March, 1919), 36.
[12] Quoted in *ibid.*, 37.

"He *did* reach Pittsburgh [said Ward] and took part in the convention for he spoke at the dinner pointing out forcefully the tremendous increased possibilities that were offered to Sigma Xi by the European war and by the inevitable destruction of productive research in European universities. He urged as the paramount need of the Society fuller knowledge of work done in its various units with much closer cooperation between chapters.

"It is not too much to say that no man has done more to initiate movements of significance to the Society [than] Professor Williston and no man has been more active for a longer period of years. It is fortunate indeed that in the period when Sigma Xi grew from a little organization to a powerful educational factor embracing in its activities the length and breadth of the nation he should have preserved constant and active interest in its work and have been willing to contribute, often at a sacrifice, to directing its policy. Historically the Society cannot look upon him as one of its founders, but as the years pass by it will recognize more and more clearly in him one of its greatest organizers and builders."

Williston's attitude on the value of the Sigma Xi was well expressed to the Yale initiates on April 2, 1917, when he said in part:

"We have been told that the mere accumulation of simple scientific facts never makes a leader in science, that, for instance, the collection of birds and bugs and brachiopods and their discrimination into species and subspecies is an inferior kind of research in natural history. But, every scientific man of repute in the past or present has begun in just that way, by the discovery and discrimination of scientific facts, however simple they may appear to others. Lamarck was a mere collector and namer of mollusks; Charles Darwin wasted years of his brilliant life in classifying cirriped crustaceans—I wonder how much those cirripeds had to do with natural selection, and I wonder how many of us would know a cirriped if we should meet one? Agassiz gave years of his life to the collection and study of poissons fossiles, and it requires no more acumen to classify fossil fishes than living bugs, for I have tried both. The collection and discrimination of mosquitoes was once a puerile pursuit. But, had there been no collectors and classifiers of mosquitoes, yellow fever would still be ravaging our seaports, and perhaps the Panama Canal would not now be a reality, and the safety of our nation endangered. Can any one see any possible relation between a mere entomological collector and the destruction of great cities by war? Had not Loewenhoek, in mere curiosity, found those organisms we call bacteria, and others wasted their time in studying and classifying them, there would have been no Pasteur, and antitoxins unknown. Is there no relation between such trivial pursuits, as some of our friends would call them, and typhoid fever?

"I say, and say with deep conviction, that the ability displayed in the observation and discrimination of what often appear to us to be trivial things may be as great as that required for the formulation of far-reaching laws in science. Even the tyro can draw conclusions, that is, recognize laws, when facts are numerous enough, and the best of us can do nothing without facts. And the discovery of natural laws is sure to come when facts are numerous enough. It is the trained student who anticipates them.

" . . . It is not *what* he does but *how* he does it that makes the leader in science as in everything else, for there is nothing small in science. . . .

"Research ability I would define as the ability to observe, to discriminate, and to judge, coupled with an intelligence that is always asking the reason why. Given this ability to observe and to understand, and its possessor has the foundation for success, whether in science, in arts or in the everyday affairs of life. Every day life is but a continual round of original research for every successful physician, lawyer, statesman or business man. And this is the highest aim of our society, to encourage the training of such students. . . .

"Has the Sigma Xi done all that it should in the past to encourage the applied sciences? Shall we give greater encouragement to the student who counts the bristles in a mosquito's proboscis or the plasmodia in its stomach than to him who applies that knowledge to the prevention of yellow fever? Does it require less ability, less research to observe, to discriminate, to judge in the construc-

242

tion of an airplane or a talking machine than to trace the fibers of a cerebral ganglion, or reconstruct the backbone of a dinosaur? Have we done what we should? Or shall we frankly restrict ourselves to the encouragement of research in pure science, and leave its application for others to further, to encourage? I believe that the decision is now before us, and upon our answer depends much of the future of our society. Trained as a young man in two professions of applied science, and the most of my life given to research in science so pure that its application to things practical seems remote in the extreme, perhaps my sympathies with both are more pronounced than usual. I can see no difference in the quality of research that I gave to locating a railroad line, the treatment of a patient with measles, or the reconstruction of a paleozoic reptile. It would be a misfortune for us, I earnestly believe, to restrict ourselves to the encouragement of research in pure science.

"A great future, I am sure, for science in America is its application, and the greater efficiency we reach in making use of the many discoveries of pure science for the amelioration and improvement of our conditions as a nation, the higher will be the honors, the greater encouragement we shall receive in the discovery of new facts and of new laws; the more honorable, the more appreciated will be the profession of the research student in pure science. . . ."[13]

Largely because of Williston, membership in the Society of the Sigma Xi is recognized as among one's highest honors.

[13] "The Future of the Sigma Xi," *Science*, Vol. XLVI, No. 1181 (1917), 149–51.

CHAPTER 16

The Last Years

For his paleontological work Williston's move to Chicago had been well worth while. For other reasons it had not. The sudden drop in salary after the first year was a disheartening blow and enforced an unwelcome separation of the family. Annie and the children went to her parents in New Haven for a year, and Williston stayed at the faculty club.

Professionally, the paleontologist was widely known, and during his Chicago days welcome honors came in. Williston had long yearned to go to Europe, to visit museums and to meet his colleagues there. His first opportunity was to visit England only; in 1907 the London Geological Society sent special invitations to its thirteen foreign members (Williston had been elected in 1902) to attend its centennial observation.

Williston thoroughly enjoyed the sea voyage to England and his tours with the group to Weymouth, Oxford, Cambridge ("so many things that I could not tell them in an hour"[1]), and Stratford-on-Avon. He spent time at the British Museum and he explored London thoroughly: "The city reminds me of what a well built American city was twenty five years ago."[2]

The trip was but a taste of what he truly wanted, and that opportunity came in March of 1913, when he was a delegate to the Ninth International Congress of Zoology at Monaco. From Naples he toured Pompeii, the National Museum, the Aquarium and the zoological garden. On he went to Rome for a few days of sightseeing and then four days of meetings at Monaco. But that was only a beginning, for Williston traveled next to Zurich and on to Stuttgart where Eberhard Fraas entertained him. He visited a number of

[1] Postcard from Williston to his daughter Hyla, October 5, 1907.
[2] Letter to Annie, September 22, 1907.

244

museums in Germany and conferred with Friedrich von Huene and Ferdinand Broili. He delighted in finding low-priced hotels and meals, and he guarded his funds zealously to make sure that he had enough to buy souvenirs for his family. In Ulm, where he paused en route to view the highest church in Europe, he "stopped in at one of the peasants' eating places and got a stein of beer, a biscuit and some Swiss cheese for which I paid all of 33 pfennigs (8 cents!)."[3]

In Germany his facility in the language was greatly admired. Williston had picked up a bit of the language in childhood and had probably learned it thoroughly while working in Marsh's laboratory from the janitor and possibly from George Baur, and he was always proud of his command of it. As he wrote Annie from München:

"Two or three times lately I have been asked how long I have lived in America! They generally take me for a German! When I tell them I have lived three hundred years in America they can't understand why it is that I have such a good German accent."[4]

Germany was a delight to him, because of significant specimens in the museums and the cordiality of the paleontologists. Just before leaving there he wrote Ruth: "I have seen *so much* in the last six weeks, that it seems like *six months*. Have read almost nothing. And it has been so interesting and pleasant that it seems almost like a dream."[5]

From Germany Williston stopped briefly at Brussels, Antwerp, and Paris before crossing the channel to England. He was surprised to find the Natural History Museum in London closed to the public:

"And what do you suppose for—the Suffragettes! They have been raising what Mary Lease advised the Kansas farmers to do a few years ago! [Raise less corn and more hell.] The other day they tried to dynamite a mansion, and even made plans to wreck St. Paul—and the Museum—and so they closed up there today. They seem to be in very deadly earnest, and things are getting

[3] Letter to Annie, April 20, 1913.
[4] *Ibid.*
[5] Letter from Frankfurt, April 29, 1913.

serious. I cant [*sic*] say that I blame them very much. There are one and a half millions more women than men in England, and they are demanding the same right to live as the men, and I don't see why they shouldn't have it."[6] So the man who had once argued the mental superiority of man over woman to the Old and New Club in Lawrence was now ready to change his tune—at least to his outspoken daughter Dorothy.

On this second visit to London, he again toured the sights of the city extensively—until he felt himself as familiar with it as with Chicago—and he studied specimens at the Museum. By mid-May he was finally tiring of so much sightseeing but he still considered the trip "the greatest vacation of my whole life."[7]

To provide a fitting end to his successful trip, Williston attended the 1913 Yale commencement and there received his third degree from that university—an honorary doctor of science. Yale thus recognized each of Williston's three professions: medicine, with the M.D. in 1880; entomology, with the Ph.D. in 1885; and paleontology, with the Sc.D. in 1913. The tribute with the Sc.D. read: "For services in carrying on further than ever before the knowledge of the history of the life on earth in geological times, the home of Dana and Marsh is proud to confer on you this degree." Marsh would probably have agreed by that time had he been still living.

Sad days were ahead for the family, but, in spite of his medical background, Williston would not face the truth for some time. His second daughter, Hyla (then not quite twenty-five), was critically ill in the spring of 1914, but he considered it the result of an abscess only, though he worried considerably about her frailty. As she slowly recovered, he wrote to Hathaway: "Both the doctors have tried to make me believe that she had something else the matter with her besides the abscess, that her fever was due to tuberculosis, and that her chances of getting better were very small. But they were surely mistaken."[8]

[6] Letter to Dorothy, May 10, 1913.
[7] Letter to Hathaway, May 13, 1913.
[8] Letter of May 2, 1914.

The summer of 1914 was a pleasant one in the East for the family, where all except Ruth were able to spend time with Hathaway in New Haven and at Haddam. Williston had bought his first automobile, a Maxwell, and it was used liberally for all errands anyone could think of, "to the tune of five thousand miles over the rocks and sands of Haddam town and the outlying districts."[9]

But the doctors had not been mistaken, and Williston finally believed them. So the family began another long, sad separation that fall when Annie took Hyla to Socorro, New Mexico in the desperate hope that the dry mountain air would cure her tuberculosis. Sam entered New Mexico School of Mines there, and Eugenie joined them in April of 1915. Annie began her long vigil hopefully, counting each small improvement in Hyla's appetite and appearance, but noting too the persistence of the cough.

One welcome honor arrived amidst the family worry, announced by Charles Schuchert on April 21, 1915:

"I just sent you a telegram of congratulations upon your election to the National Academy and I feel so good over it that I must write you more about it. You and Millikin [Robert A. Millikan] got the highest Preferential votes and were tied and as the former begins his name with an earlier letter in the alphabet was voted in first. It was a foregone conclusion that you would go in even if no one spoke in your favor but two of us set you right before the Academy. When the final vote was announced we were all glad to see you go in so easily and with such a high vote. We put you in as a paleontologist but as all the zoologists know you of course they added their votes to the geologists and paleontologists. Your old Yale friends are looking after your welfare.

"Let this good news cheer you on to more good work and to an uplift in your family and the health of your children."

Annie took time from her New Mexico vigil for a typically wifely comment: "I am truly glad that at last you are to be elected a member of the National Academy, for you have certainly worked hard & deserve it. I wish it had come years ago but better late than never."

[9] Guest book of the Haddam property, entry by Dorothy, October 26, 1914.

All the family spent part of the summer of 1915 in Socorro, and it proved to be their last together. Williston took Sam with him to visit the Baldwin beds at Abiquiu for fossils, and all of them entertained Hyla as much as the doctor would allow. Williston reverted to his earlier cooking days and helped make grape juice and pickled and spiced apples. President Judson offered to extend his vacation if desired, but in September, though dreading the long lonesome winter, the professor returned to his classes. Ruth was teaching school in nearby Oak Park, Illinois, and Dorothy was a reporter on a Chicago newspaper.

The hopes of all rose as Hyla seemed to improve, but the hopes were false. She died peacefully in her sleep March 10, 1916. Williston was in Socorro then, knowing that the end was near. The loss hit both parents very hard, even though they had been preparing for it. Hyla had long been her father's favorite, perhaps because of another problem: she had been born with a thigh bone out of its socket, and by the age of two years she had one leg distinctly shorter and that foot smaller than the other. Annie always had to buy her two pairs of shoes to match sizes. Hyla never participated fully in the children's games of running and climbing. Surprisingly, she never became an avid reader either; in fact, she disliked books and only completed the first year of high school. Home projects she did enjoy, cooking, sewing, embroidery, crocheting, and wood-burning as a hobby. Such a deformity as hers can now be readily corrected if recognized promptly, but in her day it created a complex of problems for all the family.

While staying in Socorro through the summer of 1916, Williston took advantage of the thoughtful gift from his entomological friend, J. M. Aldrich, of pins and corks to renew his interest in flies, and he collected daily in the nearby mountain country. From that came his final paper on the Diptera (1917). To distract himself further from his sorrow he wrote "Recollections," which opened in this mood:

"It happens now, in the spring of 1916, in Socorro, New Mexico, where my daughter Hyla, whom I loved so dearly, has recently died, that I have nothing to occupy my time, nothing to keep my thoughts from the past, with their memories, pleasant and sad.

"I begin to feel that there are not many more years of work before me, and to regret that I have not accomplished more. When I compare my actual accomplishments with my youthful ambitions I feel that I have not done all that I might, for the world and for my children. But, the way has often been hard, and I am thankful to be spared so long and to have done what I have.

"And so, what I shall write in these pages will be chiefly for them. Perhaps they will think more kindly of me when I am gone for what I have tried to do."

A letter he received from his vertebrate paleontology students just before Hyla's death should have made him feel that his time had been well spent:

"We, the members of your class in Vertebrate Paleontology, take this opportunity of expressing our very sincere appreciation of your guidance in our work of the past year. That we realize our good fortune in having been thus associated with the man who is recognized by all as foremost, not only in his own field but eminent among all scientists, is not questioned. We are confident also, that in later years it will be an increasing source of pleasure to recall the hours spent under your leadership. We wish you to know how grateful we have been for the helpful suggestions you have given from your long experience and for the sincere interest in our welfare which has been so constantly evident."

Other honors came to Williston in the last years of his life: fellowship in the American Academy of Arts and Sciences in Boston, on May 12, 1915; honorary fellowship (one of seven only) in the Entomological Society of America in 1916; one that probably pleased him greatly from his first alma mater—membership in the Kansas State Agricultural College chapter of Phi Kappa Phi fraternity, on September 23, 1916; and membership in the American Philosophical Society on April 20, 1918.

Did such honors please Williston? There is no doubt that they did. As he told the group of initiates of the Yale chapter of the Sigma Xi:

"It is human nature to seek honors. Scientific men, like all others, from the humblest to the greatest, welcome them, whether it be membership in the Sigma Xi or in the National Academy of Sciences. When honors come as rewards for meritorious work accomplished they cheer and encourage; and they stimulate ourselves and others to higher efforts. We would not, if we could, abolish honors for scholarship from our society, we would not restrict them to accomplished research."[10]

Soon clouds were gathering again for the family, for Williston was not well. The first inkling was even before Hyla's death when he had a physical examination and was advised to have an operation for gallstones, which he apparently did not do. By January of 1918 he was in considerable pain, but he continued his classes, to the great admiration of his students. Once when he collapsed in class, his alarmed students brought five doctors to the scene within ten minutes. Williston believed that his illness was mostly liver trouble. By midsummer he decided to enter the hospital, and there surgery revealed a hopeless spread of cancer. Samuel Wendell Williston died August 30, 1918, in the Presbyterian Hospital in Chicago. His fourth daughter Eugenie, a nursing student, attended his final hours with her mother and later that same day received her university degree, under flags at half mast for her father. Williston was buried in Manhattan, Kansas.

The special tragedy of Williston's death was that he had long dreaded cancer, probably because his father had died of cancer of the lip, and he had tended his father in Manhattan, Kansas, in the final years, going back and forth often from Lawrence.

Annie Williston lived for a year in Chicago and then moved to the family home in New Haven for many years; she outlived her husband by 42 years. Some of Williston's interests passed to his children. Ruth, who never married, became a teacher of botany for many years at Oak Park High School in Illinois (she died in 1961). Dorothy was, and is, an avid gardener; she married George G. Shor, who worked for Hearst newspapers for many years. Eugenie, also an enthusiastic gardener, married a medical doctor,

[10] "The Future of the Sigma Xi," *Science*, Vol. XLVI, No. 1181 (1917), 150.

Walter C. Earle; he helped eradicate malaria in Puerto Rico for the Public Health Service. Samuel became a mining engineer and geologist. He acquired his father's paleontological library, which he has recently given to the University of Kansas. Other items— medical, biographical, and personal—have also been given to that university by members of the family.

The death of Williston left the University of Chicago without a professor of paleontology. Paul Miller continued to collect and prepare specimens as curator of vertebrate fossils. Charles H. Behre took the introductory classes in paleontology after the war. In 1923, Alfred S. Romer became associate professor and later professor of paleontology until 1934. Intensive work on Permian amphibians and reptiles continued to be the major direction of study under both Romer and later E. C. Olson.

For the writing of memorials to Williston in various scientific journals Annie had sent to several of his colleagues the manuscript of "Recollections," which intrigued each person who saw it. Several suggested that it should be published, and an attempt was made to publish a memorial volume to Williston that would incorporate the manuscript and an analysis of his professional work, a bibliography of his works, and contributed papers in paleontology, geology and entomology by close associates and students. William K. Gregory became the secretary of the Williston Memorial Committee, and a number of distinguished colleagues offered to contribute papers and costs toward publishing the volume. E. S. Riggs, a former student, was to write a summary of Williston's life.

By the spring of 1920 problems of the cost of publishing the volume had arisen. The committee tried to secure enough advance subscriptions to guarantee five hundred copies to the publisher. But this proved impossible and the memorial volume was never published.

Another valuable volume of Williston's was published, however: the manuscript he was writing at the time of his death, *Osteology of the Reptiles*. Gregory, who completed the volume as a lengthy labor of love, summarized the history of the work in his foreword to it:

"In accordance with Williston's wishes the writer undertook to put his last work in shape for the publisher and to see it through the press. For the long delay since 1918 there have been too many causes to be profitably set forth in detail. The University of Chicago Press, which had published Williston's earlier books, repeatedly found itself unable to accept this one notwithstanding its good will, and private publishers proposed conditions that were not acceptable, either to the Williston Memorial Committee, or to Professor Williston's family. After much unsuccessful correspondence in various directions, the sad plight of Williston's still unpublished work came to the notice of Professor Thomas Barbour of Harvard University, and through his good offices the Harvard University Press now has the honor of publishing the 'Osteology of the Reptiles.' "

Alfred S. Romer undertook a complete revision of *Osteology of the Reptiles*, which was published in 1956, and he dedicated it to both Williston and Gregory.

This biography may be considered a contribution to the intent of the Williston Memorial Committee, though undoubtedly quite different from what they had visualized. I welcome the opportunity to have now become acquainted myself with S. W. Williston, and to present at last the manuscript "Recollections" and what further biographical material I have been able to locate fifty years later.

CHAPTER 17

Retrospect

THE life of a remarkable scientist has been presented in the preceding pages, from the child who wondered about fossil clam shells on the top of Blue Mont near Manhattan, Kansas, and read Shakespeare; to the youth whose heart yearned to be back at college while he surveyed for the railroad; to the young man who wooed his wife with self-torment and who sought relief from the despotism of O. C. Marsh in a new field of science; to the man who gloried in the freedom of research and teaching until the pressure of trying to be expert in too many fields in one lifetime forced him to withdraw to a new location where he could concentrate on one subject.

Social scientists are now trying to define the characteristics of a scientist in childhood; educators are pushing science courses at steadily earlier ages; parents are drumming the importance of grades into their children. Williston's life had none of these: his father disapproved of schooling (though his mother urged it), his early years were spent mainly on Latin and Greek (good for memory), and his keen interest in science developed slowly from a late adolescence. Times *have* changed and science courses are valuable at an early age, as Williston himself advocated in the 1890's. But science courses do not create scientists.

Williston's characteristics in later life have been defined by those who knew him personally:

"Professor Williston was a born naturalist, one of those who can not help studying nature. His interests were broad, not being confined to a single small department of research. He attained world-wide fame in two fields as widely apart as vertebrate paleontology and entomology, but his interests were not confined to these subjects alone. He was interested in all of nature, in whatever phase it presented itself to him.

"Genuine research, as conducted by such a man as Professor Williston, involves the persistence into manhood of that quality of childhood which always asks the question, 'Why?' Professor Williston was never satisfied with the mere recording of his observations upon the fossils or insects which he studied. He continually set his mind to answer the question, 'Why?' concerning the features which he observed. Every new suture which he discovered in the skulls of the ancient reptiles and amphibians which he knew so well and every modification in their skeletons had to be reasonably interpreted in terms of the evolution of the creatures or in their life-habits before he was satisfied with his work."[1]

That was the scientist. Here, from one of his first students, E. C. Case, who went on to great eminence himself, is the man:

"In speaking to you of Dr. Williston as a teacher I find myself hesitating between two strong inclinations. On the one hand I would pay tribute to the depth of learning, the skill in presentation, and the enthusiasm and sympathy which brought every student under his spell and made his very technical subject a most fascinating study to all who attended his classes. In all verity he stirred the dead bones; he clothed the skeletons in flesh, and the long-stilled forms passed in procession through their proper environment before our eyes, revealing the evolution of each group as in a panorama; and all this without sacrificing one necessary detail or one item of the truth to make the story more attractive.

"On the other hand I am tempted to relate a succession of anecdotes, many of them tinged with humor, that would reveal to you the real man as he was disclosed to us, his students, in the classroom and in the trying intimacies of remote camps. For the Doctor, as we liked to call him, was a very human person; with all his store of knowledge, his high position in the scientific world, and the honors which came to him, he remained a simple-mannered, kindly, big-hearted man, always ready to respond to every request for

[1] Stuart Weller, "Samuel Wendell Williston," University of Chicago *University Record* (January, 1919), 102–103.

help, be it the simple question of a tyro or the difficult problem of a colleague. In his office he would turn from his professional work or from the study of some intricate problem to solve the little personal troubles of a student, and in the field, in the 'shadow of a great rock in a thirsty land,' after a lunch of coarse camp food washed down with drink from a canteen filled with muddy water, he would slip into an informal lecture, suggested by some chance happening of the day or some new-found specimen, which would have graced in its content the hall of any learned assemblage.

"I believe that the 'Mark Hopkins and a log' idea of a university was never more nearly realized than in Dr. Williston. His knowledge of men and things was so wide and his acquaintance with many branches of science so intimate that in the heat of a barren fossil field or under the stars at night by the side of a camp fire, some bird, or flower, or fossils, some insect—'one of mine, I named it in 187-odd,' he would say—would start a talk that held his little band of student assistants enthralled until hunger, thirst, and sleep were forgotten.

"Dr. Williston was very human. He made mistakes, not many relative to the amount of work he did, but a few, and his students sometimes rejoiced a little that they had caught their chief in a rare slip, but there was such quick recognition of error, with acknowledgment and credit given in generous measure where it was due, that it always brought us closer together. There were rare outbursts of good, honest wrath when things or men went wrong. I think some of us may tingle a little even yet, though the happening may have been years ago, but once the trouble was located, be it of weather or roads, or plain stupidity in students, vigorous action or kindly advice set all to rights or taught the philosophy which bears cheerfully what may not be mended. . . .

"One thing he strove to teach his students—that the reward of the work was the result accomplished, that the discovery of truth was greater than any recognition which might come to the successful searcher. Few men have named more new forms of life than he, and yet he cared little for any credit that came to him as the author of a new name. He repeatedly declared to me, 'I don't care whether they are named or numbered, just so we know what we are talking about.' Few men have attained a greater mastery of their subject or reached a more dominant position in their chosen branch of science, and yet he was singularly free from the touch of dogmatism which frequently, and perhaps excusably, comes in the later years of a master's life. Only a few months before he died he wrote to me in half-comic despair concerning some intricate problem of the morphology of the Permo-Carboniferous vertebrates, 'The more we study these things, the more we don't know anything about them.' ...

"I can voice no better tribute from his students than this: We admired and respected the scientist, we revered the teacher, but we loved the man."[2]

In 1913, Williston wrote an introspective letter to his former student and friend, C. E. McClung: "It is now thirty-seven years since I published my first scientific attempt: I know that I have not done as much as I hoped to do in life, when I was young and ambitious, and I sometimes wonder whether what I have done amounts to much. But it is too late now for regrets and I know that I have had a good time—many happy hours with bugs and bones."[3]

Williston concluded in "Recollections" in 1916:

"And here these notes may with propriety end. My life as I look back on it has had many discouragements and many pleasures. I have made many mistakes as I now can see, and I have not accomplished what I might have done. If I may extenuate my errors, I will urge that for a country boy, with but little help and wholly without influence, the road to success was very hard. Perhaps I was too wilful and headstrong to heed advice had I had advice, I don't know. Perhaps for me experience was the best teacher, and an easy path in youth might have been the cause of failure. But it *was* hard, and I have more than once been very discouraged. I have drifted along somehow, with one underlying ambition to *learn*.

[2] "Dr. Williston as a Teacher," University of Chicago *University Record* (January, 1919), 97–101.

[3] McClung, "Samuel Wendell Williston," *Sigma Xi Quarterly*, Vol. VII, No. 1 (March, 1919), 17.

"My plans and ambitions may seem fickle, first as an engineer, next as a physician, as a chemist, entomologist, paleontologist. I have tried various things where were they steadily pursued would have been better. In reality there was only one ambition to do research work in Science. And I have realized that ambition in a measure. I have published about 300 books and papers totaling about 4000 pages. But the chief satisfaction that I find now in looking back over my life is that I have been the means, to some extent at least, of assisting not a few young men to success, [in] medicine and in science."

Williston's Publications

BOOKS AND MONOGRAPHS

Synopsis of the North American Syrphidae. Washington, Bulletin of the United States National Museum, No. 31, 1886, 335 pp.

Synopsis of the Families and Genera of North American Diptera, with Bibliography and New Species, 1878–88. New Haven, J. T. Hathaway, 1888, 84 pp.

"Diptera III," in *Biologia Centrali-Americana,* ed. F. D. Godman and O. Salvin, London, Dulau and Co., 1899, 1–89.

Manual of the Families and Genera of North American Diptera. 2d ed. New Haven, J. T. Hathaway, 1896, 167 pp.

Manual of North American Diptera. 3d ed. New Haven, J. T. Hathaway, 1908, 405 pp.

American Permian Vertebrates. Chicago, University of Chicago Press, 1911, 145 pp.

Permocarboniferous Vertebrates from New Mexico. (With E. C. Case and M. G. Mehl.) Washington, Carnegie Institution of Washington, Publication 181, 1913, 81 pp.

Water Reptiles of the Past and Present. Chicago, University of Chicago Press, 1914, 251 pp.

The Osteology of the Reptiles (ed. William King Gregory). Cambridge, Harvard University Press, 1925, 300 pp.

ARTICLES

"The American Antelope," *American Naturalist,* Vol. XI (October, 1877), 599–603.

"On the Habits of *Amblychila cylindriformis,*" *Canadian Entomologist,* Vol. IX (September, 1877), 163–65.

"The Prairie Dog, Owl, and Rattlesnake," *American Naturalist,* Vol. XII (April, 1878), 203–208.

"Mode of Advent of *Anthrenus scrophulariae,*" *Psyche,* Vol. II (1878), 126.

258

"Note on the Habits of Some of the Rarer Cicindelidae," *Transactions of the Kansas Academy of Science*, Vol. VI (1878), 32–33.

"On the Adult Male Plumage of Wilson's Phalarope (*Steganopus Wilsoni* Sab.)," *Transactions of the Kansas Academy of Science*, Vol. VI (1878), 39.

"*Spermophilus richardsoni*," *Transactions of the Kansas Academy of Science*, Vol. VI (1878), 39–40.

"American Jurassic Dinosaurs," *Transactions of the Kansas Academy of Science*, Vol. VI (1878), 42–46.

"An Anomalous Bombylid," *Canadian Entomologist*, Vol. XI (November, 1879), 215–16.

"A List of Birds Taken in Southern Wyoming," *Forest and Stream* (April 7, May 23, May 30, 1879).

"Indian Figures in Western Kansas," *Kansas City Review of Science*, Vol. III (1879), 16.

"Comments on 'Are Birds Derived from Dinosaurs?' " [by B. F. Mudge], *Kansas City Review of Science*, Vol. III (1879), 457–60.

"Some Interesting New Diptera," *Transactions of the Connecticut Academy of Arts and Sciences*, Vol. IV, Part 2 (1880), 243–46.

"*Eristalis tenax*," *Canadian Entomologist*, Vol. XIII (1881), 176.

"New or Little Known Genera of North American Syrphidae," *Canadian Entomologist*, Vol. XIV (April, 1882), 77–80.

"*Drosophila ampelophila, Loew*," *Canadian Entomologist*, Vol. XIV (April, 1882), 138.

"Contribution to a Monograph of the North American Syrphidae," *Proceedings of the American Philosophical Society*, Vol. XX, No. 112 (May, 1882), 299–332.

"The North American Species of *Conops*," *Transactions of the Connecticut Academy of Arts and Sciences*, Vol. IV (March, 1882), 325–42.

"Ueber *Mallota cimbiciformis* Fall," *Berliner Entomologische Zeitschrift*, Vol. XXVII, No. 1 (1883), 171–72.

"The North American Species of Nemestrinidae," *Canadian Entomologist*, Vol. XV (1883), 69–72.

"The Screw-worm Fly, *Compsomyia macellaria*," *Psyche*, Vol. IV (November–December, 1883), 112–14.

"On the North American Asilidae (Dasypogoninae, Laphrinae): With a New Genus of Syrphidae," *Transactions of the American Entomological Society*, Vol. XI (December, 1883), 1–35.

"Dipterous Larvae from the Western Alkaline Lakes and their Use as

Human Food," *Transactions of the Connecticut Academy of Arts and Sciences*, Vol. VI (July, 1883), 87–90.

"North American Conopidae: *Stylogaster, Dalmannia, Oncomyia,*" *Transactions of the Connecticut Academy of Arts and Sciences*, Vol. VI (July, 1883), 91–98.

"*Scopolia sequax*, n. sp.," in *Notes on Injurious Insects*, Entomological Laboratory, Michigan Agricultural College (1884), 5–6.

"Collection and Preservation of Diptera," *Psyche*, Vol. IV (January–February, 1884), 130–32.

"Protective Secretions of Species of *Eleodes*," *Psyche*, Vol. IV (1884), 168–69.

"Diptera," in *Standard (Riverside) Natural History*, Vol. V (1884), 403–33.

"Eine Merkwuerdige neue Syrphiden-Gattung," *Wiener Entomologische Zeitung*, Vol. III (1884), 185–86.

"Note on the Genus *Merapioidus* Big.," *Wiener Entomologische Zeitung*, Vol. III, No. 9 (November, 1884), 282.

"On the Classification of North American Diptera (First Paper). Syrphidae," *Bulletin of the Brooklyn Entomological Society*, Vol. VII (February, 1885), 129–39.

"Notes and Descriptions of North American Xylophagidae and Stratiomyidae," *Canadian Entomologist*, Vol. VII, No. 7 (July, 1885), 121–28.

"On the Classification of North American Diptera (Second Paper)," *Entomologica Americana*, Vol. I, No. 1 (April, 1885), 10–13.

"Variations in Diptera," *Entomologica Americana*, Vol. I (1885), 20.

"On the Classification of North American Diptera (Third Paper)," *Entomologica Americana*, Vol. I, No. 6 (September, 1885), 114–20.

"*Exorista infesta*, n. sp.," *Fourteenth Report of State Entomologist of Illinois*, for 1884 (1885), 65.

"Ueber einige Leptiden-Charakteren," *Stettiner Entomologische Zeitschrift*, Vol. XLVI (1885), 400–401.

"On the North American Asilidae (Part II)," *Transactions of the American Entomological Society*, Vol. XII (January, 1885), 53–76.

"North American Conopidae: *Conclusion*," *Transactions of the Connecticut Academy of Arts and Sciences*, Vol. VI (March, 1885), 377–94.

"On Two Interesting New Genera of Leptidae," *Entomologica Americana*, Vol. II, No. 6 (September, 1886), 105–108.

"Dipterological Notes and Descriptions," *Transactions of the American Entomological Society,* Vol. XIII (October, 1886), 287–307.

"Catalogue of the Described Species of South American Syrphidae," *Transactions of the American Entomological Society,* Vol. XIII (November, 1886), 308–24.

"Ueber *Ornithocheirus hilsensis* Koken," *Zoologischen Anzeiger,* Vol. IX (1886), 282.

"Oscar Harger," *American Naturalist,* Vol. XXI (1887), 1133–34.

"North American Tachinidae: *Gonia," Canadian Entomologist,* Vol. XIX (1887), 6–12.

"Catalogue of the Described Species of South American Syrphidae. Additions and Corrections," *Entomologica Americana,* Vol. III (1887), 27–28.

"An Interesting New Genus of South American Tachinidae," *Entomologica Americana,* Vol. III (1887), 151–53.

"Table of the Families of Diptera," *Transactions of the Kansas Academy of Science,* Vol. X (1887), 122–28.

"Notes and Descriptions of North American Tabanidae," *Transactions of the Kansas Academy of Science,* Vol. X (1887), 129–42.

"Report on Rivers Pollution" (with H. E. Smith and W. G. Daggett), *Annual Report of the Connecticut State Board of Health,* for 1887 (1888), 175–266.

"A New South American Genus of Conopinae," *Canadian Entomologist,* Vol. XX (1888), 10–12.

"An Australian Parasite of *Icerya purchasi," Insect Life,* Vol. I (1888), 21–22.

"*Hilarimorpha* and *Apiocera," Psyche,* Vol. V (September–October, 1888), 99–102.

"Diptera Brasiliana ab H. H. Smith Collecta. Part I, Stratiomyidae, Syrphidae," *Transactions of the American Entomological Society,* Vol. XV (October–December, 1888), 243–92.

"A New Cattle-pest," *American Naturalist,* Vol. XXIII (1889), 584–90.

"Report on Rivers Pollution" (with H. E. Smith and T. G. Lee), *Annual Report of the Connecticut State Board of Health,* for 1888 (1889), 237–90.

"The Dipterous Parasites of North American Butterflies," in *Butterflies of the Eastern United States and Canada,* by S. H. Scudder, Cambridge, 1889, 1912–24.

261

"A New Species of *Haematobia*," *Entomologica Americana*, Vol. V (1889), 180–81.

"Note on *Haematobia serrata* R. Desv.," *Entomologica Americana*, Vol. V (1889), 197.

"*Leucopis bellula*, n. sp.," *Insect Life*, Vol. I (1889), 258–59.

"Note on the Genus *Lestophonus*," *Insect Life*, Vol. I (1889), 328–31.

"The Cause of the Bad Smell is in the Reservoir," letter to Meriden (Connecticut) *Journal* (November 1, 1889).

"Notes on Asilidae," *Psyche*, Vol. V (August–December, 1889), 255–59.

"Note on the Pelvis of *Cumnoria* (*Camptosaurus*)," *American Naturalist*, Vol. XXIV (1890), 472–73.

"*Uroglena volvox* Ehr.," *Microscope*, Vol. X (1890), 81–82.

"The Sternalis Muscle," *Proceedings of the Academy of Natural Sciences of Philadelphia*, for 1889 (1890), 38–41.

"Chalk from the Niobrara Cretaceous of Kansas," *Science*, Vol. XVI (1890), 249.

"Structure of the Plesiosaurian Skull," *Science*, Vol. XVI (1890), 262, 290.

"On the Structure of the Kansas Chalk," *Transactions of the Kansas Academy of Science*, Vol. XII (1890), 100.

"A New Plesiosaur from the Niobrara Cretaceous of Kansas," *Transactions of the Kansas Academy of Science*, Vol. XII (1890), 174–78.

"The Skull and Hind Extremity of *Pteranodon*," *American Naturalist*, Vol. XXV (1891), 1124–26.

"Note on Syrphids Reared from Cactus," *Entomological News*, Vol. II (1891), 162.

"Kansas Mosasaurs," *Science*, Vol. XVIII (1891), 345.

"Catalogue of the Described Species of South American Asilidae," *Transactions of the American Entomological Society*, Vol. XVIII (May, 1891), 67–91.

"Volcanic Dust in Kansas and Indian Territory," *American Geologist*, Vol. X (December, 1892), 396.

"*Copestylum marginatum* and *Volucella fasciata*," *Entomological News*, Vol. II (1892), 162.

"Note on the Habits of *Ammophila*," *Entomological News*, Vol. III (1892), 85–97.

"A New Species of *Criorhina* and Notes on Synonymy," *Entomological News*, Vol. III (1892), 145–46.

"Kansas Pterodactyls, Part I," *Kansas University Quarterly*, Vol. I,

No. 1 (July, 1892), 1–13. (Abstract in *American Naturalist*, Vol. XXVII [1893], 37).

"Kansas Mosasaurs, Part I. *Clidastes*" (with E. C. Case), *Kansas University Quarterly*, Vol. I, No. 1 (July, 1892), 15–32.

"Diptera Brasiliana, Part II. *Conops*," *Kansas University Quarterly*, Vol. I, No. 1 (July, 1892), 43–46.

"On Biological Nomenclature," *Science*, Vol. XX (November 4, 1892), 58.

"Higher Professional Requirements," Address to Kansas Pharmaceutical Association, May 18, 1892, published in *Western Druggist* (1892).

"Report on the Examination of Certain Connecticut Water Supplies" (with H. E. Smith and T. G. Lee), for Connecticut State Board of Health (1892).

"Diptera of Death Valley, California," in "North American Fauna," *Bulletin of the Division of Ornithology and Mammalogy*, United States Department of Agriculture, No. 7 (1893), 253–59.

"Description of a Species of *Chlorops* Reared from Galls on *Muehlenbergia mexicana* by F. M. Webster," *Bulletin of the Ohio Experiment Station*, Technical Series, Vol. I (1893), 153–57.

"A List of Species of Diptera from San Domingo," *Canadian Entomologist*, Vol. XXV (1893), 170–71.

"The North American Psychodidae," *Entomological News*, Vol. IV (1893), 113–14.

"Note on *Meromacrus rondani*," *Entomological News*, Vol. IV (1893), 114.

"*Belvosia*, a Study," *Insect Life*, Vol. V (1893), 238–40.

"On the Apioceridae and their Allies," *Kansas University Quarterly*, Vol. I, No. 3 (January, 1893), 101–18.

"Diptera Brasiliana, Part III," *Kansas University Quarterly*, Vol. I, No. 3 (January, 1893), 119–22.

"New or Little-known Diptera," *Kansas University Quarterly*, Vol. II, No. 2 (October, 1893), 59–78.

"Kansas Pterodactyls, Part II," *Kansas University Quarterly*, Vol. II, No. 2 (October, 1893), 79–81.

"Kansas Mosasaurs, Part II," *Kansas University Quarterly*, Vol. II, No. 2 (October, 1893), 83–84.

"Notes on Tachinidae," *Psyche*, Vol. VI (1893), 409–10, 492.

"On the Systematic Position of the Diptera," letter to *Science*, Vol. XXII, No. 564 (November 24, 1893), 292.

"E. P. West," *Transactions of the Kansas Academy of Science,* Vol. XIII (1893), 68–69.

"*Bibio tristis,* n. sp.," *Transactions of the Kansas Academy of Science,* Vol. XIII (1893), 113.

"The Niobrara Cretaceous of Western Kansas," *Transactions of the Kansas Academy of Science,* Vol. XIII (1893), 107–11.

"An Interesting Food Habit of the Plesiosaurs," *Transactions of the Kansas Academy of Science,* Vol. XIII (1893), 121–22. (Abstract in *American Naturalist,* Vol. XXVIII [1894], 50.)

"*Calotarsa ornatipes* Towns," *Canadian Entomologist,* Vol. XXVI (1894), 116.

"Notes on the Habits of *Rhynchocephalus sackeni* Will.," *Entomological News,* Vol. V (1894), 47.

"On the Genus *Erax,*" *Entomological News,* Vol. V (1894), 136–37.

"The American Genera of Sapromyzinae," *Entomological News,* Vol. V (1894), 196–97.

"Restoration of *Aceratherium fossiger* Cope," *Kansas University Quarterly,* Vol. II, No. 4 (April, 1894), 289–90.

"On Various Vertebrate Remains from the Lowermost Cretaceous of Kansas," *Kansas University Quarterly,* Vol. III, No. 1 (July, 1894), 1–4.

"A New Turtle from the Benton Cretaceous," *Kansas University Quarterly,* Vol. III, No. 1 (July, 1894), 5–18.

"Notes on *Untiacrinus socialis* Grinnell" (with B. H. Hill), *Kansas University Quarterly,* Vol. III, No. 1 (July, 1894), 19–21.

"Restoration of *Platygonus,*" *Kansas University Quarterly,* Vol. III, No. 1 (July, 1894), 23–29.

"On the Genus *Dolichomyia* with the Description of a New Species from Colorado," *Kansas University Quarterly,* Vol. III, No. 1 (July, 1894), 41–43.

"A New Dicotyline Mammal from the Kansas Pliocene," *Science,* Vol. XXIII (1894), 164.

"An Explanation of the Rope of Maggots," *Science,* Vol. XXIII, No. 574 (1894).

"Ancient Sea-Serpents," *Youth's Companion* (September 13, 1894), 399–400.

"A New Tachinid with Remarkable Antennae," *Entomological News,* Vol. VI (1895), 29–32.

"New or Little Known Extinct Vertebrates," *Kansas University Quarter-*

ly, Vol. III, No. 3 (January, 1895), 165–76. (Abstract by M. Schlosser in *Archiv fur Anthropologie,* Vol. 25 [1895], 183).

"Exotic Tabanidae," *Kansas University Quarterly,* Vol. III (1895), 189–95.

"Semiarid Kansas," *Kansas University Quarterly,* Vol. III, No. 4 (April, 1895), 209–16.

"Dialysis and *Triptotricha,"* *Kansas University Quarterly,* Vol. III (1895), 263–66.

"New Bombyliidae," *Kansas University Quarterly,* Vol. III (1895), 267–69.

"Note on the Mandible of *Ornithostoma,"* *Kansas University Quarterly,* Vol. IV (1895), 61.

"Two Remarkable New Genera of Diptera," *Kansas University Quarterly,* Vol. IV (1895), 107–109.

"On the Rhopalomeridae," *Psyche,* Vol. VII (1895), 183–87.

"Rhopalomera xanthops, n. sp." *Psyche,* Vol. VII (1895), 213.

"A New Genus of Hippoboscidae," *Entomological News,* Vol. VII (1896), 184–85.

"Descriptions of Dipterous Parasites," in *The Gypsy Moth,* by E. K. Forbush and C. H. Fernald, Boston, Massachusetts State Board of Agriculture, 1896, 387–91.

"Bibliography of North American Diptera, 1878–1895," *Kansas University Quarterly,* Vol. IV (1896), 129–44, 199–204.

"Fissicorn Tachinidae," *Kansas University Quarterly,* Vol. IV (1896), 171–72.

"On the Skull of *Ornithostoma,"* *Kansas University Quarterly,* Vol. IV (1896), 195–97.

"On the Dermal Covering of *Hesperornis,"* *Kansas University Quarterly,* Vol. V (1896), 53–54.

"On the Diptera of St. Vincent (West Indies)," (Dolichopodidae and Phoridae by J. M. Aldrich), *Transactions of the Entomological Society of London,* Part III (September, 1896), 253–446.

"Diptera Brasiliana, Part IV," *Kansas University Quarterly,* Series A, Vol. VI (1897), 1–12.

"Restoration of *Ornithostoma (Pteranodon),"* *Kansas University Quarterly,* Series A, Vol. VI (1897), 35–51.

"Notice of Some Vertebrate Remains from the Kansas Permian," *Kansas University Quarterly,* Series A, Vol. VI (1897), 53–56. (Also in *Transactions of the Kansas Academy of Science,* Vol. XV [1897], 120–22.)

"A New Plesiosaur from the Kansas Comanche Cretaceous," *Kansas University Quarterly*, Series A, Vol. VI (1897), 57.

"*Brachysaurus*, a New Genus of Mosasaurs," *Kansas University Quarterly*, Series A, Vol. VI (1897), 95–98.

"On the Extremities of *Tylosaurus*," *Kansas University Quarterly*, Series A, Vol. VI (1897), 99–102.

"Restoration of Kansas Mosasaurs," *Kansas University Quarterly*, Series A, Vol. VI (1897), 107–10. (Also in *Scientific American Supplement*, Vol. XLIV [1897], 18162.)

"Range and Distribution of the Mosasaurs, with Remarks on Synonymy," *Kansas University Quarterly*, Series A, Vol. VI (1897), 177–85.

"A New Labyrinthodont from the Kansas Carboniferous," *Kansas University Quarterly*, Series A, Vol. VI, No. 4 (October, 1897), 209–10.

"Vertebrates from the Kansas Permian," *Science*, New Series, Vol. V (1897), 395.

"[Review of] *Insect Life*, by John Henry Comstock," *Science*, New Series, Vol. VI (October 29, 1897), 670–71.

"Science in Education," *Science*, New Series, Vol. VI (1897), 863–72. (Also in *Transactions of the Kansas Academy of Science*, Vol. XVI [1899], 16–24.)

"The Kansas Niobrara Cretaceous," *University Geological Survey of Kansas*, Vol. II (1897), 235–46.

"The Pleistocene of Kansas," *University Geological Survey of Kansas*, Vol. II (1897), 297–308.

"Contribution to a Symposium on the Classification and Nomenclature of Geologic Time-divisions," *Journal of Geology*, Vol. VI (1898), 342–45.

"Restoration of Kansas Cretaceous Animals," *Kansas University Quarterly*, Series A, Vol. VII (1898), frontispiece.

"The Sacrum of *Morosaurus*," *Kansas University Quarterly*, Series A, Vol. VII (1898), 173–75.

"Editorial Notes" [Note on Nuchal Fringe and Scales of *Platecarpus*], *Kansas University Quarterly*, Series A, Vol. VII (1898), 235.

"Saber-toothed Cats," *Popular Science Monthly*, Vol. LIII (1898), 348–51.

"Miocene Edentates," *Science*, New Series, Vol. VIII, No. 187 (1898), 132.

"Notes and Descriptions of Mydaidae," *Transactions of the Kansas Academy of Science*, Vol. XV (1898), 53–58.

"The Pleistocene of Kansas," *Transactions of the Kansas Academy of Science,* Vol. XV (1898), 90–94.

"Notice of Some Vertebrate Remains from the Kansas Permian," *Transactions of the Kansas Academy of Science,* Vol. XV (1898), 120–22.

"Addenda" to "The Upper Cretaceous of Kansas," by George I. Adams. *University Geological Survey of Kansas,* Vol. IV, Paleontology, Part I (1898), 28–32.

"Birds," *University Geological Survey of Kansas,* Vol. IV, Paleontology, Part II (1898), 41–63.

"Dinosaurs," *University Geological Survey of Kansas,* Vol. IV, Paleontology, Part III (1898), 65–71.

"Crocodiles," *University Geological Survey of Kansas,* Vol. IV, Paleontology, Part IV (1898), 73–78.

"Mosasaurs," *University Geological Survey of Kansas,* Vol. IV, Paleontology, Part V (1898), 81–347.

"Introduction" and *"Desmatochelys lowii," University Geological Survey of Kansas,* Vol. IV, Paleontology, Part VI (1898), 349–69.

"Prof. Benjamin F. Mudge," *American Geologist,* Vol. XXIII (June, 1899), 339–45.

"Some Additional Characters of the Mosasaurs," *Kansas University Quarterly,* Series A, Vol. VIII (1899), 39–41.

"A New Genus of Fishes from the Niobrara Cretaceous," *Kansas University Quarterly,* Series A, Vol. VIII, No. 3 (July, 1899), 113–15.

"Bibliography to 1899," *Kansas University Quarterly,* Series A, Vol. VIII (1899), 169–74.

"A New Species of *Sagenodus* from the Kansas Coal Measures," *Kansas University Quarterly,* Series A, Vol. VIII, No. 4 (October, 1899), 175–81.

"Notes on the Coraco-scapula of *Eryops* Cope," *Kansas University Quarterly,* Series A, Vol. VIII, No. 4 (October, 1899), 185–86.

"Editorial Notes" [book reviews], *Kansas University Quarterly,* Series A, Vol. VIII, No. 4 (October, 1899).

"Some Prehistoric Ruins in Scott County, Kansas," *Kansas University Quarterly,* Series B, Vol. VII, No. 4 (April, 1899), 109–14.

"On the Genus *Thlipsogaster rondani," Psyche,* Vol. VIII (1899), 331–32.

"Science and Politics," *Science,* New Series, Vol. IX (January 20, 1899), 114–15.

"The Red-beds of Kansas," *Science*, New Series, Vol. IX (February 10, 1899), 221.

"Some Pueblo Ruins in Scott County, Kansas" (with H. T. Martin), *Transactions of the Kansas State Historical Society*, Vol. VI (1899), 124–30.

"Relations of the State Board of Health to the Public," Address to Kansas State Board of Health (1899).

"Medical Education," Address to Women's Medical College of Kansas City (May, 1899).

"The Geology of Kansas," in *The Earth and its Story*, by Angelo Heilprin, New York, Silver, Burdett and Co., 1900, 269–88.

"Some Fish Teeth from the Kansas Cretaceous," *Kansas University Quarterly*, Series A, Vol. IX (January, 1900), 27–42.

"Cretaceous Fishes: Selachians and Pycnodonts, Dercetidae," *University Geological Survey of Kansas*, Vol. VI (1900), 237–56, 380–82.

"Supplement" to Diptera, in *Biologia Centrali-Americana*, ed. F. D. Godman and O. Salvin, London, Dulau and Co., 1900–1901, 217–332.

"The Dinosaurian Genus *Creosaurus*, Marsh," *American Journal of Science*, Fourth Series, Vol. XI, No. 62 (February, 1901), 111–14.

"The Teaching of Physiology in the Public Schools," *Science*, New Series, Vol. XIII (1901), 827–28, 991.

"A New Turtle from the Kansas Cretaceous," *Transactions of the Kansas Academy of Science*, Vol. XVII (1901), 195–99.

"An Arrowhead Found with Bones of *Bison occidentalis* Lucas, in Western Kansas," *American Geologist*, Vol. XXX (November, 1902), 313–15.

"On the Skeleton of *Nyctodactylus*, with Restoration," *American Journal of Anatomy*, Vol. I (1902), 297–305.

"On the Cranial Anatomy of the Plesiosaurs," *American Journal of Anatomy*, Vol. I (1902), 518.

"On the Hind Limb of *Protostega*," *American Journal of Science*, Fourth Series, Vol. XIII (1902), 276–78.

"On the Skull of *Nyctodactylus*, an Upper Cretaceous Pterodactyl," *Journal of Geology*, Vol. X (1902), 520–31.

"[Review of] *Bibliography and Catalogue of the Fossil Vertebrata of North America*, by O. P. Hay," *Journal of Geology*, Vol. X (1902), 918–19.

"Restoration of *Dolichorhynchops osborni*, a New Cretaceous Plesiosaur," *Kansas University Science Bulletin*, Vol. I (1902), 241–44.

"Notes on Some New or Little-known Extinct Reptiles," *Kansas University Science Bulletin*, Vol. I (1902), 247–54.

"On Certain Homoplastic Characters in Aquatic Air-Breathing Vertebrates," *Kansas University Science Bulletin*, Vol. I (1902), 259–66.

"Winged Reptiles," *Popular Science Monthly*, Vol. LX (1902), 314–22.

"[Review of] *Dragons of the Air, an Account of Extinct Flying Reptiles*, by H. G. Seeley," *Science*, New Series, Vol. XV (1902), 67–68.

"[Review of] *Animals of the Past*, by Frederic A. Lucas," *Science*, New Series, Vol. XV (1902), 586–87.

"A Fossil Man from Kansas," *Science*, New Series, Vol. XVI (1902), 195–96.

"The Laramie Cretaceous of Wyoming," *Science*, New Series, Vol. XVI (1902), 952–53.

"[Review of] *History of Geology and Palaeontology to the End of the Nineteenth Century*, by Karl Alfred von Zittel," Chicago *Tribune* (August 20, 1902).

"Higher Education in Kansas," Address to University of Kansas Chapter of the Sigma Xi (June 7, 1902).

"North American Plesiosaurs, Part I," *Field Columbian Museum Publication 73*, Geological Series, Vol. II, No. 1 (April, 1903), 1–77.

"On the Osteology of *Nyctosaurus* (*Nyctodactylus*), with Notes on American Pterosaurs," *Field Columbian Museum Publication 78*, Geological Series, Vol. II (1903), 125–63.

"[Review of] 'New Ichthyosauria from the Upper Triassic of California,' by J. C. Merriam," *Journal of Geology*, Vol. XI (1903), 515–16.

"[Review of] 'On the Skull of a True Lizard (*Paliguana whitei*) from the Triassic of South Africa,' by R. Broom," *Journal of Geology*, Vol. XI (1903), 516.

"The Fossil Man of Lansing, Kansas," *Popular Science Monthly*, Vol. LVII (1903), 463–73.

"On the Structure of the Plesiosaurian Skull," *Science*, New Series, Vol. XVII, No. 442 (1903), 980.

"Specialization in Education," *Science*, New Series, Vol. XVIII, No. 448 (July 31, 1903), 129–38.

"The Society of the Vertebrate Paleontologists of America," *Science*, New Series, Vol. XVIII (1903), 827–28.

"Some Osteological Terms," *Science*, New Series, Vol. XVIII (1903), 829–30.

"Index" and "Supplement" to Diptera, in *Biologia Centrali-Americana*, ed. F. D. Godman and O. Salvin, London, Dulau and Co., 1903.

"Presidential Address," to Sixth Biennial Convention of the Society of the Sigma Xi (1903).

"Wilbur Clinton Knight," *American Geologist*, Vol. XXXIII (January, 1904), 1–6.

"The Temporal Arches of the Reptilia," *Biological Bulletin*, Vol. VII, No. 4 (September, 1904), 175–92.

"The Fingers of Pterodactyls," *Geological Magazine*, Vol. I (1904), 59–60.

"The Relationships and Habits of the Mosasaurs," *Journal of Geology*, Vol. XII, No. 1 (January–February, 1904), 43–51.

"Notice of Some New Reptiles from the Upper Trias of Wyoming," *Journal of Geology*, Vol. XII, No. 8 (November–December, 1904), 688–97.

"The Stomach Stones of the Plesiosaurs," *Science*, New Series, Vol. XX (1904), 565.

"Is Man the End of Evolution?" *Independent*, Vol. LVIII (1905), 1172–77.

"[Review of] 'On the Evolution of the Proboscidae,' and 'The Barypoda, a New Order of Ungulate Mammals'," *Journal of Geology*, Vol. XIII (1905), 88.

"[Review of] 'A New Marine Reptile from the Trias of California'," *Journal of Geology*, Vol. XIII (1905), 183.

"[Review of] 'New Zeuglodonten aus dem unteren Mitteleocen vom Mokattam bei Cairo'," *Journal of Geology*, Vol. XIII (1905), 183–84.

"[Review of] *'Teleorrhinus browni*—a New Teleosaur in the Fort Benton'," *Journal of Geology*, Vol. XIII (1905), 184.

"The Hallopus, Baptanodon, and Atlantosaurus Beds of Marsh," *Journal of Geology*, Vol. XIII, No. 4 (May–June, 1905), 338–50.

"On the Lansing Man," *Proceedings of the International Congress of Americanists*, Thirteenth Session (1905), 85–89. (Also in *American Geologist*, Vol. XXXV [June, 1905], 342–46.)

"Phylogeny and Classification of the Reptilia," (Abstract), *Science*, New Series, Vol. XXI (1905), 294.

"New Locality for Triassic Vertebrates," (Abstract), *Science*, New Series, Vol. XXI (1905), 297–98.

"A New Armored Dinosaur from the Upper Cretaceous of Wyoming," *Science*, New Series, Vol. XXII (1905), 503–504.

"North American Plesiosaurs: *Elasmosaurus, Cimoliasaurus,* and *Polycotylus,*" *American Journal of Science,* Fourth Series, Vol. XXI, No. 123 (March, 1906), 221–36.

"The Classification of the Culicidae," *Canadian Entomologist,* Vol. XXXVIII (1906), 384–88.

"American Amphicoelian Crocodiles," *Journal of Geology,* Vol. XIV, No. 1 (January–February, 1906), 1–17.

"Some Common Errors in the Nomenclature of the Dipterous Wing," *Psyche,* Vol. XIII (December, 1906), 154–57.

"The Great Plains," Address to Geographical Society of Chicago, *School of Science and Mathematics,* Vol. VI, No. 8 (November, 1906), 641–51.

"The Antennae of Diptera; a Study in Phylogeny," *Biological Bulletin,* Vol. XIII, No. 6 (November, 1907), 324–32.

"Dipterological Notes," *Journal of the New York Entomological Society,* Vol. XV (1907), 1–2.

"The Skull of *Brachauchenius,* with Observations on the Relationships of the Plesiosaurs," *Proceedings of the United States National Museum,* Vol. XXXII (June 15, 1907), 477–89.

"The First Reviser of Species," *Science,* New Series, Vol. XXV, No. 646 (May 17, 1907), 790–91.

"What is a Species?" *American Naturalist,* Vol. XLII, No. 495 (March, 1908), 184–94.

"Lysorophus, a Permian Urodele," *Biological Bulletin,* Vol. XV (1908), 229–40.

"The Cotylosauria," *Journal of Geology,* Vol. XV, No. 2 (February–March, 1908), 139–48.

" 'The Oldest Known Reptile'—*Isodectes punctulatus* Cope," *Journal of Geology,* Vol. XVI, No. 5 (July–August, 1908), 395–400.

"North American Plesiosaurs: *Trinacromerum,*" *Journal of Geology,* Vol. XVI, No. 8 (November–December, 1908), 715–36.

"[Review of] 'Triassic Ichthyosauria, with Special Reference to the American Forms,' by J. C. Merriam," *Journal of Geology,* Vol. XVI (1908), 775–77.

"The Evolution and Distribution of the Plesiosaurs," (Abstract), *Science,* New Series, Vol. XXVII (1908), 726–27.

"A New Group of Permian Amphibians," *Science,* New Series, Vol. XXVIII, No. 714 (September, 1908), 316-17.

"[Review of] *The Fossil Turtles of North America*, by O. P. Hay," *Science*, New Series, Vol. XXVIII (1908), 803-804.

"Its Function and Duties," Letter to Kansas Agricultural College *Alumnus* (June 17, 1908).

"New or Little-known Permian Vertebrates: *Pariotichus*," *Biological Bulletin*, Vol. XVII, No. 3 (August, 1909), 241–55.

"Francis H. Snow, the Man and Scientist," University of Kansas *Graduate Magazine*, Vol. VII (January, 1909), 128–34.

"The Faunal Relations of the Early Vertebrates," *Journal of Geology*, Vol. XVII, No. 4 (July–August, 1909), 389–402. (Also in *Outlines of Geologic History*, by B. Willis and R. D. Salisbury, Chicago, University of Chicago Press, 1910, 163–74.)

"New or Little-known Permian Vertebrates: *Trematops*, New Genus," *Journal of Geology*, Vol. XVII, No. 7 (October–November, 1909), 636–58.

"The Origin of the University of Kansas School of Medicine," *Journal of the Kansas Medical Society*, Vol. IX, No. 6 (June, 1909), 212–15.

"Discussion of 'Dinosaur Societies' by R. S. Lull," *Science*, New Series, Vol. XXIX (1909), 194.

"The Skull and Extremities of *Diplocaulus*," *Transactions of the Kansas Academy of Science*, Vol. XXII (1909), 122–31.

"Has the American College Failed to Fulfill its Function?" *Volume of Proceedings*, National Education Association (1909), 526–33.

"The Skull of *Labidosaurus*," *American Journal of Anatomy*, Vol. X, No. 1 (January, 1910), 69–84.

"*Cacops, Desmospondylus*; New Genera of Permian Vertebrates," *Bulletin of the Geological Society of America*, Vol. XXI (June, 1910), 249–84.

"Introduction" to "The Occurrence of a Sauropod Dinosaur in the Trinity Cretaceous of Oklahoma," by Pierce Larkin, *Journal of Geology*, Vol. XVIII, No. 1 (January–February, 1910), 93.

"*Dissorophus* Cope," *Journal of Geology*, Vol. XVIII, No. 6 (1910), 526–36.

"A Mounted Skeleton of *Platecarpus*," *Journal of Geology*, Vol. XVIII, No. 6 (1910), 537–41.

"New Permian Reptiles: Rachitomous Vertebrae," *Journal of Geology*, Vol. XVIII, No. 7 (1910), 585–600.

"The Birthplace of Man," *Popular Science Monthly*, Vol. LXXVII (1910), 594–97. (Also in *The Paleontologic Record* [1910], 85–88.)

"*Varanosaurus* species, a Permian Pelycosaur," (Abstract), *Science*, New Series, Vol. XXXII (1910), 223.

"Man in Evolution," Address to the Kansas Chapter of the Society of Sigma Xi (June, 1910).

"A New Family of Reptiles from the Permian of New Mexico," *American Journal of Science*, Fourth Series, Vol. XXXI (1911), 378–98.

"Restoration of *Seymouria baylorensis* Broili, an American Cotylosaur," *Journal of Geology*, Vol. XIX, No. 3 (April–May, 1911), 232–37.

"[Review of] 'Ueber *Erythrosuchus*, Vertreter der neuen Reptilordnung Pelycosimia,' by F. von Huene," *Journal of Geology*, Vol. XIX, No. 7 (October–November, 1911), 661–64.

"The Wing-finger of Pterodactyls, with Restoration of *Nyctosaurus*," *Journal of Geology*, Vol. XIX, No. 8 (November–December, 1911), 696–705.

"[Review of] *The Age of Mammals in Europe, Asia and North America*, by Henry Fairfield Osborn," *Science*, New Series, Vol. XXXIII, No. 842 (1911), 250–52.

"Permian Reptiles," *Science*, New Series, Vol. XXXIII, No. 851 (April, 1911), 631–32.

"Bibliography: Samuel Wendell Williston," New Haven, J. T. Hathaway (1911), 1–19.

"A Description of the Skulls of *Diadectes lentus* and *Animasaurus carinatus*" (with E. C. Case), *American Journal of Science*, Fourth Series, Vol. XXXIII (April, 1912), 339–48.

"Restoration of *Limnoscelis*, a Cotylosaur Reptile from New Mexico," *American Journal of Science*, Fourth Series, Vol. XXXIV (November, 1912), 457–68.

"Evolutionary Evidences," in Symposium on Ten Years Progress in Vertebrate Paleontology, *Bulletin of the Geological Society of America*, Vol. XXIII (June, 1912), 257–62.

"The Permo-Carboniferous of Northern New Mexico" (with E. C. Case), *Journal of Geology*, Vol. XX, No. 1 (January–February, 1912), 1–12.

"[Review of] Grundzuge der Paläontologie, by Karl A. von Zittel," *Journal of Geology*, Vol. XX, No. 1 (January–February, 1912), 91–93.

"[Review of] 'Beitrage zur Kenntnis der Oligozänen Landsäugetiere aus dem Fayum (Aegypten),' by Max Schlosser," *Journal of Geology*, Vol. XX (1912), 93–94.

"[Review of] 'Osteology of *Pteranodon*,' by George F. Eaton," *Journal of Geology*, Vol. XX (1912), 288.

"Primitive Reptiles: A Review," *Journal of Morphology*, Vol. XXIII, No. 4 (December, 1912), 637–63.

"[Review of] *A Revision of the Cotylosauria of North America*, by E. C. Case," *Science*, New Series, Vol. XXXV, No. 907 (1912), 779–80.

"A Vote on the Priority Rule by the American Society of Zoologists, Central Branch" (with C. C. Nutting and H. B. Ward), *Science*, New Series, Vol. XXXVI (1912), 830–33.

"New Plesiosaurian Genus from the Niobrara Cretaceous of Nebraska" (with R. L. Moodie), (Abstract), *Bulletin of the Geological Society of America*, Vol. XXIV (1913), 120–21.

"*Ostodelepis brevispinatus*, a New Reptile from the Permian of Texas," *Journal of Geology*, Vol. XXI, No. 4 (May–June, 1913), 363–66.

"The Primitive Structure of the Mandible in Amphibians and Reptiles," *Journal of Geology*, Vol. XXI, No. 7 (October–November, 1913), 625–27.

"The Skulls of *Araeoscelis* and *Casea*, Permian Reptiles," *Journal of Geology*, Vol. XXI, No. 8 (November–December, 1913), 743–47.

"[Review of] 'The Skeleton of *Ornithodesmus latidens*,' by R. W. Hooley," *Journal of Geology*, Vol. XXI, No. 8 (November–December, 1913), 754–56.

"The Pelycosaurian Mandible," *Science*, New Series, Vol. XXXVIII, No. 980 (1913), 512.

"An Ancestral Lizard from the Permian of Texas," *Science*, New Series, Vol. XXXVIII, No. 988 (December 5, 1913), 825–26.

"*Broiliellus*, a New Genus of Amphibians from the Permian of Texas," *Journal of Geology*, Vol. XXII, No. 1 (January–February, 1914), 49–56.

"Restorations of Some American Permocarboniferous Amphibians and Reptiles," *Journal of Geology*, Vol. XXII, No. 1 (January–February, 1914), 57–70.

"The Osteology of Some American Permian Vertebrates," *Journal of Geology*, Vol. XXII (May–June, 1914), 364–419. (Also in *Contributions from Walker Museum*, Vol. I (July, 1914), 105–162.)

"American Permocarboniferous Reptiles and Amphibians," *Papers of IXth Congrès International de Zoologie* at Monaco, 25–30 March, 1913 (1914), 120–21.

"The American Land Vertebrate Fauna and its Relations," *Science*, New Series, Vol. XL (1914), 777–78.

"[Review of] *Letters and Recollections of Alexander Agassiz, with a*

Sketch of his Work and Life, edited by George R. Agassiz," *Yale Review,* Vol. III, No. 4 (1914), 818–20.

"New Genera of Permian Reptiles," *American Journal of Science,* Fourth Series, Vol. XXXIX (1915), 575–79.

"The First Discovery of Dinosaurs in the West," in *Dinosaurs,* by W. D. Matthew, American Museum of Natural History Handbook Series No. 5 (1915), 124–31.

"Trimerorhachis, a Permian Temnospondyl Amphibian," *Journal of Geology,* Vol. XXIII, No. 3 (April–May, 1915), 246–55.

"A New Genus and Species of American Theromorpha, *Mycterosaurus longiceps,*" *Journal of Geology,* Vol. XXIII, No. 6 (September–October, 1915), 554–59.

"Origin of the Sternum in the Reptiles and Mammals," (Abstract), *Bulletin of the Geological Society of America,* Vol. XXVII (1916), 152.

"Osteology of Some American Permian Vertebrates, II," *Contributions from Walker Museum,* Vol. I, No. 9 (1916), 163–92.

"Synopsis of the American Permocarboniferous Tetrapoda," *Contributions from Walker Museum,* Vol. I, No. 9 (1916), 193–236.

"The Skeleton of *Trimerorhachis,*" *Journal of Geology,* Vol. XXIV, No. 3 (April–May, 1916), 291–97.

"Sphenacodon, Marsh, a Permocarboniferous Theromorph Reptile from New Mexico," *Proceedings of the National Academy of Sciences,* Vol. II (1916), 650–54.

"Camptopelta, a New Genus of Stratiomyidae," *Annals of the Entomological Society of America,* Vol. X (1917), 23–26.

"Report of the Committee on Nomenclature, Appendix C, Comments," *Bulletin of the Geological Society of America,* Vol. XXVIII (1917), 985–86.

"Labidosaurus Cope, a Lower Permian Cotylosaur Reptile from Texas," *Journal of Geology,* Vol. XXV, No. 4 (May–June, 1917), 309–21.

"The Phylogeny and Classification of Reptiles," *Journal of Geology,* Vol. XXV, No. 5 (July–August, 1917), 411–21.

"Ogmodirus martinii, a New Plesiosaur from the Cretaceous of Kansas" (with R. L. Moodie), *Kansas University Science Bulletin,* Vol. X, No. 5 (January, 1917), 61–73.

"The Future of the Sigma Xi," Address to Yale Chapter of the Society of Sigma Xi, *Science,* Vol. XLVI, No. 1181 (August 17, 1917), 147–52.

"Evolution of Vertebrae," *Contributions from Walker Museum,* Vol. II

(1918), 75–85. (Abstract in *Bulletin of the Geological Society of America,* Vol. XXIX [1918], 146.)

"Osteology of Some American Permian Vertebrates, III," *Contributions from Walker Museum,* Vol. II (1918), 87–112.

"[Review of] *Organic Evolution, a Text-book,* by Richard Swann Lull," *Journal of Geology,* Vol. XXVI (1918), 285–86.

"[Review of] *Geology of the Navajo Country: A Reconnaissance of Parts of Arizona, New Mexico, and Utah,* by Herbert E. Gregory," *Journal of Geology,* Vol. XXVI (1918), 287–88.

"Additional Papers [to Bibliography of S. W. Williston], 1911–1917," New Haven, J. T. Hathaway (1918), 2 pp.

"The Progress of Science Since the Foundation of the Kansas Academy of Science," *Transactions of the Kansas Academy of Science,* Vol. XXIX (1920), 53–61.

"The Culture of Hardy Flowering Bulbs in Eastern Kansas," Address to Kansas State Horticultural Society, Thirty-fourth Annual Meeting, n.d.

"Flies as Carriers of Disease," (journal and date unknown, page proof bound in Williston's publications).

"Heredity and Disease," Address to the Kansas Medical Society, Thirty-fifth Annual Meeting, n.d.

Bibliography

NEWSPAPERS

Kansas City *Star.*
Lawrence *Daily Journal.*
New York *Herald.*
University of Kansas *University Courier.*

BOOKS

Bonner, Thomas N. *The Kansas Doctor.* Lawrence, University of Kansas Press, 1959.

Colbert, Edwin H. *Dinosaurs.* New York, E. P. Dutton & Company, 1961.

———. *Men and Dinosaurs.* New York, E. P. Dutton & Company, 1968.

Curran, C. H. *North American Diptera.* New York, Ballou Press, 1934.

Fisher, D. Jerome. *The Seventy Years of the Department of Geology, University of Chicago.* Chicago, University of Chicago Press, 1963.

Gould, Charles N. *Covered Wagon Geologist.* Norman, University of Oklahoma Press, 1959.

Hyder, Clyde Kenneth. *Snow of Kansas.* Lawrence, University of Kansas Press, 1953.

Matthew, W. D. *Dinosaurs.* New York, American Museum of Natural History Handbook, Series No. 5, 1915.

Miller, Nyle H. *Kansas: A Students' Guide to Localized History.* New York, Teachers College, Columbia University, 1965.

Osborn, Henry Fairfield. *Cope: Master Naturalist.* Princeton, Princeton University Press, 1931.

Ostrom, John H., and John S. McIntosh. *Marsh's Dinosaurs.* New Haven, Yale University Press, 1966.

Romer, Alfred S. *Osteology of the Reptiles* (revised). Chicago, University of Chicago Press, 1956.

———. "The Texas Permian Redbeds and Their Vertebrate Fauna," in T. S. Westoll, ed. *Studies on Fossil Vertebrates,* London, 1958.

277

Schuchert, Charles, and Clara M. LeVene. *O. C. Marsh: Pioneer in Paleontology*. New Haven, Yale University Press, 1940.

Sterling, Wilson, ed. *Quarter-Centennial History of the University of Kansas, 1866–1891*. Topeka, Geo. W. Crane & Co., 1891.

Sternberg, Charles H. *The Life of a Fossil Hunter*. New York, Henry Holt & Company, 1909.

Stevens, W. C. "Reminiscences," *The Fiftieth Anniversary of the Founding of the Kansas Chapter of the Society of the Sigma Xi*. University of Kansas, 1941.

Storr, Richard J. *Harper's University: The Beginnings*. Chicago, University of Chicago Press, 1966.

ARTICLES

Aldrich, J. M. "Samuel Wendell Williston," *Entomological News*, Vol. XXIX (November, 1918), 322–27.

———. "Samuel Wendell Williston: The Entomologist," *Sigma Xi Quarterly*, Vol. VII, No. 1 (March, 1919), 19–21.

Bailey, E. H. S. "Doctor Samuel Wendell Williston," University of Kansas *Graduate Magazine*, Vol. XVII, No. 2 (November, 1918), 35–37.

———. "Samuel Wendell Williston: A Kansas Tribute," *Sigma Xi Quarterly*, Vol. VII, No. 1 (March, 1919), 26–28.

Case, E. C. "Dr. Williston as a Teacher," University of Chicago *University Record* (January, 1919), 97–101.

Johnston, G. F. "Medical Registration," *Journal of the Kansas Medical Society* (1902), reprinted in Centennial Issue of the Journal, Vol. LX, No. 5 (May, 1959), 83–84.

Knight, Wilbur C. "The Wyoming Fossil Fields Expedition of July, 1899," *National Geographic Magazine*, Vol. XI, No. 12 (December, 1900), 449–65.

Lull, Richard Swann. "Samuel Wendell Williston," *Memoirs of the National Academy of Sciences*, Vol. XVII, 5th Memoir (1924), 113–41.

McClung, C. E. "Samuel Wendell Williston: A Student Appreciation," *Sigma Xi Quarterly*, Vol. VII, No. 1 (March, 1919), 9–18.

———. "Samuel Wendell Williston," *Bios*, Vol. XIV, No. 1 (March, 1943), 35–37.

Olson, Everett C. Untitled memorial to Paul C. Miller, *Society of Vertebrate Paleontologists News Bulletin* (December 31, 1945), 20–21.

Osborn, Henry Fairfield. "Joseph Leidy," *National Academy of Sciences Biographical Memoirs*, Vol. VII (1913), 339–70.

————. "Samuel Wendell Williston," *Journal of Geology*, Vol. XXVI, No. 8 (November–December, 1918), 673–89. (Almost identical article in *Geological Society of America Proceedings for 1918*, 66–76.)

Penrose, R. A. F., Jr. "The Early Days of the Department of Geology at the University of Chicago," *Journal of Geology*. Vol. XXXVII (1929), 320–27.

Romer, Alfred S. "Review of *Late Permian Terrestrial Vertebrates, U.S.A. and U.S.S.R.*, by Everett C. Olson," *Copeia*, No. 1 (1964), 250–53.

Stieglitz, Julius. "Samuel Wendell Williston in the Society of the Sigma Xi," *Sigma Xi Quarterly*, Vol. VII, No. 1 (March, 1919), 22–25.

Ward, Henry B. "Samuel Wendell Williston: The Great Apostle of Sigma Xi," *Sigma Xi Quarterly*, Vol. VII, No. 1 (March, 1919), 29–38.

Weller, Stuart. "Samuel Wendell Williston," University of Chicago *University Record* (January, 1919), 102–105.

ADDITIONAL MEMORIALS TO WILLISTON NOT CITED ABOVE

Anonymous. "Samuel Wendell Williston," *The Canadian Entomologist*, Vol. LI (February, 1919), 39–41.

Brown, Barnum. "Samuel Wendell Williston (1852–1918) by One of his Students," *American Museum Journal*, Vol. XVIII, No. 7 (November, 1918), 611 and frontispiece.

Dictionary of American Biography. New York, Charles Scribner's Sons, 1928–1937.

Dictionary of Scientific Biography. Charles Scribner's Sons (in press).

Encyclopaedia Britannica. 1955 edition.

Essig, E. O. *A History of Entomology*. New York, Hafner Publishing Company, 1931, 796–800.

Lillie, Frank Rattray. "Samuel Wendell Williston, 1852–1918: Dr. Williston's Work in Entomology, in Medicine, and as Student of the Evolution of Life," University of Chicago *University Record* (January, 1919), 92–97.

Osborn, Henry Fairfield. "Samuel Wendell Williston: The Man and the Paleontologist," *Sigma Xi Quarterly*, Vol. VII, No. 1 (March, 1919), 2–8.

Osborn, Herbert. *Fragments of Entomological History*. Columbus, Ohio, published by the author, 1937, 189, 318.

————, T. H. Parks, and J. J. Davis. "Resolutions on the Death of Dr. S. W. Williston," *Annals of The Entomological Society of America*, Vol. XII, No. 1 (March, 1919), 56–57.

279

Index

Abiquiu, N. Mex.: 220–21, 248
Agassiz, Alexander: 95
Aldrich, J. M.: 101, 115, 165, 190, 236, 248
Amblycheila cylindriformis: 100, 130
American Academy of Arts and Sciences: 249
American Naturalist: 120
American Permian Vertebrates: 220
American Philosophical Society: 249
American Scientist: 240

Bailey, E. H. S.: 143–44
Baker, Charles Laurence: 210, 217
Baldwin beds, N. Mex.: 220, 222, 248
Baldwin, David: 86, 97, 220
Ball, E. E.: 213
Ballou, William Hosea: 117
Barber, Marshall: 171
Barbour, Erwin H.: 141 & n., 142, 184
Barbour, Thomas: 252
Baumgartner, W. J.: 130
Baur, George: 122, 184, 206, 245
Beebe, J. W.: 144
Behre, Charles H.: 211, 251
Belemnites: 92, 95
Bell, Simeon: 166 & n.
Biologia Centrali-Americana: 165–66, 236–37
Birds, toothed (Odontornithes): 71, 75–84, 87, 120, 145–46
Bison: 52, 67, 72, 75
Black Walnut House (Manhattan, Kans.): 14–15
Blue Mont (Manhattan, Kans.): 14, 253
Blue Mont College (Manhattan, Kans.): 15–16
Blue River, Kans.: 10, 14, 16
Blue Valley Railroad (Kans.): 51
Branson, Edwin Bayer: 211–12 & n.
British Museum (Natural History): 244–46

Broili, Ferdinand: 245
Broom, Robert: 224 & n.
Brous, Harry A.: 55ff., 72, 77, 82–83, 90, 99–100, 102
Brown, Barnum: 141 & n., 180, 198
Brown, Lucy: 186–88
Brown, N. H. (on 1903 fossil trip): 213
Brown, W. H. (Kansas student): 198
Buffalo Park, Kans.: 61, 74, 82–83
Burgess, Edward: 101
Butterfield Overland Express: 17 & n.

Cacops bonebed (Texas): 219–20
Canfield, James H.: 186, 188
Cañon City, Colo.: 85ff., 184, 222
Carlin, William E.: 86, 91, 93
Carpenter, Mr. (on railroad survey): 27ff., 32
Carruth, William Herbert: 186
Case, Ermine Cowles: 138 & n., 141–42, 144, 215, 220, 254
Chamberlin, Thomas C.: 205–208
Civil War: 16–18
Como, Wyo.: 85–87, 89–95, 101, 143, 213, 218
Cooper, George: 72, 76–77, 90
Cope, Edward: 3, 6, 22, 77, 82–83, 94, 97–98, 102, 137–38, 140, 184, 217, 224; and Kansas fossils, 55, 68–69; and O. C. Marsh, 57, 68–71, 117–23; background of, 67–71; and Sternberg, 73–74, 78; discovery of dinosaurs by, 84ff.
Coues, Elliott: 99 & n.
Craddock bonebed (Texas): 217, 219
Cretaceous fossils: 57, 90, 145–46; *see also* by fossil type
Crinoids: 75, 81
Crumbine, Samuel J.: 171
Curran, C. H.: 236 & n.

Dana, James Dwight: 62, 88, 246